This is a phenomenal book. A good shot of history, equal parts anthropology and media analysis and a dash of wit and wisdom. This is the most sensible and balanced approach to alcohol consumption I have ever read. It should be required of all college students.

– Ken Albala, History, *University of the Pacific*

Instantly engaging, Janet Chrzan's historical and cross-cultural overview of views and practices related to alcohol as a "nurturing beverage" or "dangerous drug," brings to life the value of anthropological analysis to university students. Making a compelling case for alcohol as a "total social fact," enmeshed as it is with so many other facets of social life, Chrzan masterfully portrays the social meanings of alcohol use.

– Andrea Wiley, Anthropology, *Indiana University, Bloomington*

This lively and accessible book bubbles with intriguing details about the history and culture of alcohol consumption from the earliest archaeological evidence to contemporary U.S. college students' arresting drinking diaries. It is an engaging introduction to anthropology which encourages critical thinking about the practices and meanings of campus drinking."

– Carole Counihan, Anthropology, *Millersville University*

This book should be required reading for any college student who has pre-gamed, bar-hopped, tail-gated, shot-gunned, played beer-pong, or done a beer bong. Janet Chrzan puts American drinking cultures in theoretical and comparative perspective, offering practical advice for limiting the harms of alcohol while still enjoying it sociably.

– Jeffrey M. Pilcher, History, *University of Minnesota*

Janet Chrzan has captured the all-encompassing hold of alcoholic beverages on our species from prehistoric villages to the modern college campus. Whether drinker or abstainer, we come away from this book with a better understanding of what drives us toward or away from this most paradoxical and universal of substances. By turns, alcohol can be viewed as inspirational and socializing, nutritional and medicinal, relaxing and restorative, or dangerous and destructive

– Patrick McGovern, Ph.D. Scientific Director, Biomolecular Archaeology Laboratory *University of Pennsylvania Museum of Archaeology and Anthropology*

As a food historian who appreciates the long view of history, I heartily welcome this refreshing and highly useful book on the social implications of alcohol. With a balanced selection of material past and present, this is the perfect classroom guide to the basic issues and mores that have defined the role of alcohol down through time. It enlightens the student, invites self-examination, and hopefully provides a lasting framework for dealing with alcohol as a potent and yet highly deceptive medium for socialization

– Dr. William Woys Weaver, Director, *The Keystone Center for the Study of Regional Foods and Food Tourism*

Janet Chrzan has written a probing, insightful (and incidentally often very amusing) study of alcohol use, alcoholism, intoxication, social drinking, and the role alcohol plays in many cultures, including, most specifically, our own. Her broad look at the problematic role of alcohol in American history is fascinating on its own; peeling back the layers of meaning in alcohol use and the social messages it conveys, she reveals a context that can frame much more of our social habits and beliefs.

– Nancy Harmon Jenkins, author of *The New Mediterranean Diet* and many other books about Mediterranean food, wine, and culinary traditions

The Routledge Series for Creative Teaching and Learning in Anthropology
Editor: Richard H. Robbins, SUNY Plattsburgh

This series is dedicated to innovative, unconventional ways to connect under-graduate students and their lived concerns about our social world to the power of social science ideas and evidence. Our goal is to help spark social science imaginations and, in doing so, open new avenues for meaningful thought and action.

ALCOHOL

Alcohol: Social Drinking in Cultural Context critically examines alcohol use across cultures and through time. This short text is a framework for students to self-consciously examine their beliefs about and use of alcohol, and a companion text for teaching the primary concepts of anthropology to first or second year college students.

Janet Chrzan received a Ph.D. in Nutritional Anthropology from the University of Pennsylvania in 2008.

ALCOHOL

Social Drinking in Cultural Context

Janet Chrzan

Routledge
Taylor & Francis Group

NEW YORK AND LONDON

First published 2013
by Routledge
711 Third Avenue, New York, NY 10017

Simultaneously published in the UK
by Routledge
2 Park Square, Milton Park, Abingdon, Oxon OX14 4RN

Routledge is an imprint of the Taylor & Francis Group, an informa business

Library of Congress Cataloging in Publication Data

Chrzan, Janet.
Alcohol: social drinking in cultural context / Janet Chrzan.
    p. cm. — (The Routledge series for creative teaching and learning
in anthropology)
Includes bibliographical references and index.
1. Drinking of alcoholic beverages–History. 2. Alcoholic beverages–
Social aspects. I. Title.
HV5020.C46 2013
364.1'3–dc23   2012029043

ISBN: 978-0-415-89249-0 (hbk)
ISBN: 978-0-415-89250-6 (pbk)
ISBN: 978-0-203-07138-0 (ebk)

Typeset in Baskerville
by Cenveo Publisher Services

Printed and bound in the United States of America by
Edwards Brothers Malloy on sustainably sourced paper

CONTENTS

SERIES FOREWORD

The premise of these short books on the anthropology of stuff is that stuff talks, that written into the biographies of everyday items of our lives—coffee, T-shirts, computers, iPods, flowers, drugs, coffee, and so forth—are the stories that make us who we are and that makes the world the way it is. From their beginnings, each item bears the signature of the people who extracted, manufactured, picked, caught, assembled, packaged, delivered, purchased and disposed of it. And in our modern market-driven societies, our lives are dominated by the pursuit of stuff.

Examining stuff is also an excellent way to teach and learn about what is exciting and insightful about anthropological and sociological ways of knowing. Students, as with virtually all of us, can relate to stuff, while, at the same time, discovering through these books that it can provide new and fascinating ways of looking at the world.

Stuff, or commodities and things are central, of course, to all societies, to one extent or another. Whether it is yams, necklaces, horses, cattle, or shells, the acquisition, accumulation and exchange of things is central to the identities and relationships that tie people together and drive their behavior. But never, before now, has the craving for stuff reached the level it has; and never before have so many people been trying to convince each other that acquiring more stuff is what they most want to do. As a consequence, the creation, consumption, and disposal of stuff now threatens the planet itself. Yet to stop or even slow down the manufacture and accumulation of stuff would threaten the viability of our economy, on which our society is built.

This raises various questions. For example, what impact does the compulsion to acquire stuff have on our economic, social, and political well-being, as well as on our environment? How do we come to believe that there are certain things that we must have? How do we come to value some commodities or form of commodities above others? How have we managed to create commodity chains that link peasant farmers in Colombia or gold miners in Angola to wealthy residents of New York or teenagers in Nebraska? Who comes up with the ideas for stuff and how do they translate those ideas into things for people to buy?

Why do we sometimes consume stuff that is not very good for us? These short books examine such questions, and more.

Alcohol, of course, occupies a special place in the pantheon of stuff, particularly for most college-age students who occupy the liminal space between prohibition and legality. Yet, as Janet Chrzan beautifully illustrates in *Alcohol: Social Drinking in Cultural Context*, alcohol enjoys a fascinating history from a way of storing grain to a sacred liquid surrounded by rules and prohibitions. It is, as she points out, the only dose-dependent drug, one which has always been made safe by social conventions for use. Consequently she exposes the social structures of modern society, particularly those of student culture, that frame the appropriate (and inappropriate) use of alcohol to allow people to act within appropriate (and generally safe) boundaries.

This book explores social drinking in the Western world by examining how people think about drinking and how that affects how they use alcohol. Chrzan is quick to point out that the book is not about a need to regulate alcohol or a treatise on the effects of alcohol on the body, or, for that matter, the problems that alcohol can cause. Rather the book tells the story of how alcohol has been and is thought about, and how these thoughts affect its use. It is, she notes, a biocultural review of how cultures, including those of students, determine proper alcohol intake.

Chrzan uses college student ethnographic reports of parties and other drinking occasions to understand how young adults use alcohol and to counter the public perception of college-age drinking as dangerous and out of control. Instead, by examining its history and cultural range, along with its use by students, Chrzan helps us understand alcohol use as a tool for social and psychological development. More importantly, the book provides students an opportunity to rethink their culture-bound notions of drink, and to engage in a process of placing their own beliefs and behaviors in a cultural and historical perspective.

Richard Robbins, State University of New York, Plattsburgh

PREFACE

I really enjoy bars. I love the sounds of a bar – the clink of glasses, the murmur of conversation, the occasional loud gusts of laughter, the thunk as a pint of beer hits a table, the ice-rattling rhythm of a cocktail being shaken. Bars, pubs, taverns, lounges, whatever the name – people gather in them to talk, to relax, to make new friends and find lovers. Bars enhance communities by providing a place where people can gather informally, share news, make plans and create new alliances. As an anthropologist, I know that one of the best ways to find out about a new community is to understand how people use bars. Are they respectable, welcome and open to all – a real community hub – or are they considered dodgy places for the down and out and the morally suspect? Do they cater to everyone by serving food and other drinks, or do they open only at night, to serve a crowd mostly interested in intoxication? Are they segregated by age or gender? And finally, what are the community norms for how to drink while in a bar? Should patrons gulp quickly while standing, or sip quietly and long while chatting with friends or playing chess or checkers? Are patrons welcoming to strangers, or do they ignore them? Are drinkers expected to stay relatively sober, or are they given license to become visibly drunk?

And, of course, a bar is not merely a gathering place but exists because it serves alcohol, which is a legal intoxicant in most cultures. Bars are places where people can become drunk, high, squishy, 'faced', pixilated, 'effed-up', etc. They sell a substance that alters the consciousness of the user. Bars sell a drug. Admittedly, it's usually a legal drug, but it's still a drug. Since intoxication alters social interactions, the kinds of encounters that occur in bars are different than everyday human sociality. Sometimes intoxication promotes good fellowship and warm feelings, at other times it encourages anger and even violence. Because of this tension social drinking remains a site of ambiguity in all cultures that use alcohol. This book explores social drinking in the Western world by examining how people think about drinking and how that affects how they use alcohol. This is not a book about alcoholism or a treatise on the need for alcohol regulation, nor is it a scientific text about the effects of alcohol on the body and mind. Nor does this volume celebrate alcohol through stories of wine appreciation or by downplaying the problems that alcohol can cause. And unfortunately, this book is not a comprehensive volume on alcohol use – that is far too large a topic for one book. Instead, this book is a short history of the cultural categories and beliefs that influence alcohol use in the Western world and is designed to make the reader consider how alcohol is thought about and how those thoughts affects use. Using evidence from anthropology, history, literature and archeology, this book presents a biocultural review of how some cultures determine proper alcohol intake. Biocultural is an anthropological term that describes research that assumes that biology affects socio-cultural functions and that socio-cultural patterns of behavior also affect biology. Alcohol has biological relevance because it causes a shift in mental state and an alteration in balance and physical functioning, but also because it contains calories. In the modern, presumably well-fed world these calories are a nuisance that contributes to overweight, but they may have been vitally important to health in the past. Beer, wine and cider allow farmers to store grain and fruit well past harvest date, potentially ensuring a source of calories when other food stores run low. The cultures that developed fermentation and used alcohol as a food also developed rules of use that decreased the dangers presented by alcohol as a drug. The widespread availability of cheap and strong distilled spirits starting in the eighteenth century created a shift in how alcohol was perceived, making it more of a drug and less of a food. Today we consider alcohol a drug first and foremost, and this affects how we use it.

This book also makes use of college student ethnographic reports of parties and other drinking occasions to better understand how young adults use alcohol. The public perception of college-age drinking is that it is dangerous and out of control, but the diaries and ethnographic descriptions indicate that most students don't abuse alcohol regularly, don't get drunk frequently, nor do they present a regular danger to themselves or others. Alcohol use is revealed as a tool for social and psychological development that helps students accomplish a number of critical developmental tasks. This observation does not underestimate the dangers of youth and young adult drinking, but asserts that the sociality of drinking plays a role in the development of personal identity and the social and community lives of young adults. I use a harm reduction approach to suggest that the more we understand about how and why we drink (or use intoxicants in general) the more likely we are to use them wisely and well. Harm reduction means to accept the reality of use and to work with the user to make that use as safe as possible. Because alcohol is legal, I am convinced that if young adults choose to use alcohol they must learn how to use it safely. I hope that the reader uses this book to better understand how our culture contributes to our individual understanding and use of this particular intoxicant and can use this information to adopt drinking behaviors that ensure that the pleasures of intake are not swamped by the dangers of abuse.

ACKNOWLEDGMENTS

Many people helped write this book, most of all my superb, patient and very helpful editor Richard Robbins. I thank him for suggesting the project and for being immensely supportive even through delays. I also wish to thank Steve Rutter and Samantha Barbaro of Routledge, who were helpful at all stages of creation. Several reviewers read the manuscript prior to publication; I greatly appreciated the insightful suggestions provided by Michele Gamburd of Portland State University, Rachel Black of Boston University and Mac MacDevitt. Like all books, this one is at heart a collaboration. It would not have existed without the Department of Anthropology and the Office of Alcohol and Other Drug Initiatives at the University of Pennsylvania, which sponsored the course that led to this text, or without the support of Stephanie Ives, Julie Lyzinski Nettleton and Kate Ward-Gaus, the directors and associate director of the alcohol and drug health education program. Kate Ward-Gaus was my collaborator and co-teacher for many years, and her vision and deep understanding of alcohol use opened my eyes to the social lives of intoxicants and informs every page of this book. But the errors are mine alone.

The greatest debt is owed to my students and teaching assistants, who provided the ethnographic observations and descriptions of college drinking. The many students who took the course taught me as much, and possibly more, than I ever taught them. The candor and self-reflection of the students and teaching assistants made the harm reduction approach meaningful to all of us. The researchers and employees of the Museum of Anthropology and Archeology were immensely helpful, especially Patrick McGovern, whose advice was invaluable. This book would not have been written without the guidance and intellectual support of Willam Woys Weaver and Don Yoder; their knowledge of the history of food and drink is unparalleled. I am also indebted to the many members of the Association for the Study of Food and Society and the Society for the Anthropology of Food and Nutrition, whose conversations enlightened me, encouraged me and set me straight when I had followed too closely a flight of fancy. Many thanks are also due to William Fitts, who took many of the photographs that illustrate this volume. And finally, I thank everyone with whom I've ever raised a glass … those experiences in social drinking were distilled to become this volume.

Above all I must thank my husband, Larry Chrzan, who supported me literally, emotionally and editorially throughout every page of this book. He read every chapter and made superb suggestions, corrected purple prose and eliminated many superfluous semi-colons. He made this book possible. Thank you.

1

INTRODUCTION

Why is Drinking Interesting?

Wine does not intoxicate men; men intoxicate themselves.

Chinese proverb

SCENE ONE

It's Saturday night on campus, and you are a rising senior returning after summer break. While walking through the main walkway of your college at about 9pm you notice a girl (God, they are getting younger looking every year!) vomiting into a bush. She's having a hard time holding herself up, keeps pitching forward into the leaves of the shrubbery and there is vomit in her hair. You shake your head and walk past, remembering how stupid you were at New Student Orientation when you were a freshman and glad you aren't stupid enough anymore to get sick in public.

SCENE TWO

It's later that night and you are pre-gaming with your friends, playing beer pong and taking shots of vodka and kahlua before you go to a house party. It's the same group you've been hanging out with for the last three years – you have lots of war stories – and you are winning the beer pong game. Your house added some new rules and the losers of each round have to drink a shot of the vodka mix when they step down from the table. The living room of your house is littered with red solo cups, small clear plastic cups for shots, and the floor is sticky from a spilled bottle of kahlua. At midnight you all decide it's time to go to the party and everyone troops outside. You realize that even though you won the game you are really feeling the booze – must have been the sympathy shots you took with the losers – you are totally dizzy and feel ill. You lean over the rail of the front porch and vomit into the bushes, glad you got that taken care of before you got to the party. Boot and rally. Grabbing another beer to wash the taste out of your mouth and closing one eye to make it easier to see, you follow your friends down the street, hoping your roommate remembers how to get to the party.

SCENE THREE

It's 7pm on Initiation night at your sorority, when parents meet all the new sisters. The parents are in the living room with appetizers and glasses of alcohol-free punch, chatting while waiting for their daughters to be formally 'presented'. The 4pm initiation ceremony was quite a surprise – your hands were bound, you were blindfolded with a scarf and a pillow case was placed over your head. You were then made to walk up and down stairs and around the chapter house for about a half hour until you were completely confused and didn't know where you were. You finally ended up in what felt like a big room and you could hear lots of girls talking. You were pushed into position and told to stand still during the ceremony, which consisted of a lot of questions about the history of the house and then a group rendition of the chapter's anthem. The pillow case was ripped off your head and your big sister stood in front of you with a big glass of tequila; you realized you were in the basement. All the bigs were in front of their littles in a circle, and were chanting "drink, drink, drink!" as they held the glass to their little's mouths. Your hands were tied so you couldn't hold the glass, but you were glad that your big let you take big breaths in between gulps of the fiery liquid. After everyone finished the drinks hands were untied and the pledges pronounced Active Members. Your big took you upstairs into her suite and she and her roommates had more drinks for their littles, so you got ready for the party while singing along to favorite songs and taking shots. When it was time to go downstairs to meet all the parents you realized your legs were wobbly and that you couldn't walk down the stairs. Shit, you were trashed. Could your parents smell the booze on your breath? Your big sister gave you some Listerine to gargle with and then held you up when you wobbled downstairs. Shit, how were you going to make it through the ceremony, reception and dinner without your parents figuring out you were totally faced?

Student and Youth Drinking

How many of you can see yourself in those examples, or had a similar experience or two in college? Why are these episodes so believable? And finally, why do college students drink so much?

The drinking habits of students and youth have been deplored for thousands of years, providing humorous and moral tales at least as far back as the Greeks, who wrote drunken youth into comedic drama as a stock figure symbolizing callow licentiousness. Student intoxication is even credited with the creation of the legal and independent status of the university, as it supposedly arose from a drunken brawl in the twelfth century at the University of Paris. The apocryphal story involves a student riot caused by a dispute with a tavern-keeper. The students were thrown out of the tavern, but returned to destroy the business, and the riot that ensued damaged many buildings in Paris. In retaliation several students were captured and killed by the town watch. The student response was to go on strike, thereby causing economic losses to the townspeople who relied on college incomes. After two years the students returned, but only after the Pope granted the university self-governance under the protection of the Papacy. This freed the students from discipline by town magistrates and cemented the right of universities to self-governance. The perceived lack of control over student behavior and student misconduct has plagued relations between 'town' and 'gown' ever since. Many students assume that universities are safe areas free of supervisory control, or spaces of potential discipline-free transgression. At some colleges this is described as a 'bubble' that constructs a spatially defined zone where students are welcome to do as they please in safety and freedom. The experience of being a student in a kind of municipal 'free zone' can be encouraged by university police departments that often look the other way when students transgress civic rules, including public drunkenness. When the bubble penetrates nightlife zones it becomes a liminal space where time-out activities are normalized, which reinforces the belief that the college years are a period where drunken excesses are safe and normal (Sperber, 2000: 192–200; Wolburg, 2001; Chatterton and Hollands, 2003: 126–147; Grazian, 2008; Dowdall, 2009).

The belief that the college years are a time when out-of-control and intoxicated actions are acceptable has been reproduced by the media again and again, most evocatively in the movie *Animal House* and in television shows such as *Greek*, *The Real World*, and *Jersey Shore*. John Belushi's iconic downing of a bottle of bourbon in *Animal House* has come to symbolize the college experience. The advertising poster for the 2008 film *College* featured an image of a young man vomiting into a toilet with the accompanying text "Best. Weekend. Ever." The series *Greek* used a red solo cup as the logo for the show, with the cup mimicking a hot tub – with beer instead of water. The theme of fun drunkenness is reinforced with three attractive 'co-eds' popping out of the cup-as-hot-tub, arms in the air and bodies displayed. Accompanying them in the 'tub' are two very preppy-looking white males, one wearing a button-down shirt and the other bare-chested, presumably naked. On the outside of the red cup are three nerdy-looking males trying to get into the cup/tub. They are on the outside and aren't preppy, cool and white: one is fat, one is Black and one is wearing a pink inner tube that looks, from a distance, like a pink tutu. The message is crystal clear (if perhaps covered in foam): college is fun, girls are easy, and if you're a preppy white guy you are going to have a great time. The intricacies of the college social hierarchy are perfectly on display, and it's clear that anyone who is not attractive, fun-loving and drunk (and willing to get naked in a hot tub) isn't welcome.

Why Anthropology and Alcohol?

I first became interested in the anthropology of alcohol when I moved from San Francisco to the East Coast. I had always considered my California peer group to be on the high end of alcohol intake because we loved cocktails and parties, and everyone drank wine with dinner. I didn't know anyone who had problems with booze, but I knew a lot of people who drank a fair bit. But in my new city people drank more when they partied and there was more drunkenness. Whole evenings were devoted to drinking rather than to 'having a cocktail' and doing another activity, and this seemed common among students and townspeople. I realized that I was dealing with very different cultural norms about how alcohol fits into social life, and it seemed to be an 'all or nothing' activity rather than a pleasant addition to an evening with friends.

Then I was asked to teach a harm-reduction medical anthropology course on alcohol to undergraduates. As I explored the anthropological, sociological and medical literature on drinking I realized the vast diversity in drinking habits around the world, and how lucky I had been to have grown up in a Mediterranean drinking culture. While I had enjoyed alcohol during my college years, few people at my California university seemed to place as much importance on drinking as did the students I was teaching. My students were exhibiting the binge behaviors more common among Northern European cultures, and were often getting in trouble and experiencing consequences caused by intoxication. To help students situate their use historically and culturally – and to question their beliefs about how they should drink – I had them keep diaries and write ethnographies of college parties. They had to go to the party sober and experience it as if it was another culture, which probably wasn't too difficult given that for many it was the first time they had experienced a party without being intoxicated. Their reflections about what they witnessed provided opportunities for in-class discussions about boundaries, drunkenness, acceptable behavior and keeping safe while drinking. These discussions also made crystal clear that how students drank was a product of their culture, and that most regarded alcohol as a drug and used it as such. Many had no concept that there was any other way to use alcohol or that people in other places and times had been able to enjoy alcohol in moderation without consequences. Their drinking was a product of student culture that made no sense to me, having been brought up in another culture with different drinking habits. Teaching the class cemented my understanding that drinking alcohol was a deeply cultural act with variations determined by social expectations.

Anthropology studies human beings holistically, from biology to psychology. Anthropologists usually divide this examination into four 'fields' of study – physical, socio-cultural, linguistic and archeological – but recognize that all four areas are important to understanding human cultural systems. Each of these fields has connections to other disciplines as well; physical anthropologists often do research in biology, public health or medicine, socio-cultural anthropologists study how belief systems and cultural structures affect individuals and societies, and linguistic anthropologists are interested in how language, images and folklore shape culture – and how culture shapes language use and perception of the world. And everyone knows that archeologists dig up old stuff: human remains, clay pots and treasure from ancient civilizations. But anthropologists also understand that their particular area is just one part of an interconnected discipline that explores how human cultures function and influence the individuals within them. Individuals are understood to have singular identities and personalities shaped by the knowledge and history of their culture. Individuals do not stand alone – they inhabit the past and create the future because they represent the embodied knowledge of prior generations and transmit these cultural practices to their children.

Drinking alcohol is both a physical and a cultural act. The physical response is well known and almost everyone can recognize when someone is drunk. Once an individual has experienced alcohol he or she understands its biological effects intimately, from the first burn upon the lips to the giddy feeling of intoxication. But drinking alcohol is also a deeply cultural act and every society has different rules for use. Anthropology acknowledges that wide cultural variations exist for almost every form of social practice, and each culture's beliefs and forms of behavior render its rules rational. Cultures have overlapping norms of belief and behavior across multiple fields of human action that mutually reinforce the 'rightness' of specific ways of seeing the world and interacting with others. For instance, religious and socio-economic structures and beliefs support many different cultural practices in addition to those tied directly to religion, social structure and economics. Each culture's rules present a reasonably holistic cultural package to those who have learned how to be human in that society. As a result, there is much variation in rules and expectations of alcohol from culture to culture – this can make drinking with someone from another culture quite an adventure. But because alcohol also has distinct and predictable physical effects there is similarity across cultures as well. Dwight Heath has spent decades studying how different cultures use alcohol, and he maintains that there are predictable rules that operate in every culture that uses alcohol:

1. In most societies, drinking is a social act, embedded in a context of values, attitudes and other norms.
2. These values, norms and attitudes influence the effects of drinking, regardless of how important biochemical, physiological and pharmacokinetic factors may also be to the experience of drinking.

3. The drinking of alcoholic beverages tends to be hedged with rules. Often such rules are the focus of exceptionally strong emotions and sanctions.
4. The value of alcohol for promoting relaxation and sociability is emphasized in many populations and most populations treat alcohol intake as an act of celebration or something appropriate for celebrations.
5. The association of drinking with any kind of specifically associated problems is rare among cultures throughout both history and the contemporary world.
6. When alcohol-related problems do occur, they are clearly linked with modalities of drinking, and usually also with values, attitudes and norms about drinking. What is normal for consumption defines the abnormal that is considered a problem. Societies that consider drunkenness shameful or disgusting usually have less incidence of intoxication.
7. Attempts at prohibiting alcohol use (like Prohibition) have never been successful except when couched in terms of sacred or supernatural rules.
8. In cultures where drinking is considered heroic, masculine or desirable it tends to be embraced. These positive evaluations may provide little defense against the risks and dangers of excessive drinking.
9. Societies in which alcohol is disallowed to the young, and in which alcohol is considered to enhance the self by conferring sex appeal or power, tend to have youth who drink too much, too fast, for inappropriate or unrealistic reasons.

Heath (2000: 196–198)

American beliefs about alcohol tend to grant it heroic status, restrict it from youth and tolerate drunken behavior. According to Heath's observations, it is a cultural trifecta almost perfectly designed to encourage abuse among youth. And predictably, in the United States alcohol has been regarded as both a blessing and a curse. During the colonial period beer and cider were important sources of nutrients and fluids for men, women and children and were considered to be necessary beverages for all ages. The rise of Temperance changed American ideas about alcohol during the nineteenth century. While the original intent of the Temperance organizers was to encourage drunkards to reform by giving up hard alcohol (spirits), over time it morphed into a political and religious movement to outlaw production, distribution and use of alcohol entirely. Beliefs about alcohol shifted from a healthful and enjoyable beverage to a dangerous and seductive drug. That belief predominates in the United States today, even though alcohol is legal in all 50 states and bars and liquor stores are present in most cities and towns.

Re-imaging alcohol as a drug ignores many thousands of years of more positive human use. Alcohol has been an important agricultural product and a good source of calories since grain and grape were first fermented. Archeological and historical evidence suggests that alcohol was considered a food by most cultures until distilled spirits, which have a far higher alcohol content, became a common tipple. Alcohol has been incorporated into religious and secular rituals and has been used to produce, consolidate and display economic and social power. While the dangers of alcohol always have been recognized, the value of the social and nutritional functions to early agricultural societies guaranteed that alcohol remained on the table and that appropriate social rules were developed to limit its danger to individuals and communities. Because early farmers may not have produced grains in great enough quantities to allow frequent beer or wine production, and since most rural and traditional societies expect people to drink together and in public, it is possible that abuse and addiction were infrequent. Alcoholism may very well have been almost unknown in ancient societies, although the consequences of over-use and abuse would have been obvious. Early texts do not hesitate to describe the joys and dangers of drunkenness, and to assign shame to bad behavior enabled by drink.

The nature of our relationship with alcohol changed after the development of distillation, and especially when hard alcohol became an important economic trade item. For the first time in history alcohol was cheap and concentrated enough to encourage easy intoxication on a regular basis – only a few shots and the drinker could be nearly insensible. The low alcohol content of beer means that drinking a sufficient volume for extreme intoxication may overwhelm the capacity of the stomach and cause vomiting. Wine is stronger than beer, and most wine-drinking cultures have social rules about how, when, where and how much to drink. Spirits are cheap to produce, easy to store and trade, and enable fast and dangerous drinking. The Temperance Movement in the United States initially was intended to end intake of spirits, not beer and wine, because its founders perceived that hard alcohol acted differently in the body and mind than did the traditional lower-alcohol beverages.

The United States is one of a handful of countries that have implemented a secular ban on alcohol sales. Trade in alcohol has been legal since 1933 but many of the ideas encouraged by the Temperance Movement are still present and active among our people; alcohol is viewed by many as a dangerous drug and roughly 30 percent of adults choose not to drink. Prohibition (the period during which trade in alcohol was made illegal in the United States after the enactment of the Eighteenth Amendment in 1920) fueled a nation-wide cocktail culture that glorified speakeasies, jazz clubs, sophisticated nightlife and the martini. Hollywood romanticized drinking from the 1930s through the 1980s, when the neo-temperance movement once again made alcohol déclassé. But bars, nightclubs and drinking events remain an important part of American social lives and national identity, and taking a first legal drink at age 21 remains an important rite of passage. Alcohol advertising is found in every form of media, and teens and youth recognize promotional characters such as the Budweiser frogs and Captain Morgan. Even though alcohol is proscribed to those under 21, it is widely understood and accepted that teens and young adults drink illegally. Because drinking has become such an expected part of college life and because many college students are not yet old enough to legally drink, college drinking is considered to be a national problem by parents and university administrators. To college students, drinking is an easy way to have a great time with friends, meet possible romantic partners and prove maturity, all at once. Sure, there are consequences, and sometimes people get sick, or get into a fight, or fall down and get hurt. But it's all good fun, the student says. But surveying the typical wreckage of a college campus on a Saturday morning, it's tempting to ask: "Are college students drinking too much?"

This book examines alcohol intake in Europe, the United States and among college students by exploring how cultural patterns influence drinking habits. Evidence from archeology, history, literature and ethnography is used to argue that how we drink is influenced by cultural expectations of social behavior. In looking at the history of the Old World it is clear that alcohol functioned as a food item as well as an intoxicant, and because it was an important source of calories its use was bounded by rules about intake and behavior in order to decrease the dangers of abuse. Current drinking patterns in the Unites States are influenced by our particular social development as a colony established at the same time that spirits became a common drink; unlike European cultures that had a tradition of using beer and wine as everyday foods and could contrast such use with that of distilled alcohol, the young United States was established during the period in which spirits were causing widespread problems in both the Old and New Worlds. Additionally, drinking alcohol in the modern world of branded consumption has become a performance that signals social and economic characteristics of the self (unlike our ancestors who drank a local beer and probably not much else), so what you drink and where and how you drink it becomes a matter of great social importance. Drinking alcohol has increasingly become part of the crafting of what is sometimes labeled 'the branded self'. Modern Americans use alcohol to signal something about them-selves to others; like many consumer items it can be used to construct a sense of self while also communicating scripted personal qualities to other people. In the modern consumerist world, alcohol use – much like language, clothing and other purchased and displayed goods – becomes a semiotic text manipulated to convey social meanings. Why and how this came about and how it influences current drinking is the focus of this book.

Starting at the beginning of time – or at least the beginning of fermentation – Chapter 2 examines archeological and textual evidence for alcohol use in

Europe and the Near East. Greek wine culture is used to highlight the development of social boundaries and mores that inhibit misuse of alcohol among Mediterranean peoples. Chapter 3 moves to Western Europe to chronicle how alcohol and its paraphernalia (glasses, mixing bowls and drinking horns) were used to convey power among Celtic and Germanic tribes and how those cultural expressions are preserved in rituals and social habits among modern peoples. In Europe and early America alcohol, especially beer and cider, was an important source of calories and was considered to be a form of food; the advent of widespread distillation shifted categorization of alcohol from food to mere – and dangerous – drug. This shift in perception about alcohol is explored in Chapter 4, which looks at the history of American drinking to better understand why and how we have come to think of alcohol as we do today. Chapter 5 uses sociological and anthropological theory to place drinking within cultural concepts of time and space to explain how phrases such as "what happens in Vegas stays in Vegas" came to be meaningful to almost all Americans. These themes are continued in Chapter 6 through an analysis of alcohol advertising and how advertising provides a model for everyday use that calls upon the past to define appropriate utilization, while creating new expectations and patterns of consumption to increase sales. Finally, Chapter 7 explores the drinking habits of college students to lay bare why they drink, how they drink and what it accomplishes for them. College drinking is understood to be one expression of a larger cultural model for appropriate drinking behavior, rather than a time-defined period of excess that stands outside of normative (adult) patterns of use.

This book examines drinking habits from prehistory to the present by focusing on how we think about alcohol and how that affects how and why we drink. Beliefs and practices developed in the ancient and early modern world have influenced how people perceive and use alcohol, even in modern America. Attitudes formed in earlier times influence what we do on Friday night today – and why we do it. Through history and across cultures alcohol has been useful for far more than mere intoxication – it has been a food, a muse, a way to demonstrate economic and political power, and not least of all, a key ingredient in courting rituals. Ancient and modern cultures have recognized the power of alcohol to bind friends and create joy as well as cause damage and addiction. In this book we'll look at the culture of drinking so we can better understand our own use of alcohol.

2

ALCOHOL IN THE ANCIENT WORLD

Man, being reasonable, must get drunk;
The best of life is but intoxication.

Lord Byron, *Don Juan*, 1819

Wine lays bare the heart of man.

Athenaeus, *The Deipnosophists*, Book 2: 38

In the Beginning ... There Was Beer?

Much of what we know about how ancient peoples thought about the world comes to us in the form of stories. Archaic Greece becomes real in the words of Homer, the ancient Near East is partly knowable because of *The Epic of Gilgamesh* and the Old Testament offers tales about the lives of early Israelites. Fragments of poems, stories and hymns dating back millennia are a portal into extinct cultures because human beings make sense of their lives and experiences through the telling of tales that explain how the world works. To be able to tell a story requires the cognitive ability to project meaning, awareness and intent onto characters that are subjectively different than the self. The mental ability to be objective requires a far more complex awareness than do simple reactions to environmental stimuli and is a very special characteristic of being human.

Evidence that human beings could objectify the world around them is seen late in our evolutionary history, which does not mean that it didn't occur earlier; lack of evidence may be due to natural destruction of artifacts. Ancient cave paintings in Europe and Africa demonstrate that humankind realized the objectivity of existence by 30,000 years ago, and paint and possible jewelry fragments 100,000 years old from the African sites Border Cave and Klasies River Mouth Cave suggest that early people could think objectively about their bodies. It is reasonable to assume that storytelling is also ancient, but until the invention of the written word stories could not be transmitted for posterity. *The Epic of Gilgamesh* dates to approximately 2000 BC and is from Sumer, an ancient city-state in Mesopotamia. The story of Gilgamesh is important because it proposes that intoxication makes us human.

The protagonist, Gilgamesh, is an authoritarian and abusive king whose subjects pray to the gods for change. In response, the gods send a half man/half beast named Enkidu who lacks self-awareness and knowledge of clothing, language and civilized eating. Enkidu must be tamed before he can become a friend (a metaphor for taking on culture) so Gilgamesh tempts him with sex, beer and bread – three very powerful and iconic symbols of being social.

> Enkidu knew nothing about eating bread for food, and of drinking beer he had not been taught.
> The harlot spoke to Enkidu, saying:
> "Eat the food, Enkidu, it is the way one lives.
> Drink the beer, as is the custom of the land."
> Enkidu ate the food until he was sated,
> he drank the beer-seven jugs!—and became expansive and sang with joy!
> He was elated and his face glowed.
> He splashed his shaggy body with water, and rubbed himself with oil, and turned into a human.
>
> *Gilgamesh Epic Two, Old Babylonian Version,* in Maureen Kovacs (Trans.)
> *The Epic of Gilgamesh,* 1985: 16

Enkidu becomes human through awareness of self ("he became expansive and sang with joy") and because he adopts the habits of humanity by consorting with a woman, eating bread, drinking beer and bathing. He is then transformed into a young man who becomes Gilgamesh's companion and whose friendship tempers the king's bad behavior.

Certainly the metaphor of how culture is acquired, and how culture makes us human, is important to this tale. But even more important is how Enkidu becomes aware of himself through intoxication. Implied in this passage is that self-awareness is promoted by a difference in subjectivity. Descartes famously reasoned "Cogito ergo sum" and embedded in "I think, therefore I am" is the awareness of thinking, which implies an awareness of the self doing the thinking. Enkidu becomes subjective through awareness of a different state of mental activity when his sense of self was altered by intoxication. Perhaps the ancient Sumerians thought that self-knowledge could come about through intoxication because it promotes seeing the world and the self differently; drugs are used in many cultures to open up the mind to enhanced awareness. The text reveals that the Sumerians had a sophisticated knowledge of cognitive awareness, perhaps indicating long association with intoxication and an appreciation of the value of such experiences.

Alcohol and Consciousness

In *Uncorking the Past,* Patrick McGovern suggests that intoxication may have played a significant role in the development of human culture and art (McGovern, 2009: 16). Although we lack proof of intentional fermentation until the Neolithic, he notes that cave art indicates that early peoples might have been enjoying alcoholic beverages. Not far from Lascaux, France, is a 20,000 year old carved bas relief of a bountiful female figure holding a horn with the wide end pointed toward her face (the *Vénus à la corne de Laussel* from the Collection Musée d'Aquitaine). If the image was designed to convey the idea that the figure was blowing the horn to make music, the narrow end would be closest to her mouth. But she appears to be raising the horn to her lips; the angle is exactly what would be expected just prior to taking a sip. One of the earliest and most natural receptacles for holding liquids (after cupped hands) would be an animal horn. The horn later becomes a symbol of alcoholic intake – we find them as burial goods in many cultures and to this very day horn-shaped cups are sold for harvest-period drinking parties throughout Europe. Through much of the ancient world the *rhyton* (the Greek name for a horn-shaped cup) was used exclusively for alcohol and in religious ritual or to display political power. That the horn depicted in the ancient French bas relief was for drinking alcohol is of course pure supposition, but is reasonable given the later history and cultural significance of the horn-shaped cup.

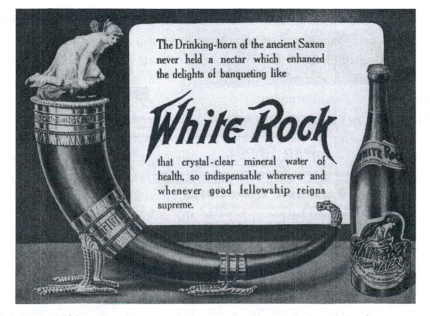

Figure 2.1 **Early 1900s advertisement that uses the iconography of the horn to promote a brand of bottled water.** (*Source:* Collection of the author.)

McGovern argues that intoxication could lead to forms of cultural expression such as music and art, as suggested by cave paintings and bone flutes found in the ancient caves. His reasoning is conjectural but worth considering; he argues that intoxication can encourage community bonding through social rituals (including music-making and art) and foster the development of religious mythology through altered states of mind. And who is to say he is wrong? Certainly many religions have utilized intoxicants to create visions for shamans and worshipers. In many cultures hallucinations are considered messages from the divine, and so it is reasonable to imagine ancient people developing religious practices in response to altered states of being. McGovern states "I contend ... that the driving forces in human development from the Paleolithic period to the present have been the uniquely human traits of self-consciousness, innovation, the arts and religion, all of which can be heightened and encouraged by the consumption of an alcoholic beverage with its profound effects in the human brain" (McGovern, 2009: 17). Katherine Milton, a physical anthropologist who has studied human and primate dietary physiology, reasons that human societies adopted the use of alcohol as part of an overall dietary regime and that the sweet taste of fermented beverages may have encouraged intake. She also suggests that because humans are self-aware they may wish for relief from subjectivity: "Humans also appear to be the only animals with a highly developed sense of self-awareness and thus they may be the only animals that might wish to escape from their own consciousness. Ethanol offers humans this psychopharmacologic effect" (Milton, 2004: 312).

Alcohol and Agriculture

The earliest evidence of intentional brewing has been found in China, at a Neolithic site called Jiahu. Dating to 7000–5600 BC, Jiahu yielded pots that contained residues of a potent beverage made of grape and hawthorn fruit wine, honey mead and rice beer (McGovern et al., 2005; McGovern 2009: 19). Archeological discoveries from the site indicate that rice was cultivated and that the village was settled and agricultural. By 9000 years ago humans in China had developed complex agricultural systems that produced enough extra grain that some could be used for alcohol. Accompanying the production of alcohol was a diversification of pottery forms and probable social (and perhaps religious) rituals that utilized intoxicants. Pat McGovern worked with Sam Calagione of Dogfish Head Brewery to recreate the Jiahu recipe using hawthorn fruit, muscat grapes, honey and rice malt. 'Chateau Jiahu' is a bit odd in flavor but pairs well with food – you could (almost) replicate the effect by mixing a robust white wine with sake and beer, adding honey, a few drops of bitters and allowing a second fermentation until it becomes mildly bubbly.

Other areas of the old world have yielded early examples of beer-brewing and wine-making, especially the Near East and the Anatolian peninsula. Archeological studies at Hajji Firuz Tepe in Iran provided pots containing wine and beer residues dating to 5400–5000 BC, causing scholars to hypothesize that wine-making radiated out of Anatolia along with *Vitis vinifera*, the domesticated grape species most typically used to produce wine (McGovern, 2009: 74–75). This supposition is supported by the earliest known word for wine (*woi-no*), which comes from the proto-Indo-European language of eastern Turkey. *Woi-no* later morphs into *oinos* in Greek and *vinum* (pronounced wee-num) in Latin. The English word 'wine' was derived from the Latin.

The Near East was the epicenter of the domestication of wheat and barley and a very likely site for the development of beer-brewing. Solomon Katz and Mary Voigt (Katz and Voigt, 1986) have argued that beer-making might have jump-started early farming because beer and bread were essential for the development of early societies. The archeological record indicates that both bread and beer were important to early Near East cultures, and Katz and Voigt suggest that there are very good cultural and nutritional reasons for a society to make beer. When considering their arguments, it's important to understand that because of the brewing technologies available at the time the beer available probably had an alcohol content of only two or three percent, so getting thoroughly drunk would have been very difficult. Certainly a state of tipsiness would have occurred, but not the sort of

Figure 2.2 **Wine set from Tell-es Sa'idiyeh, tomb 101 (late Bronze Age, 1300–1200 BC).** (*Source*: Courtesy of the University of Pennsylvania Museum of Archaeology and Anthropology.)

inebriation caused by shots of tequila or a few martinis, because stomach capacity would have inhibited extreme intoxication. Katz and Voigt also maintain that there are some excellent nutritional reasons for drinking beer. Beer is high in easily absorbed calories, which is good if you are a hard-working farmer. Drinking a few beers provides far more fuel quickly and with less physiological effort than chewing and digesting bread. Beer provides B vitamins and protein (from yeast bodies), decreases phytate ingestion (in comparison with bread) and increases zinc absorption. High levels of phytate in grain-based diets can inhibit absorption of zinc, which can constrain physical growth and cause delays in sexual maturation. Beer also provides a reasonably safe form of fluid intake in settled environments where sewage may have fouled the water supplies.

In most ancient agricultural sites both bread and beer are found and both probably evolved from gruels. Bread and beer are linked in the cuisines of the early farming peoples because bread-baking and beer-making are similar and the same grain can be a source of gruel, bread, beer or (later in time) whiskey; only the processing differs (Dietler, 2006). Beer-making requires that grain be soaked, malted and allowed to ferment, while bread requires grinding, fermentation with yeast and baking, although not all breads are made with yeast (Brothwell and Brothwell, 1969: 94–104). Furthermore, in the Near East and in Egypt some forms of early beer were made by crumbling bread loaves into water and adding yeast to start fermentation (Katz and Maytag, 1991; Cantrell, 2000: 620; Nelson, 2005: 10–11). It is no accident that most bread-based cultures are also beer-drinking cultures, since the ecology of grain production would channel the development of regional cuisines. Soils good for growing grain tend to be too good for grape production, and drinks made from the grains used for daily breads or gruels would be favored for the making of intoxicants. In addition, most bread is dry and bread-eaters tend to add oil or butter and to drink fluids with a bread meal in order to wash down the grain products. Until quite recently much of Northern Europe relied on bread and beer for daily calories, often (and hopefully) accompanied by small portions of vegetables and meat. Beer and bread have been natural partners for most grain-producing peoples from the start of agriculture, since beer provides a pleasurable means to help masticate bread.

Alcohol and Community Cohesion

The mild intoxication created by beer can also improve social relations and provide psychological benefits that encourage community development. Katz and Voigt (1986) reason that cultures that drink beer become more cohesive because of the elevating effects of small amounts of alcohol, and that the resulting good feelings would encourage social bonding and interaction in work, warfare and religion. Pointing out that every group that uses alcohol also creates complex rules and rituals for its use, Katz and Voigt propose that beer-making may have played a role in domestication of grain because cultures that relied on wild plants for supply of ritually important grains may have taken steps to ensure a ready supply through deliberate distribution of seed. Above all, they reason that population groups that use beer would have had a Darwinian selective advantage in relation to other groups and would have been more likely to survive and persist in early environments due to increased calorie and nutrient intake, and better physical and social health.

The importance of mind-altering substances to the development of early cultures cannot be ignored since almost all societies have adopted some form of intoxicant. Often their employment of a drug is not recreational, as we think of such use today. Sherratt (1995: 15) explains "the use of psychoactive substances covers a spectrum of practices which from a modern, Western point of view might be described as religious, medical and secular. And where only one such substance is available to a society, it may indeed combine all three aspects – although 'secular' uses are likely to be subject to contextually appropriate use and prescription." Ancient use probably transcended modern categorical dichotomies such as 'food' and 'drug', and intoxicants would have played multiple economic and social roles within each cultural field of action. Utilization became widespread because it developed into a social marker constructed by practical choice of substance (appropriate choice and preparation), level of experience (learning how to produce an appropriate response, socially and pharmacologically), and the social assignment of contextual meaning to the act

Figure 2.3 **Glass wine cup from Syria-Palestine (300 AD).** (*Source:* Courtesy of the University of Pennsylvania Museum of Archaeology and Anthropology.)

of consumption. Users gain cultural and social capital from knowing what, how, when, why and how much to take of available intoxicants, as well as how to react appropriately when under the influence.

For example, many people in the United States admire those who know about wine and can choose the right vintage, pair it with foods, appreciate flavors and aromas, and talk about it intelligently. Wine is secular (with a meal, at a party), religious (Sabbath and Passover dinners, Catholic and Protestant communion), and medicinal (reputed to aid in the production of 'good' lipids in the bloodstream). We, as cultural agents, instinctively know when someone is using wine appropriately, and more important, we know when they are not. The person who is knowledgeable about wine is thought of as sophisticated and worldly; using wine properly is one of the markers of a 'successful' person because becoming a connoisseur requires effort, time and *lots* of money. So in the Western world 'knowing about wine' has become a marker of someone who is culturally and economically successful, and using wine a sign of celebration and cultural capital. Wine sales are fueled by cultural acceptance and admiration. No doubt a similar process occurred in the ancient world and encouraged the further use of alcohol in social and religious settings.

Sherratt agrees with Katz and Voigt's argument that alcohol improves social cohesion, and writes "to consume a certain substance in a certain way embodies a statement, but this assertion can be either accepted or controverted by others involved in the process of social reproduction. 'Acceptable practice' thus evolves through a constant network of negotiations and serves to define the identities of individuals and groups" (Sherratt, 1995: 12). Intoxicant use becomes a marker for group belonging, and can map subtle gradations of social categorization and power; knowledge and use of wine is a perfect example of this process. With whom you drink (and equally important, those with whom you'd never share a pub table) mark important social boundaries because each social category is defined in relation to other categories, and all members of a society understand the rules and the boundaries (see Douglas, 1987a, for a superb explanation of this process). Alcohol serves as a social boundary-maker for religious groups (Christians use wine in religious worship, while Muslims abjure all use of alcohol), social categories (people tend to drink in groups marked by age, gender and family), and even economic classes (the rich and the poor often drink very different beverages out of choice as well as necessity). All of these practices become central to processes of identity creation and, because they are material habits that contribute to creation of the self within the society, become permanently embedded in cultural life. They become necessary to the creation and maintenance of the social self because they help to define how individuals negotiate social rules. As Enkidu the wild man demonstrated, we drink because it socializes us.

The earliest use of alcohol by *Homo sapiens* is literally buried in the mists of time. The material culture – brewing and storage vessels, drinking cups, carvings and images that attest to use – remains, but the reasons for drinking, the beliefs that surround intake and the social boundaries of drinking behavior are lost forever. We can, however, reconstruct possible scenarios through the writings of early people, by analogy with current behavioral patterns and by analysis of material culture, and even reconstruct early beverages. We do know that alcohol use provides benefits in addition to inebriation, and that it allows for social practices that define and bring together groups of people, and we know that early people accepted intoxication for its own sake. We also know that early people valued alcohol as food, fluid, ritual object and psychological release and that they left us tantalizing stories about how they thought about drunkenness. But unfortunately we will never *really* know what it was like to 'drink like a Babylonian'.

Wine in Ancient Greece

The peoples of the Mediterranean began to emerge from barbarism when they learnt to cultivate the olive and the vine.

Thucydides, fifth century BC

Two spirits there be that in man's world are first of worth.
Demeter one is named; she is the Earth—
Call her which name thou will!—who feeds man's frame
With sustenance of things dry. And that which came
Her work to perfect, second, is the Power
From Semele born. He found the liquid show
Hid in the grape. He rests man's spirit dim
From grieving, when the vine exalteth him.

Euripides, *The Bacchae* (Murray, 1906: 94)

To the Ancient Greeks wine was so central to existence that they had a god of wine. Dionysus, the god of the vine, of rejuvenation and of the underworld, was one of the 12 Olympian gods whose whims and desires determined Greek culture, economy and religious practice (Dalby, 2003; Graves, 1960: 19–21). When a Greek placed cup to lip he was not merely enjoying an intoxicating beverage, he was drinking a god (Johnson, 1989: 47–58). Wine was an object of religious veneration and an essential economic product used as food, medicine and to inspire poetry, good fellowship and lust. With oil and wheat it formed the backbone of the Mediterranean economy, and it encouraged the growth of

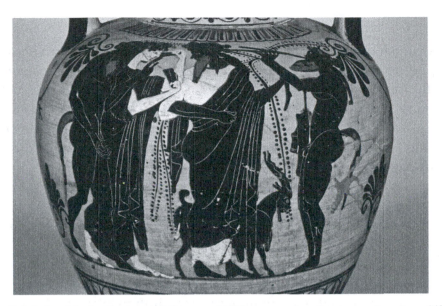

Figure 2.4 **Attic black figure amphora of Dionysus, bacchante and satyr (525–500 BC).** (*Source:* Courtesy of the University of Pennsylvania Museum of Archaeology and Anthropology.)

sophisticated trade relationships, the development and expansion of a mercantile naval fleet, and even the military organization and naval resources necessary to protect that mercantile fleet. Wine was a cornerstone of Greek religion, economy, social life and diet.

Each spring the Greeks threw a festival to honor Dionysus with drama contests, dancing, feasts and drinking. During the festival the entire population stopped work to enjoy municipal entertainment, dances and other revelry, much of it bawdy or intended to turn the everyday upside down in rituals of reversal. Plays often covered taboo or comic subjects (Bowie, 1995; Konstantakos, 2005) such as women and slaves taking over the government or displays of public drunkenness by scholars and politicians. The streets of Athens were filled with intoxicated partiers. Spring festivals of this type occur in many cultures and are often rituals of rebirth that herald a new year and a new growing season. They are also rituals of reversal, or structure and anti-structure (Turner, 1969) in which good becomes bad, bad is good, and citizens can let loose and behave in an abandoned manner for a prescribed period of time. Examples of such modern-day rituals include Carnival, Mardi Gras and Spring Break, and in each participants are allowed to act outside of character for a period of time without social consequence. Among the Greeks, revelers could get drunk in public, insult politicians and mock the gods – all without social consequences because of intoxication. It was an early version of "what happens in Vegas stays in Vegas" … "what happens at the Dionysian Festival stays in Athens"!

Symposia, Drama and Drunkenness

We know what the Greeks valued and what they condemned in part because the plays performed during the Festival portrayed drunkenness as comedic and shameful and associated intoxication with unmanly and lower-class behavior. The dramas of the Festival functioned to represent 'good Greek citizenship' by marking antisocial activities such as drunkenness and gender reversals as humorous, disgusting and ridiculous. For instance, in one play, the author Eubulus has Dionysus define the limits of responsible drinking by a chronicle of what goes wrong when too much is enjoyed:

> Three kraters only do I propose for sensible men, one for health, the second for love and pleasure and the third for sleep; when this has been drunk up, wise guests make for home. The fourth krater is mine no longer, but belongs to hubris; the fifth to shouting; the sixth to revel; the seventh to black eyes; the eighth to summonses; the ninth to bile; and the tenth to madness and people tossing the furniture about.

Quoted in Davidson (1997: 47–48)

The clear demarcation between good drinking and bad is that fourth cup, the one that no longer belongs to the god but to the hubris of man, who challenges the gods for supremacy and control. To the Greeks, the appropriate management of the tension between civility and control and their obverse was the essential quality of the good citizen, and so intoxication served to mark the differences between good and bad behavior and the good and bad person.

One way a Greek male was able to prove himself a good citizen was by behaving with honor in symposia, which were male-only events devoted to drinking, conversation, poetry and story-telling. Knowing how to behave in a symposium was a learned process and young men were specifically educated in proper comportment (Booth, 1991). They had to know how to converse, how to sing and make poetry, and how to drink appropriately (Pellizer, 1990; Vetta, 1999). The symposiarch, usually the eldest or most elite man at the party, would decide how many 'kraters' of wine were to be drunk, how much water should be used to dilute the wine and the theme of the poetry or stories to be told. A krater was a large bowl used to mix water and wine, often decorated with drinking or martial images. The first cup of wine was poured uncut, and dedicated to Agaithos Daimon (the high god), and then three kraters were mixed to be shared. The first was dedicated to the Olympians, the second to the Homeric warriors and the third honored Zeus. These ritualized toasts marked the party as a formal occasion in which participants honored the gods, emulated the Archaic heroes and appropriated some of the gravitas and grandeur of those so honored

(Murray, 1983 and 1991). Equality was the core value of the symposium and all participants were expected to drink the same amount and entertain each other with witty stories and tales of adventure. As the night wore on the drinkers enjoyed the songs and acrobatics of hired performers, and some would slip into sleep or sneak out with a comely flute girl – for the symposium was an acknowledged space for elite men to engage in (semi)public sex (Pellizer, 1990). On some occasions the event degenerated into a *komos*, a raucous party that spilled out of the house with flute players and dancers leading the now-merry band of aristocratic drunks into the surrounding streets, slave boys following with wine jugs and amphorae to slake the revelers' thirst (Murray, 1990; Rosler, 1995; Vetta, 1999; Smith, 2003: 1–46).

We know so much about Greek symposia because in addition to plays and poetry about drinking, the Ancient Greeks left behind painted pottery and drinking equipment with symposium images (Lissarrague, 1990). The symposium is a simulacrum of the banquet that occurs after a battle, and so all signs of war are to be banished (Vetta, 1999). Shields and swords are shown hanging on the walls to demonstrate that the drinkers have no need of weaponry.

Figure 2.5 **Youth playing *kottobos*, a Greek drinking game.** (*Source*: Courtesy of the University of Pennsylvania Museum of Archaeology and Anthropology.)

Wine glasses are shared because the drinkers are brothers in cups, if not arms, but perhaps the cups stand metaphorically for the arms (Murray, 1983, 1990 and 1991). Wine is watered and served in shallow bowls that require some measure of sobriety to use without spilling. Davidson argues that the deep rhyton-shaped cups found in taverns were so reviled that they were often painted or sculpted with monsters, deformed humans, barbarians and slaves to signify that they rendered men insensible (Davidson, 1997: 53–69). Deep cups were never permitted in symposia because they negated the symbolic values of the event. The symposium stands as the primary example of the good side of wine (and indeed, the good or civilized side of people), and the evening's flirting with drunkenness serves to highlight the self-control and moderation expected of a good Greek citizen. Just as war creates heroes, peace provides stable governance and wealth, as demonstrated in this passage by Aristophanes, from *The Acharnians*:

> Never will I welcome War into my home, never will he sing Harmodius reclining by my side, because he's nothing but a troublemaker when he's drunk. This is the fellow who burst upon our prosperity, like a komast, wreaking all manner of destruction, knocking things over, spilling wine and brawling, and still, when we implored him repeatedly, "Drink, recline, take the cup of friendship" still more did he set fire to our trellises, and violently spilled the wine from our vines.
>
> Quoted in Davidson (1997: 49)

Wine stands here as a symbol of prosperity as well as of destruction; War spills wine from the vines, destroying the economy, and refuses the symposium cup of friendship and vow of equality and peace. But wine allows War his destructive capacities because he is rendered insensible with intoxication. The good citizen must carefully mediate between these two extremes.

Wine in Greek Agriculture and Economy

In contrast to the dangers of symposium drinking, there is very little written about daily drinking with meals. Probably when wine was part of a meal it was considered to be food, so the dangers of intoxication were lessened in comparison with the drug-like intake of the symposium. The Greek myths about the founding of Athens underline the importance of wine as a food, since each of the primary food commodities were attributed to the favor of a god. Dionysus brought wine and Demeter, the Mother-Goddess and Goddess of the Harvest, brought grain to the Greeks; like Dionysus she is also a goddess of birth and death, and of the seasons. Olive oil, the final tripod of the Greek economy, was given by Athena, the Goddess of Wisdom. Wine, grain and olive oil formed the core of the Greek economy and diet, and the Greek states exported these commodities through the Mediterranean and beyond. To this day Greece is a primary producer of wine and olive oil, with 129,000 hectares under vines (as of the year 2000), producing 3.5 million hectoliters annually (Budd, 2003). In 2010 wheat was the first, olive oil the fifth and wine the seventh most important crops for Greece (CIA World Factbook, 2010). Olive oil remains the primary cooking oil and modern Greeks drink approximately 30 liters of wine per person each year (Budd, 2003).

The importance of all three foods to the diet and health of the Greeks cannot be underestimated. The ecology of the Greek peninsula and islands is dry and rocky. While reading Homer may encourage us to think that the Greeks lived on meat, bread and wine, the more prosaic truth was probably wheat gruel, beans, greens and wine (Dalby and Grainger, 1996; Amouretti, 1999). The land is dry and hilly, perfect for the cultivation of grapes and olive trees but not for the production of meat and grain. Since olives can be grown on the most inhospitable of hillsides and vines grow best in poor and rocky soil, better soils can be used to farm grain, pulses and vegetables. In Mediterranean regions the cultivation of olives and grapes provides a means to profit from scrubland. Both olive oil and wine, once processed, are valuable and rather compact export commodities; a common weight of oil or wine is far more valuable than a similar weight of grain. It was this trading opportunity that fueled the growth of Greek maritime trade, and made the early Greek city states wealthy and powerful.

Oil, grain and wine were augmented by side dishes made of beans, greens, vegetables and small amounts of meat or fish. While bread is commonly imagined to be the primary staple in most grain-growing regions, grains are frequently cooked as a pilaf or porridge, similar to the way rice is used in Chinese cuisine. The Greeks even had words to distinguish this staple food (*sitos*) from the accompaniment (*opson*) (Davidson, 1997). As with many diets based on grains the meal could be dry, and needed to be washed down with plenty of liquid – usually watered wine. Unfortunately, very little is written about wine used as food; perhaps the Greeks preferred to ponder only the dangerous qualities of wine, although this may be a simple skewing of data given that much of the information about drinking comes from dramas written for the Dionysian contests and the iconography of sympotic ware. Regardless, the Greeks wrote little about domestic meals, and there is very little information about daily wine-drinking, even though wine accompanies meals in the Homeric texts. Even in Plato's *Laws*, a work that covered aspects of health and diet, wine is referred to as a drug, as something to be consumed in moderation, rather than as a liquid to accompany food (Skiadas and Lascarato, 2001).

However, like all agricultural peoples in wine-growing regions, the Greeks drank wine with meals and like most Mediterranean people (and some peasant vintners today) they took their wine mixed with water. Here is a quote from Homer about a gift of wine to Odysseus: "Maron drew off for me sweet unmixed wine ... and whenever he drank the honeyed red wine, filling a cup he poured it into twenty measures of water, and a marvelous sweet smell rose from the mixing bowl" (quoted in Dalby and Grainger, 1996: 30). While they didn't understand germ theory, most ancient farming peoples recognized that plain water could be unsafe; it has only been since the advent of modern sewage and water treatment centers that water has been taken neat on a regular basis. Just as in the recent past, wine-making areas would have relied on watered wine (or, technically, wined water) for drinking throughout the day (Kelly-Blazeby, 2006: 55). Unfortunately, we have no handy dietaries for the Ancient Greeks or manifests of allotted foods as we do with other feudal agricultural peoples, and we have few accounts of Greek wine intake from archeologists or dietitians; almost all of our information comes from classicists interested in the ancient texts (Kelly-Blazeby, 2006). Regrettably, the ancient Greek writers were more concerned with the moral and political lives of drinkers than their nutriture.

Wine and Diet

To understand the role that wine may have played in diet we can triangulate by analogy with Roman and Cypriot records. Both regions possess a long history of wine production and share a climate similar to that of Greece (see Purcell, 1985, for a discussion of everyday use of wine during the Roman Empire). According to Tchernia (1986) who analyzed the wine allowance given to academics in Ancient Rome, senior scholars were given about 470 gallons a year while the rank and file were allotted 104 gallons annually (Fleming, 2001: 57). However, these amounts might have been part of salary and not meant to be drunk by the recipient. Rome was a patronage society and the wine allotment could have been meant for further division and sharing, considerably decreasing any individual amount. Tchernia (1986) used trade records to estimate that adults in Rome drank approximately 48 gallons per year; Fleming reworks these data using age structures to argue that likely Roman intake was closer to 23 gallons per head, a figure more in line with current Italian drinking habits (Fleming, 2001: 59). That's roughly eight ounces per day, or two small glasses of wine. However, this figure is for an urban population, and one that might not have been entirely dependent on wine for safe water supplies since Roman aqueducts supplied the city with potable water. Two glasses per day might not have been typical for rural populations competing with livestock and other humans for safe sources of liquid.

The island of Cyprus possesses similar ecological and farming conditions to Greece, and is a clear Mediterranean analog to other parts of the Greek archipelago. William Woys Weaver has analyzed late medieval estate records from the wheat-producing manor Psimolofou and reports that the wine allotment for working families in 1317 was 576 liters per year, while the bailiff received 240 liters per month and the justice of the peace 288 liters.

Clearly these amounts were not meant to be drunk by one person, but to be shared among family, retainers and servants (Weaver, 2008: 31–32). Given that this wine was purchased for the estate rather than produced, we must assume it was meant for the estate workers to consume rather than sell. What we do not know is how far the ration had to be shared; if it can be assumed that the head of the family shared his wine we can estimate his intake by a simple calculation of household age structure. If we hypothesize that such a worker would have used approximately one quarter of the wine himself, leaving one eighth for his wife, one quarter each for two adolescent or adult-aged working sons and the remaining eighth for other women or children, he might have drunk 144 liters per year. If each liter contains 33.8 ounces, then he could have had 13 ounces of wine a day, or approximately a scant three (small, modern-sized) glasses. This is 50 percent more than Fleming's calculation for the Roman urban classes, but consistent with the increased fluid needs of an agricultural worker (assuming, of course, that the wine would have been watered). While these figures are speculative, they do illustrate the importance of wine to the daily dietary intake of calories and liquid, for 13 ounces of wine could have provided approximately 260 calories, at 20 kcal per ounce. The more important service would have been rendering water supplies safe and palatable.

Even though these wine intake calculations are not from Ancient Greece they suggest a way to calculate the strength of Greek alcoholic beverages. Given that Greece is hot and dry, most wines would have been quite strong since heat produces high-sugar grapes and relatively strong wines. Because yeast dies when alcohol reaches roughly 16 percent, most Greek wines would have been in the range of 14 percent, similar to the high-alcohol red wines of Napa Valley. Watered at a ratio of three to one the wines would approximate modern commercial beers. Watered at a ratio of five to one would ensure a very mildly alcoholic beverage of approximately 2–3 percent, which is similar to the 'small beer' drunk by everyone in early modern Europe and Colonial America. In other words, it would have been unlikely to have caused drunkenness and social disruption, and would not have required morality texts to warn against excess intake. However, even if the wine served at a symposium was roughly equivalent to modern lager, anyone who has ever gone to college can tell you that cheap beer of 3.2 percent, if imbibed in sufficient volume, can cause all of the negative outcomes listed in Eubulus's play. Imbibing unwatered wine, drinking in taverns or out of deep cups as do foreigners, barbarians, women (allegedly) and slaves (Davidson, 1997: 53–69; Nelson, 2005: 38–40), failing to share a cup with others, or even mixing too many kraters at a symposium could render a drinker insensate, out of control and potentially dangerous. And that was what worried the aristocratic Greeks, since losing control was considered a symbol of bad citizenship and of 'conduct unbecoming to a gentleman'.

Figure 2.6 **Apulian white ground horse-headed rhyton, fourth century BC.** (*Source:* Courtesy of the University of Pennsylvania Museum of Archaeology and Anthropology.)

Conclusion

To the Ancient Greeks, appropriate use of wine defined the dichotomy between civilized behavior and alcoholic excess, and between peace and discord. It would not be amiss to argue that for the Greeks, wine was a 'total social fact' as theorized by Durkheim (1897 [1997]) and Mauss (1924 [1990]): an entity that interpenetrates multiple fields of social, legal, economic, political, medicinal and religious cultural action. Because wine was so important to the Greek economy, its role in Greek life was far greater than a mere intoxicant. Wine was an indispensible element of social, religious and political life and was endlessly discussed in drama, poetry and song. Greek doctors recognized the value of wine in treatment of medical conditions; Galen (discussed in Standage, 2005: 82–83) and Hippocrates (see Hippocrates *Regiment* ca. 460–370 BC) list many functions of wine as medicine in their treatises about medical care, as do other contemporary medical practitioners. Wine provided calories and a means to purify water, and allowed the Greeks to utilize land that otherwise would be barren. Given all these benefits, it is no wonder that the god of wine, Dionysus, was welcomed into the Olympian pantheon by Zeus himself (Graves, 1960: 19). The Greeks, as well as their gods, understood and appreciated the positive aspects of wine.

The Greeks also had no delusions about the negative properties of wine or the dangers of mindless intoxication. Philosophers and playwrights devoted page after page to exposing the problems of overindulgence, creating dramas that were the classical world's equivalent of Public Service Announcements about the dangers of drunkenness. Drunkenness was a popular comic theme that exposed the drunkard as a fool; the root of the term 'comedy' comes from *komos* (*komodia*), the Greek word for a drunken party. That the Greeks could embrace the good and worry about the bad in wine was possible because they possessed a nuanced understanding of the action of wine in the body – they recognized that alcohol was dose-dependent, and that the dose was up to the drinker. This is one of the most important reasons why alcohol is a popular, and usually legal 'drug'; unlike many intoxicants (cocaine, LSD, mushrooms, heroin, etc.) alcohol's effects are predictable, which gives alcohol a truly privileged status as a psychotropic (Sherratt, 1995). One, two or three drinks and the party is harmonious; more, and the revelry threatens to devolve into arguments, violence and behavior that hurts the drinker and society. It was this awareness that allowed the Greeks to embrace wine's benefits while warning about the excess that rendered it dangerous, and explains why their best philosophers wrote morality plays about intoxication. Because man is social, he is capable of learning the appropriate rules for intake in order to derive pleasure and health from wine while avoiding the dangers of intoxication. Because man is moral, he is able to know the difference between good and bad use of alcohol. And because wine tests the character of man it was of interest to the humanist philosophers, who realized alcohol use could define the boundaries of what it means to be human.

3

BARBARIANS AND BEERPOTS

European Drinking from the Celts to Victoria

The Gauls are exceedingly addicted to the use of wine and fill themselves with the wine which is brought into their country by merchants, drinking it unmixed, and since they partake of this drink without moderation by reason of their craving for it, when they are drunken they fall into a stupor or a state of madness. Consequently many of the Italian traders, induced by the love of money which characterizes them, believe that the love of wine of these Gauls is their own godsend. For these transport the wine on the navigable rivers by means of boats and through the level plain on wagons, and receive for it an incredible price; for in exchange for a jar of wine they receive a slave, getting a servant in return for the drink.

Diodoros Siculus, V.26.3 (Oldfather, Trans., 1933)

While the Greeks were enjoying their aristocratic symposia and watered wine, just what were those Northern barbarians up to? From what we find in the textual and archeological evidence they seem to have been upholding a fine Hollywood tradition of fighting, wenching and getting drunk, just as the Greeks suspected. In this chapter we'll examine the history of drinking among the Germanic tribes and Early Modern Europeans, which were the cultures that provided most of the immigrants to the New World and whose habits may be influencing modern American drinking patterns today.

The historical and archeological record provides an opportunity to examine many social, political and economic functions of early European alcohol use (Dietler, 1990 and 2006). According to Arnold (1999) there are four sources of information about Old European drinking and feasting patterns. These are contemporary Greek and Roman writers' accounts, epics and tales from Ireland and Wales, contemporary legal tracts and modern-day archeological finds. Magnificent gold-encrusted horns, decorated bronze bowls, and wine and beer vessels were a symbol of hierarchical relationships and of the transmission of power through rituals that demonstrated the power of warrior chiefs (Arnold, 1999: 87). In early Europe, the reign of a king was legitimated by his acceptance of drink as a symbol of a divine rule (Enright, 1996: 1–37), as well as his capacity to entertain his followers with wine, mead, beer and meat (Dietler, 1996: 96–99). Archeological finds from Britain through Eastern European demonstrate the importance of alcohol to these tribal societies – an importance that some argue continues to influence geographical patterns of alcohol use today (Engs, 1995 and 2001).

From prehistory through the development of the modern European state, alcohol has played an important role in social, economic and political processes. As this chapter will explore, rituals using beer and wine bestowed power and rights upon kings and warriors and reveal the political importance of women in the early Celtic states. Alcohol was also used to strengthen social ties; the sense of togetherness found in the modern pub has a deep history in Western Europe, from the Greek symposia to Celtic banquets. Above all, it is clear that beer and wine provided important calories to European populations, and that because of its importance to the economy and nutrition, the cultural perception of alcohol was positive. The dangers of alcohol became far more apparent when cheap distillation allowed far stronger alcohol to be produced at very low cost. Cultural behaviors and rules were thrown into turmoil when gin, brandy and rum became the tipples of choice, and much of this confusion was carried to the New World with the colonists, who were creatures of their time and place, with drinking habits and beliefs formed by millennia of use.

Early Textual Records of Barbarian Drinking

Most of the contemporary information about Celtic life has been extracted from the work of Posidonius, a Greek historian who traveled among the Northern tribes during the first century BC. He was certainly not the first of the Greeks to chronicle Northern ways (Tierney, 1960: 193–197), but was probably the most objective. Most descriptions of Northern habits were fantastical or emphasized the otherness (or barbarianism) of the tribes; most Greeks considered beer to be impure due to the addition of yeast to start the fermentation process because they did not understand that wine production also used yeast, which is found naturally on ripe grapes (Nelson, 2005: 25–37). Posidonius writes of a Celtic culture with manners and mores very different than those of the cosmopolitan Greeks and Romans – where honor ruled life (but life was cheap), where chieftains ruled through battle and demonstrations of wealth, and where women had far more freedom and power than they did in the South. But most importantly, he left us with richly detailed descriptions of cultural habits, including those related to food and drink.

Posidonius was a geographer in addition to being an ethnographer, and was interested in how climate and ecology affected cultural patterns, habits and human character. He understood that the Gauls drank beer "because excessive cold ruins the climate of the air" and the land thus "bears neither wine nor oil" (quoted in Nelson, 2005: 48). He also chronicled that the rich drank wine unmixed, while the poor drank beer made of wheat and honey. He tells us that they ate meat and bread and drank from shared cups while seated in a circle, with the most prominent man in the center (Athenaeus 4, Kidd 1999: 36; see also Tierney 1960: 247). Posidonius provides a powerful image of Celtic feasting and one surprisingly similar to a symposium – the circle of hierarchically ranked men, the semi-martial atmosphere and the emphasis on bread, meat and alcohol. Imagine the scene: a wooden hall hung with tapestries, thick with smoke from an open fire, the smell of roasted meats and of beer-soaked hay. Underlying this would be the rich tang of wine, spiced beer and honey mead, and the metallic glimmer of the drinking vessels. The warriors boast to each other of glories in battle; the sound of loud male laughter punctuates the background banquet noise. There is music played on drums and pipes, a chorus singing poetry and ancient tales of war and love chanted by the tribe's chief bard. Perhaps a few comely dancers perform; the chieftain's daughter attracts the eye of the bravest warrior as she brings her father more wine …

Scenes of this sort are repeated in other texts over a thousand years; in *Beowulf* and *The Gododdin* tales of drinking and mead halls provide a window into Celtic and Northern politics and social organization. *The Gododdin* is an ancient set of either Welsh (Koch, 1997) or Scottish (Jackson, 1969) poems from the sixth century AD (Jackson, 1969: 3). The original poet, Aneirin, commemorates warriors' heroics; the work pre-dates almost all others from the British Isles (ibid.: ix). Like Homer's *Iliad*, it's a set of grand tales of adventure and war, but told through death dirges for the warriors killed in battle. What is remarkable about these poems is that so many of them mention alcohol in relation to warfare; mead and wine play a role in wars won, wars lost and wars causing death. To 'earn one's mead' is to participate as a warrior in a fight against a chieftain's enemies, and mead precedes the fight, follows the fight and commemorates the fight. The hero's reward is mead – either triumphant and in the flesh in the lord's mead hall, or defeated and sepulchral in Valhalla.

In poem number 21 the connection between alcohol and war is made crystal clear:

The men went to Catraeth; they were renowned
Wine and mead from golden cups was their beverage …
Three warriors and three score and three hundred, wearing the golden torques
Of those who hurried forth after the excess of reveling,
But three escaped by the prowess of the gashing sword

The two war-dogs of Aeron, and Cenon the dauntless
And myself from the spilling of my blood, the reward of my sacred song.

Skene (1868: 382)

The idea that to 'earn one's mead', or to receive banquet and drink from the chieftain, required fealty and honoring the call for a strong arm and sword is made clear in many of the poems (Jackson, 1969: 36–37). In return for fighting, the warriors were to be feted at the expense of the lord; the mead hall would honor the triumphant and drink to the dead. The lord gave his men mead, wine and torques; they gave him their lives: "wearing a brooch, in the front rank, like a wolf in fury, giving amber beads and spurs and torques at the share-out, Gwefrfawr was invaluable in return for wine from the drinking horn ..." (Jackson, 1969: 117). Among the Gauls this implicit and symbolic exchange between lord and vassal was also clear, as is shown in this passage from Posidonius (quoted by Athenaeus):

He, aiming at becoming a leader of the populace, used to drive in a chariot over the plains, and scatter gold and silver among the myriads of Celts who followed him; and that he enclosed a fenced space of twelve furlongs in length every way, square, in which he erected wine-presses, and filled them with expensive liquors; and that he prepared so vast a quantity of eatables that for very many days anyone who chose was at liberty to go and enjoy what was there prepared, being waited on without interruption or cessation.

Athenaeus 4, translation by Kidd (1999: 37)
(see also Tierney 1960: 248)

In these passages alcohol is a manifest symbol of the power of the lord to provide for his people; it is not the sum total of his provisioning, only the most culturally salient icon for the rights and responsibilities of a ruler.

Mead Hall and Political Power

In the epic poem *Beowulf*, Heorot, the mead hall of King Hrothgar, is the site of a banquet attended by the hero-warrior Beowulf before his mission to kill the monster Grendel. The king's grand new building was feast hall, mead hall and palace; it was the proof of his power and a symbol of the wealth he bestowed upon vassals. When Beowulf enters the hall he is greeted by the queen Wealhtheow and given mead, a ritual that demonstrates the importance of alcohol as a symbol of kingship (and power) among the Celts. The ritualized service of mead by the queen defines the relationship of the warriors to each other, to the

Figure 3.1 **Victorian drawing of a Norse chieftain in his mead hall.** (*Source:* Fredrik Sander (1893). *Edda Sämund Den Vise.* W. Meyer, illustrator, Stockholm, Norstedt: 251.)

king and to God. As described in the translation by Seamus Heaney, the queen offers the cup first to her husband Hrothgar, then to the assembled warriors and finally to Beowulf. Beowulf then "accepted the cup, a daunting man, dangerous in action and eager for it always" and addresses her, pledging his support to slay the monster Grendel: "and I shall fulfill that purpose, prove myself with proud deed or meet my death here in the mead-hall." Pleased with his promise, the queen sits next to her husband and the party rages on into the night (*Beowulf* 608–646, translated by Heaney (2008): 41–45).

This passage is powerful as a tale as well as powerfully revealing about gender, social relations and politics among the Northern European tribes. First, similar to the prehistoric Celtic cultures (Arnold, 1999; Enright, 1996: 1–37; Ward, 2001), the power of the king is legitimated by the queen as she serves him mead; it is Wealhtheow who bestows the cup that acknowledges Hrothgar as the first drinker and therefore rightful ruler of the warrior band, and it is Wealhtheow who presents the cup to each person in the mead hall. She is no mere serving-maid but a queen 'regal' and garbed in gold and rings, "the symbolic carrier of royal authority" (Enright, 1996: 34). Her offering of cup and mead is not one of servitude but of a patron giving a gift to those who owe allegiance (Enright, 1996: 5). It is she, not Hrothgar, who petitioned for a deliverer from Grendel the monster, it is she who acknowledges Beowulf's promise to fight, and it is she – not her husband the king – who accepts his fealty and "is pleased" by his boast. Only after Beowulf speaks does she sit with her husband, which means that Beowulf was addressing Wealhtheow, not Hrothgar, when he pledged his service. According to Michael Enright (ibid.: 69–96), the symbolic and highly religious liquor ritual performed by the queen cements the bonds between lord and retainers and ensures the continuity and maintenance of the early European warband. The queen personifies the legitimacy of rule and her offering of mead signals her acceptance of the chief's rule. Royal rule flows from the queen, by way of mead, and into the body and person of the king. Alcohol was used as a symbol to establish the divine right of kings.

Figure 3.2 **Brunhilde bringing a drinking horn to Siegfried.** (*Source:* Fredrik Sander (1893). *Edda Sämund Den Vise*, W. Meyer, illustrator, Stockholm, Norstedt: 225.)

The movie version of *The Lord of the Rings* illustrates how a mead hall may have been experienced. You probably remember the scene where Aragorn and his half of the Fellowship of the Ring have traveled to the Court of Edoras in Rohan to muster the Rohirrim cavalry. On the night before they leave for Gondor a raucous beer feast is held in Meduseld, the grand hall of the king. That party is as near as we are ever to get to a real mead hall ruckus; imagine Aragorn as Beowulf or as a bright and brave warrior of the Gododdin, Theoden as Hrothgar and Meduseld as Heorot. Like Heorot, Meduseld was the feast hall of kings, roofed in gold, a place where the lord and his warriors could plan for battle, feast, drink and celebrate a victory – or mourn a defeat. And like Wealhtheow, Eowyn, the niece of King Theoden, offers a cup of drink to Aragorn – in this case, signaling her interest in him as a suitor as well as her acknowledgment of his capacities as a warrior. The scenes in the movie could have been taken straight from *Beowulf*. And this should not be surprising, for it was in the early tales of Celtic derring-do that Tolkien found his inspiration for Middle Earth and its people.

The Archeology of Barbarian Drinking: Patronage and Tribal Power

The ritual of a lady presenting a lord with a drink to define him as ruler or hero is found throughout prehistoric Europe, and especially among the Celts and Norsemen. Ancient images of well-dressed women carrying drinking horns and cups can be found throughout Norse Europe, and are often thought to be rep-resentations of Valkyries, the handmaidens of Odin who welcome dead heroes into the feasting (and drinking) hall Valhalla. Enright (1996: 69–96) argues that the Germanic tribes recognized the power and the right to rule through the liquor ritual as a symbol of the connection between lord and vassal, much as the Eucharist is a symbol of the relationship between God and man. Given the combustible nature of a chieftain-led warband and the difficulty of control-ling a group of trained and contentious (and perhaps eager to mutiny) warriors (Dodgshon, 1995), it is imperative that a chieftain manipulate symbols of lead-ership that can replace the need for constant physical proof of his right to rule. Often these symbols are material goods that have been imbued with power by cultural values (such as scepters and crowns) or they are goods which the ruler gives to his followers that highlight their respective relationships as lord and vassal; those who receive are usually hierarchically inferior to those who give (Mauss, 1990 [1924], see also Joffe, 1998 and Wells, 1980: 4–8).

In early Europe chiefs ruled, in part, through redistribution of food and drink (Arnold, 1999; Culiffe, 1988; Deitler 1990, 1995 and 1996; Wells, 1980) with actual gifts of goods as well as communal festivities. The association of a warrior class with communal alcohol use occurs in almost all cultures (except Islamic), because drinking together encourages group solidarity (Murray, 1983 and 1991). Hence the importance of the mead hall to Hrothgar; it was the seat of his power and allowed him to call together his warriors for public displays of loyalty. Similarly, in *The Gododdin* the worthy warrior Gwefrfawr gave "amber beads and spurs and torques at the shareout," in return for wine. He was providing his chief with the winnings of war in proof of his loyalty; the lord reciprocated with alcohol – a valuable commodity in and of itself (because imported) but also valuable because it was a symbol of power achieved. The lord was sharing his power with his warrior and they legitimated each other.

Archeological evidence indicates that the socio-political organization of Gaul and Germania changed over the centuries due to an influx of high-status items from Greece and Rome (Dietler, 1990, 1995 and 1996). This led to a greater reliance on feasting and drinking displays by high-status individuals and may have fueled the differentiation of class in these societies. Cunliffe (1988) and Wells (1980, 1985 and 1995) note that the redistributive economy allowed chieftains to consolidate power through the provisioning of prestige goods to followers. Gifts of imported wine and use of Roman drinking ware signaled high status and maintained it through patronage. Gaul was a primary source of the slaves necessary to the Roman economy and trade of wine for slaves (Cunliffe, 1988: 77) and metal craft (Cunliffe, 1988: 141; Tchernia, 1983; Wells, 1995) fueled Roman expansion into the region because the Empire was dependent on an annual influx of slaves to supply the vast agro-business farms that fed Rome (Cunliffe, 1988: 64; Tchernia, 1983: 97–99). Cunliffe and Wells hypothesize that tribal societies based on kinship linkages were transformed into chieftaincies in part because trade goods, especially wine, allowed high-ranking individuals to establish patronage systems in which they controlled distribution of prestige goods in return for military fealty. This kind of socio-political structure is called a 'prestige goods economy' and in the Celtic region, wine and wine vessels provided some of the most salient prestige items. These hierarchical political structures eventually led to the development of a feudal system with differing ranks of lords owing fealty to each other – and responsible for providing men and arms when called upon by the lord above them in rank. While it is not correct to state that alcohol led directly to these political developments, it would be possible to argue that alcohol stood as a symbol for the changes that occurred because its presence signaled ties of patronage, oath-making and fealty.

Using linguistic evidence, Enright demonstrates that these gifts of mead and ale within a warband were analogous to Anglo-Saxon kinship rituals that also used alcohol as a symbol of connection. In early marriage ceremonies when the bride gave a bowl of ale to her groom it indicated her desire to wed him and his acceptance marked them as married (Enright, 1996: 80–87). He cites the word *druht* as evidence of this analogy between the structures of vassalage and that of marriage; *druht* initially meant 'marriage procession' or festival meal (ibid.: 71–72, citing Kuhn 1956) and was used to express the idea of a festive party. Over the centuries the word morphs to mean an armed band of men in liege to a lord. Enright argues that the first meaning of 'festivity' is widespread enough to hypothesize that *druht* is the ancient (pre-contact) Germanic word for 'drink', and that "one notes immediately how very closely this cluster of ideas – marriage procession, drink, festival meal – accord with … the wife who gives drink to her husband and proclaims his leadership of the warband" (ibid.: 72). This linkage of ale and marriage is not new and the word 'bridal' has evolved from the old English words *bryd ealu* which means 'bride ale' and *brydealo,* meaning 'marriage feast'. In effect, there is a long-standing tradition among many Anglo-Saxon, Germanic and Celtic groups that a marriage occurs when ale is exchanged between the bride and groom (which gives additional significance to the drink Eowyn gave Aragorn). The ancient rite of a shared cup of mead is now transformed into the modern-day tradition of the wedding couple and guests simultaneously drinking from flutes of champagne after the toast: "Drink to me only with thine eyes, And I will pledge with mine; Or leave a kiss but in the cup, And I'll not look for wine" (Ben Jonson, from the poem *The Forest – Song to Celia*).

Alcohol and Female Power

Bettina Arnold's archeological examination of European beer and wine use reveals how cultural changes during the Iron Age affected gender relations and female power. She argues that there is a 'multivocality' to the patronage system, and that women's roles were not defined by service or as a node between a lord and his men, but that female power was systemic and complex (Arnold, 1999: 80). She uses both archeological and linguistic evidence to hypothesize that women wielded power in their own right. Similar to Enright's exploration of the word *druht* Arnold contrasts the meanings of the early Celtic words *laith* and *flaith* to illustrate her point: "the distribution of alcohol as a means of maintaining kingship or sovereignty was one aspect of Celtic drinking practices. Alcohol served the purpose of establishing an insular chieftain, lord or king through its consumption by the new ruler at his inauguration ceremony or 'banais regi'. The rhyme words laith, 'liquor', and flaith, 'lord or lordship' … underlie the fundamental nature of this aspect of insular Celtic kingship" (Arnold, 1999: 81)

Furthermore, the word *banais* or *banfeis* used to indicate the inauguration ceremony of *banais regi* means wife-feast or wedding, exactly as does *druht* among the Germanic tribes. To drink is to signal a bond, among marriage partners as well as lord and vassal. Among the Celts the king was anointed by the queen when she, in a public ceremony, presented him with ale from a ritual vessel (ibid.: 83, quoting Wagner, 1975). It was her craft that made the ale (the magical and holy liquid that expanded the mind and signified the power of the gods) and thus her power to award the kingdom to the king.

Both Arnold and Enright review the archeological record for evidence of gender and status, and fortunately there are many tombs in Iron Age Europe containing rich burial goods for both men and women. Enright identifies specific artifacts found in elite female tombs such as ladles and sieves used for serving mead and wine, peculiar-shaped ringed drinking cups (*drillingsfass* and *ringgefass*) used for warband liquor rituals, chatelaines carrying ritual amulets and weaving tools and staffs that resemble spinning whorls (Enright, 1996: 105–120). These artifacts are not found in male tombs (which are filled with drinking bowls, horns, swords and armor), nor are the ladles and sieves found in lower-status female burials. Enright argues that these items probably indicate that these tribes had an elite priestess class of women whose power was parallel to the male control of warfare. He argues that female power legitimized and empowered the *comitatus* (loyalty) bonds of the warband's male warriors because it was the female control of the liquor ritual that glued the warband together. Possible evidence of female socio-political power is found in an early and splendid burial for an elite woman found in Vix, France (Joffrey, 1979; Megaw, 1966). The 35-year-old woman was buried around 500 BC, at a time when Mediterranean traders were active in the northern hinterlands, and her grave included alcohol-related serving equipment made in Greece and Etruria. The most fabulous find was the Vix krater, a bronze vessel over 5 feet tall that held 300 gallons of liquid. This vessel is the largest surviving Greek bronze and was probably created in Corinth around 600 BC and transported in pieces to Vix (Megaw, 1966). The tomb contained other wine-related imported items, as well as gold jewelry, bronze vessels and a chariot. It was altogether a 'princely' burial, and one of the richest from that era (see Witt, 1997, for a diagram of the burial). However, while the woman was clearly of very high status, it has been difficult to understand her role in the late Hallstatt culture: was she a princess, a priestess or queen? We do not know. We do know that she was buried with the accouterments of a large-scale liquor ritual, of the sort that solidified the power of chieftains.

Drinking Horns and Male Political Power

Just a few years before the Princess of Vix was laid to rest, another magnificent burial from the same culture occurred in Hochdorf, Germany. Around 550 BC a tall and well-built male of 45 years of age was buried in a tomb containing magnificent drinking vessels, a chariot, and richly decorated, gold-encrusted jewelry and arms (Arnold, 1999 and 2001). The importance of alcohol was obvious because he was buried with a large cauldron that could hold 100 gallons of mead (Arnold, 2001). Over his head hung a gigantic drinking horn made of iron and gold that could hold 5.5 liters of fluid; at his feet was the cauldron and a gold drinking bowl, and hanging on the wall of the tomb near his feet were eight more 1-liter drinking horns. All of the items had been used and reused as evident from repairs. He was buried with an enormous amount of mead but no food, which Arnold argues demonstrates the cultural importance of alcohol to status display and role maintenance. She also notes that surveys of early Celtic burials demonstrate that only higher-status persons (mostly male) were buried with alcohol, feasting paraphernalia and chariots, suggesting that these were badges of office. To quote:

> Drinking equipment is not found in every wealthy Iron Age burial. It follows that this artifact complex must have particular significance beyond the obvious display of wealth. This discussion has presented evidence for a connection between Celtic drinking and feasting equipment and sovereignty or political control over others ... the term "chieftain's grave" [sic] should be applied only to those burials which contain a full range of drinking and feasting equipment, including an especially large storage vessel, in addition to the usual trappings of a wealthy Iron Age individual.
>
> Arnold (2001: 88)

The evidence that power in Iron Age Europe was tied to, and symbolized by, drinking accouterments such as elaborate vessels and drinking horns has been established by numerous authors and archeologists. Drinking vessels functioned to represent the power of the chief during redistributive feasts and drinking parties (Craven, 2007). But what of more modern times – are these symbols of power important today, and if so, how? Certainly the modern world has ways to establish hierarchy through alcohol – expensive champagne comes to mind immediately – but what of the drinking paraphernalia? Do the status items of the past hold sway over us today?

The drinking horn is an example of an item of alcohol material culture that has retained its significance. The horn can be traced to the earliest evidence of human art (for instance, the Neolithic carving of a woman with a horn described in Chapter 2) and hunting horns and horn-shaped vessels are found throughout the Ancient Near East and in Early Europe. A horn demands drunkenness since it cannot be put down and must be drained, held or passed between drinkers until finished. It is not associated with female drinking except in jest, when Greek dramatists wished to demonstrate that the world had been 'turned upside down' and women controlled politics and drank deeply from rhytons. And in Europe it is plausible to hypothesize that some element of that competitiveness, of the proof of masculinity that deep and quick drinking allows, is demonstrated by the archeological record. Only men are buried with horns and even the Princess of Vix, buried with the grandest of drinking vessels, did not possess a drinking horn. But the lord of Hochdorf had nine, and we can imagine this chief in the center of a his loyal warriors downing the contents of his 5-liter horn and daring his vassals to attempt his feat – to prove their might – by drinking as deeply and quickly as he can. Arnold states:

> The political symbolism of drinking, particularly the connection between *laith* (Irish for liquor) and *flaith* (Irish for sovereignty or lordship), appear to have been maintained through time as well. Drinking horns, such as those found at Hochdorf, are frequently referred to as symbols of authority and kingship in Irish poetry, and as late as the 15th century a 300-year-old drinking horn was cited by the Kavanagh family as the basis for their claim to the kingship of Leinster.
>
> Arnold (1999: 19)

Drinking horns are linked to military achievement, political control and masculinity throughout Early Modern Europe and to the present. Even today drinking horns are sold at shops in central Europe for use in Octoberfest rituals and cut glass versions are popular as beer bongs.

Modern Cultures and Barbarian Drinking

Residual meanings of past cultural practices influence the modern world in subtle ways, as shown by the continued importance of the drinking horn. But can the drinking patterns of the past affect the culture of drinking today? Ruth Engs (1995 and 2001; see also Holt, 2006) uses archeological and textual evidence from Europe to compare archaic and current drinking cultures.

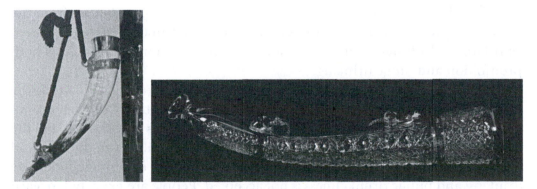

Figures 3.3 and 3.4 **Drinking horn from Innsbruck, Austria** (photographed by the author in 2006) **and a glass drinking horn** (from the author's collection, photograph by William Fitts). The glass horn is used by placing the thumb over the hole in the bottom while filling, then placing the mouth over the end and removing the thumb.

She maintains that the Southern European (Italian, Greek, Southern France and Spain) pattern of wine use, daily drinking and moderation has been carried through to modern-day Southern cultures as has the Northern pattern of feast or binge drinking of mead and ale. She calls the Southern areas the "wet cultures" because they accept wine as a part of diet and use it daily at family meals, permit all ages to drink as part of a meal and (much like the Greeks) frown upon drunkenness. She labels the Northern cultures "dry" because they are ambivalent about alcohol use, classify alcohol as a drug to be used by adults on weekends and at festivals, are tolerant of episodic drunkenness, restrict drinking at home and rarely permit children to drink. Modern Northern Europeans drink ale and spirits more than wine and often binge, and Engs suggests that this is because ancient beer and mead couldn't be stored for long, so beer cultures got into the habit of binging when it was available, and that cultural patterns of patronage and authority legitimated episodic drinking bouts. It could be argued that an 'all or nothing' production pattern led to 'all or nothing' or 'time-out' drinking.

Because of this episodic and heavy use, alcohol is perceived to be a drug among dry cultures and is considered dangerous in the North. The cultures and countries arising out of Northern origins (such as the United States) are the only ones that have enacted prohibition of alcohol. Engs examines modern European drinking patterns in relation to language group, little or no history of wine production, religion and prohibition to find that the culture complex of Germanic languages, Protestantism, binge-style drinking of ale and grain alcohol is linked to alcohol use ambivalence, prohibitionary laws and recognition of alcoholism as a prevalent disease. Likewise Roman languages, wine production history, Roman Catholicism and daily dietary use correlate with few prohibitionary impulses and far less alcoholism (or perhaps less recognition of alcoholism). Most remarkably, she notes that these characteristics have been transferred to the areas of the New World that absorbed populations from the North and the South (Engs, 2001) so that Germanic and Celtic language areas with largely Protestant populations tend to have a history and habit of both prohibition and binge drinking.

To understand how and why this might have developed we can consult the previous chapter and think about how production and habits of use determines cultural perception of use. In the South among the Greeks and Romans and the cultures they inspired, wine can be stored for years, is available all the time and is an everyday food item. Cultural norms are in place to encourage moderate drinking and public drunkenness is not accepted. People are expected to learn how to drink without getting rowdy. Southern European youth might grow up seeing members of their family drinking daily without drunkenness and then adopt those patterns of behavior without thinking. In the North alcohol is not available daily and there is a history of binge festival drinking and drunkenness without in-home use, so children are raised thinking of alcohol as a special-occasion drug for adults only. As they grow up, they adopt these patterns of use so that binge drinking becomes an emblem of adulthood, especially since pro-hibitionary laws disallow intake before majority. Alcohol is thus transformed into a mysterious and dangerous mark of maturity and used accordingly, since children learn to drink by watching adult behavior. Each generation replicates the norms of their elders and adopts the same way of framing the perception of use. And as a result alcohol continues to be food in the South but drug in the North.

The Material Culture of European Drinking

Having recently visited a mead hall, let's move forward in time to seventeenth century Holland, to visit with members of the Amsterdam Militia immortalized in a painting by Bartholomeus van der Helst (see Figure 3.5). Here we have an early-modern version of a mead hall celebration, although with the Three Musketeers in place of Celtic warriors. They are shown after their triumph, having returned to the Militia Hall to enjoy a grand feast with beer and wine, rich foods and a peacock pie. Note the crystal and gold wine goblets, the filled-to-the-brim beer glasses and the rich clothing – all signs of victory, prosperity and plenty. And if you look carefully, in the right-hand area of the painting you will see a man dressed in black velvet holding a very large silver drinking horn. Even though he's not located in the center of the painting he appears to be the most important man at the feast. And of course he is, because he is Cornelis Witsen, the Captain of the Guard, and he is shaking the hand of Lieutenant van Waveren to celebrate the end of the Eighty Year's War. In the painting the horn is a 'horn of peace' because the figure of St. George symbolizes victory over the Spanish. In this example St. George, who slew the dragon (an impossibly strong beast that is a metaphor for the Spanish Empire) is a latter-day Beowulf, the slayer of the impossibly strong monster Grendel (see Figure 3.6). And just as in the tale of Beowulf, once the monster has been vanquished, it's time to have a beer back at the mead hall, in the 'Old Hall' of the Militia headquarters in Amsterdam.

That 'horn of peace' was so important to the Dutch that to this day it holds pride of place in the Amsterdam Historic Museum, just a few blocks from where the painting is displayed. It was made in 1566 by silversmith Frederik Jans to stand as a symbol of the Militia's loyalty to Holland; the base has an image of an enclosure containing a lion, a sign of the unity of the Dutch provinces. But cal-culated in deeper cultural time we can trace the symbolism into a Jungian thicket of warrior masculinity, honor, patronage, protection and alcohol. This horn signified the bond that the Militia made to protect Amsterdam and the unified Low Country just as the horns found in burials and bards' tales chronicle

Figure 3.5 Militia Banquet **by Bartholomeus van der Helst.** (*Source:* Collections Rijksmuseum Amsterdam. Image used by permission of the Rijksmuseum Amsterdam.)

the relationship between a feudal lord and his vassals. And just as the early warriors earned their mead with derring-do on the battlefield, so have the members of the Militia earned their feast by triumphing over Spain. The link between warrior, victory and wine is millennia deep and reproduces the meanings of ancient symbols of power (such as drinking horns) generation to generation.

Figure 3.6 **Horn of St George, from the** *Militia Banquet* **by Bartholomeus van der Helst.** (*Source:* Collections Rijksmuseum Amsterdam. Image used by permission of the Rijksmuseum Amsterdam.)

During the Renaissance and later in Europe, alcohol accouterments defined status in the same manner as did gold and silver cups, drinking horns and elaborately painted kraters in the ancient world. As explored by Mary Douglas and other authors in the influential 1987 text *Constructive Drinking* (Douglas, 1987a), alcohol use constructs the world 'as it is', as 'it should be', and maps the economy by revealing owners, producers, users and even those who resist the accepted economic order. All of these messages came together in the production of the goblets and other fine drinking vessels that were made for the elite because they conferred power, defined power and displayed power to users and vassals. The 'horn of peace' of the Amsterdam Militia is only one example; in much of Europe the horn maintained its symbolism, and even today almost every museum carries at least one historic example, often covered in gold or silver and elaborately carved. Extensive collections can be found in the Nordic history museums, especially the National Museums of Denmark and Sweden. The Clan Macleod possesses Rory Mor's Horn, a thousand-year-old horn that each new clan chief must drain of claret (red Bordeaux wine) before he can assume his new post. Elaborate wine goblets made of crystal, silver, gold and precious stones also became popular during this period and can be viewed in museums in every country. The Silver Museum of the Pitti Palace, the home of the Medicis in Florence, boasts an impressive collection of goblets originally owned by the Medicis as well as a collection of precious-metal German drinking horns from the fourteenth to the sixteenth centuries collected by Ferdinando III of Lorraine. As Bettina Arnold has illuminated (1999 and 2001), there are almost no instances of horn use that are separate from the wielding of political power, especially military-political might.

Among the less-exalted middle-class but staunchly respectable Dutch burgers of Amsterdam, distinction was displayed through interior and still-life paintings that portrayed rich food and drink as part of the 'good life' that rewards the industrious. The cornucopian displays popular in seventeenth century painting emphasized an owner's wealth and taste and often carried hidden morality tales warning of the dangers of sloth, greed or lust (Barnes and Rose, 2002). The Dutch depicted drink and drinking both as positive and negative, with alcohol used to symbolize the moral message of the painting. Drink can be a part of a life well lived, as in the painting *Still Life with Gilt Cup* by Willem Claesz (see Figure 3.7), where oysters, lemons and a rich array of drinks depict a luxurious meal. The painting shows a gilt (gold over silver) goblet, a knobby-stemmed wine glass (designed to decrease the chance of a goblet slipping out of grease-laden fingers) and a beer tumbler. The large pewter pitcher was for serving beer, and the elaborate blown glass flagon for wine.

Alcohol indicated sin and dissipation in paintings of taverns and brothels that showed drinking by gamblers and patrons of prostitutes; in these scenes

Figure 3.7 Still Life with Gilt Cup, **by Willem Claesz (1635).** (*Source:* Collections Rijksmuseum Amsterdam. Image used by permission of the Rijksmuseum Amsterdam.)

Figure 3.8 **Dutch silver tea-caddy spoon (circa 1880) showing a scene from a brothel; note the tankard and beer pitcher.** (*Source:* Collection of the author, photograph by William Fitts.)

wine was taken without food and was used only to intoxicate. These images were later appropriated for coffee and tea services to illustrate the dangers of alcohol in comparison with non-intoxicating and respectable beverages.

The Pub as Community Social Center

Alcohol use can be a symbol of victory (as in the painting of the Amsterdam Militia) or of prosperity (in the table scene) but it is also an opportunity for good cheer and sociability. Because the good cheer engendered by alcohol is central to its use, our brief trip to Holland is appropriate since the Dutch are passionate about their beer and pubs. Every town in Holland boasts pubs where locals gather to drink, eat and make merry. There is even a word in Dutch, *gezellig*, indicating a cozy, friendly, open atmosphere that creates a sense of belonging and connection to other people. It implies sociality; while you could be 'cozy' wrapped up in a blanket in front of a fire, if you are alone in that setting you can't be *gezellig*, which requires good fellowship and cheer. Most of the time, if you ask a Dutch person to recommend a pub, they will discuss the various options in relation to their qualities of *gezellig*. Although a room or a house (or even a person's attitude) can be described as *gezellig*, it seems to be a quality that most clearly adheres to a public house or beer hall. The good bar in Holland is not defined by its beer list or food but by its capacity to make the patron feel welcome, physically comfortable and 'cozy' with friends. This preference for a cozy pub bridges the Channel as well, as the British also prefer their 'local' to be friendly, cozy and welcoming (Vasey, 1990; 49–73). In this manner alcohol creates social inclusion, breaks down barriers between people and encourages interaction. This is another example of how alcohol use maps both the ideal and actual world, because drinking together implies a connected social world (see Mass Observation, 1943: 17–25; Heath, 1987 and 2000; Vasey, 1990: 87–100; Schivelbusch, 1993: 188–193; Roche 2001; Dietler 2006). These examples of the sociality of drinking provide two ways to think about drinking practices: as processes that encourage either inclusion or exclusion. Of course, drinking within the military functions to unite men of the warband and promotes in-group sociality, but it also serves to separate the warriors from the citizenry. The warrior earns his mead by fighting and dying, and he is part of a band of brothers but he is separate, because of that taint of death dealt, from the farmer or the shopkeeper. He earns the right to drink from deep horns and silver vessels. On the other hand, the farmer and the shopkeeper – and maybe even the lord and warrior, on occasion – can meet each other in the ale house where social distinctions and boundaries are ignored in favor of good fellowship. The pub is a place where social barriers can dissolve in favor of good-fellowship and social inclusion.

Pubs range from high-end to low-end but usually obtain their atmosphere from the company of neighborhood regulars who make it their 'home away from home'. Pubs are considered to be a 'third place' (Oldenburg, 1989; Heath, 2000: 50–59; Putnam, 2000: 9–115) – a neutral space that is neither home (first place) or work (second place) and where the rules and hierarchies governing those locations are mediated by communal norms negotiated by local agents. According to Oldenburg (1989: 20–38) third places are neutral, open to all regardless of class, physically separate from home or work, and are places where the primary activity is conversation or social interaction. In essence, the third place is a space where predictable and negotiated forms of social interaction happen and where patrons are able to participate in the creation of social norms and activities (Vasey, 1990: 87–100). These kinds of social norms are described by Gusfield as "communal controls" since they are "normative and structured patterns of social interaction that constitute facets of situated, particular action. The … social controls of specific settings, of popular and often unofficial culture must be contrasted with the official, public controls of governments and laws as well as church officials and others in public positions" (the latter he labels "public controls") (Gusfield, 1991: 402). The pub is a place of release from established authority with freedom of expression encouraged through negotiated interactions. And according to Oldenburg and Putnam, every society needs such places because they provide a place for community consensus-building.

There is clear historical evidence that the public house in England has played this role for many centuries. In some eras the pub was a respectable gathering place for the entire community and at other times has been reviled as a den of iniquity appropriate for only the most hardened of male drunkards. For most of the pre-industrial period ale houses were more numerous than any other type of retail establishment (Clark, 1983: ix), suggesting they probably performed the very important role of a third place. The very first public houses were probably just that – ale shops operated out of homes by housewives who had a bit of extra grain and time to make ale. During the Anglo-Saxon period three types of drinking establishments were known: the ale house, the tavern and the inn (*eala-hus, win-hus* and *cumen-hus*), with the ale house lowest in status followed by the tavern (which sold wine and food), while the inn catered to better-off travelers and the wealthy (Earnshaw, 2000: 5). Ale houses date back to Roman Britain and by 1309 London had 1330 ale shops for a population of 30,000–40,000 (Clark, 1983: 21), and many of these businesses were owned and operated by women (alewives) who used the proceeds to support their families. Most of this ale would have been relatively low in alcohol and would not have lasted for long, since hops were not used regularly to preserve beer until after the fifteenth century (Clark, 1983: 32 and 96; Unger, 2004: 97–103, Hagen,

2006: 204–208). Ales brewed by alewives would have been available sporadically and advertised with an ale-stake (a long pole with a bush or twigs attached) in front of the house. These front-parlor or front-yard and often-informal pubs were present up until changes in the licensing laws in 1869 allowed local magistrates more control over the number of beer houses (Girouard, 1984: 32).

Church Ales, State Power and the Pub

Another important venue for drinking was the parish church, which held regular 'church ales' to raise money for ecclesiastic responsibilities. The church ale can be traced back as far as the early Christian period, and may have been instituted as an antidote to the drink-fests in the mead halls of the early feudal lords (Blair, 1940: 1). A church ale could be held on any day but was most often on Sunday after services or on saints' days, Whitsun and Easter (Marchant, 1888: 87–113; Blair, 1940: 1; Hagen, 2006: 242–244). They were also held as benefits for widows and orphans or as 'bride ales', which was a selling of beer to benefit a newly married couple or a church-centered party to fete the new bride (and feed the entire village) with cake and ale (Day, 2002). Connections of this sort between church and brewer were common all over Europe, especially in the Germanic and Celtic regions (Kumin, 2007: 172–178). Many of the pagan festivals that incorporated drinking seem to have been absorbed into Christianity in this manner; the end-of-year festival of lights (*Imbolg*) even preserved its ancient festival drink called *wassail*, a dish of hot spiced ale (Brears, 1993b) whose name originates from the Anglo-Saxon phrase 'good health' (*waes hal*) which was used in toasting ceremonies with drinking companions (Hagen, 2006: 240) and eventually morphed into the custom of Christmas caroling. Hot spiced ale drinks were popular during the Roman occupation of Britain and very possibly before as well (Cool, 2006: 143–147). These ale-and-feast-days provided an opportunity for the church to raise money, much in the same manner as parishes hold 'bring and buy' sales or fried-chicken dinners today. But even though the church ales raised capital for the parish, there was considerable criticism of such bawdy and gluttonous activities occurring on holy days and on hallowed ground.

The normalization of drinking as a recreational activity in Early Modern Britain must be acknowledged because it demonstrates how the cultural framing of alcohol use has changed over the centuries. In the time of the Celtic lords there was no shame in public drinking, or, if Posidonious is to be believed, in public drunkenness. During the intervening centuries drinking was fully accepted, even if drunkenness was not; the act of intake was not reviled, only drink-related negative consequences. Beer was considered a healthy and necessary beverage that could be enjoyed daily and most people would have been drinking small beer, a low-alcohol product of a second brewing of the grain mash (Cool, 2006: 142). Church ales demonstrate that the social functions of the church and the pub overlapped to some extent, as befitted two areas of intense and important social and cultural action. Kumin (2007: 176) character-izes this as a combination of two of the three nodes of early modern power: politics in the town hall, religion in the church and socio-cultural relations in the public house. The Celtic warband was an integrated power structure with politics and public life bound together in 'trink-fests' provided by the lord and legitimated by the religious power of a Celtic priestess, but later social processes were marked by a disaggregation of these nodes into three spheres of cultural control. As community control was decoupled from a unitary source (such as the warband), secular and religious approval of the rituals and community power of the public house lessened, leading to a rise in political and religious regulations designed to control or prohibit alcohol intake and the public house. Official religious and political power splits from community power, with the 'public control' of polity and church standing in opposition to the 'communal control' of the public house (Vasey, 1990: 87–90; Hunter, 2002). This power split encouraged the late modern state's attempts to regulate and control the ale house (Burnett, 1999; Earnshaw, 2000: 7–9; Nicholls, 2008; Tlusty, 2001: 80–102; Marcus, 2005; Martin, 2009: 185–214). Alcohol (and the places that serve it) became associated with non-work (non-legitimate) lower-class disorder and was seen as a direct threat to the organizing and civilizing power of state and church.

The perception that pubs were dangerous places could also have arisen from the increased availability of hard alcohol after 1700, especially in England. Even though the Dutch had traded in gin during the seventeenth century, there was little hard alcohol available at a low price until after the passage of a 1690 law that allowed commercial spirits production (Gately, 2008: 159–174). The act was passed to stabilize the price of grain and protect the farming economy, but its effect was to encourage widespread distillation of low-quality, high-proof gin. The population of England took to gin with aplomb and drank it with the same gusto and in almost the same volume as ale. The consequences were horrific, particularly in the cities, where hellish living and working conditions encour-aged liquid obliteration of misery. During the height of the 'Gin Craze' of 1730–1740 there were widespread panics caused by public drunkenness, violence and rioting. Several Gin Acts were passed to decrease availability and intake tapered off over the course of several decades, but the danger of strong drink remained obvious to all (Warner, 2002; Dillon, 2003). Public houses and other purveyors of alcohol lost status among the urban middle and upper classes and respectable people increasingly turned to private clubs and other exclusive venues in place of the public tavern. While previously alcohol had been per-ceived as a good substance that could cause problems in excess, it began to be viewed as something that in all guises could cause damage to person and society.

Regardless of changes in perception of drink, after the Reformation the social power of the pub continued to expand, untainted by competition from church ales. The operations of the ale house shifted from small, often female-owned establishments run out of homes with a domestic and homey ambience (Girouard, 1984: 24–26), to more formal pubs, inns and taverns with bars, tables and take-out counters (Clark, 1983: 273–305; Girouard, 1984: 28; Earnshaw, 2000: 11). According to Harrison (1973: 162) these drinking establishments fulfilled three major roles: transportation (the inns and taverns often operated coaching routes), recreation center and meeting hall. To this can also be added dining hall, especially for those who lacked kitchen facilities or capacities; Girouard (1984: 11 and 32) notes that pubs were places where working-class men could bring a chop to be cooked, presumably to be enjoyed with a tankard or two of house ale. Meals were more typically provided by inns and taverns, but later in the Victorian period pubs increasingly offered small meals of the porkpie and sandwich variety (ibid.: 10). This would have been in contrast to the meals served by licensed taverns and inns, which were patronized by

Figure 3.9 A *pasglass*, a seventeenth/eighteenth century Dutch pub glass used for drinking games. The players were required to take a swig that lowered the volume to exactly the next ring. Losers had to buy the round. (*Source:* Collection of the author, photograph by William Fitts.)

better-off travelers rather than the local working class (Pennington, 2002). However, there continued to be considerable overlap in function, with some inns and taverns operating as ale houses for the local population as well as hotels for the traveler (Chartres, 2002).

Jane Austen Drinks Too Much!

Respectable drinking places also provided meeting rooms for voluntary societies and clubs (Mass Observation, 1943: 270–283; Girouard, 1984: 7–12; Chartres, 2002; O'Callaghan, 2004). Before the Victorian period it was quite common for clubs and societies in both Britain and the Colonies to hold formal events in the local tavern and for families to attend assemblies (social events with dancing) in these meeting rooms. There is such a scene in Chapter 3 of Jane Austen's novel *Pride and Prejudice*, in which Mr. Darcy is first introduced to the Bennet family by his friend Mr. Bingley. Bingley takes him to a local ball held in an assembly room. In this famous scene Mr. Darcy disparages the ladies of the village and especially Elizabeth Bennet, thus setting up one of the most culturally important narrative themes in modern Western literature: a love story almost undone by pride (Darcy) and prejudice (Lizzy Bennet) but rescued when both parties see the error of their ways and succumb to mutual respect. But the initial encounter was not positive in part because Mr. Darcy was not pleased to attend a ball held in public assembly rooms rather than in a private ballroom. During the late Georgian period it was not uncommon for 'gentlemen' to patronize public houses, especially for organized events, nor would it have been improper for the ladies of that class to attend events in the meeting rooms (but not to drink in the public areas). Austen was well acquainted with such events, and describes a local assembly in a rather wicked and gossipy letter to her sister Cassandra that includes lines that indicate that Miss Austen was more familiar with Georgian norms of female behavior than her later Victorian fans would have found palatable: "I believe I drank too much wine last night at Hurstbourne; I know not how else to account for the shaking of my hand today; –You will kindly make allowance therefore for any indistinctness of writing by attributing it to this venial Error ..." (Austen, 1800). During the Victorian period the middle and upper classes increasingly retreated from public watering holes and public intake of alcohol, in part because public drinking became seen as sinful and because the clubs associated with the meeting rooms were perceived as potentially seditious by the ruling elite (Clark, 1983: 324). The respectable members of society (or those who wished to be thought of as respectable) increasingly preferred private clubs and the ballrooms of hotels for catered parties and events – a pattern which continues to this day.

The pub provided a respectable meeting place for artisans, tradespeople, apprentices and others of a less exalted social class. A. Lynn Martin has examined the writings of Roger Lowe, a Lancashire apprentice who kept a diary from 1663 through 1674 (Martin, 2006; see also Clark, 1983: 224–225). Lowe drank for three reasons: calories, recreation and leisure, and during rites-of-passage events such as weddings and christenings. Of the 470 entries, 174 chronicle drinking occurring in public houses, with 25 different ale houses named in his village and 22 in the neighboring villages. Most of the drinking occasions he wrote about were business-related or social encounters rather than the daily drinking that would have occurred with meals, so the diary probably underestimates his total intake. Ale cost two pence a quart, and Lowe usually drank between one and three quarts during a session, and Martin suggests that this was not 'small beer' but probably equivalent in strength to modern beers. On only a few occasions did he drink more than a few quarts, and then only at times of emotional turmoil. Most interesting is how intensely social his drinking was: during a recorded 174 reports of drinking he was alone only 13 times, and for the rest recorded a total of 129 named companions in addition to others not named. This demonstrates how frequently social and business affairs were conducted in ale houses and over drinks; Lowe records settling personal disputes and making business agreements over drinks as well as celebrations of all types. Most interestingly, many of his companions were women, which suggests that the ale house functioned as a social center for everyone of the working and lower middle classes and wasn't solely a male preserve.

The centrality of the public house (and the tavern) to British social and cultural life is demonstrated by the social roles provided by such establishments. Unlike the bar of today, a place which often functions to distribute a legal drug to a somewhat raffish section of society, the pub of the past served as a primary meeting place for all classes of society. It, along with the church and the great hall of the lord (or the rooms of the town hall, for those villages large enough to have one), were the only large enclosed public spaces available for community gatherings. The church was controlled by the clergy, the hall by the lord, but the public house was controlled by the people. As public space and a 'third' place it functioned as anti-authoritarian refuge from political and religious rule and provided a social space for the development of community norms of behavior and culture. The pub also represented leisure, and consequently leisure-time later came to be conflated with misrule, drinking and anti-establishment behaviors in opposition to the rules of comportment and control entrenched in politics, religion and work.

Liquid Nourishment: Beer as Food

Beer was regarded as an important part of the diet among the British and other Northern Europeans until quite recently, when its capacity to intoxicate became more culturally salient – and excessive use of spirits branded all alcohols as dangerous. Until the twentieth century, beer provided essential calories and vitamins, safe drinking fluids, and enlivened meals dominated by starchy bread and porridge. The possible volume of intake was shown in the diary of Roger Lowe, who drank roughly two quarts a day of ale purchased from taverns and alehouses. The question to ask is whether this was a normal intake pattern, and if not, what might have been a typical daily amount for the population, and how many calories would ale or beer have provided? Would the calories from ale provide an adaptive nutritional advantage to those who imbibed, as Katz and Voight (1986) have suggested, or were England and Northern Europe simply full of sodden drunks?

The ubiquity of ale (and later beer) as a daily drink and as a part of diet is unimpeachable. Almost every manor house had brewing facilities, and beer was distributed to all estate workers (Clark, 1983: 24; Brears, 1993a). The amounts allotted to workers were carefully delineated in relation to age, status and types of work, just as were the wine allotments for the Cypriot plantation workers of the thirteenth century. Amounts may seem excessive by the standards of the modern world but must be contextualized by a potentially lower alcohol content (in the case of small beer) and by the need to provide safe liquids for a population without modern municipal water systems or reliable indoor plumbing. As a consequence, the ale drunk probably provided a significant proportion of daily calories as well as B vitamins and other micronutrients available in unfiltered beer. And equally important, ale would have made palatable a diet consisting largely of dry grain-based breads and gruel offset by cheese and pickled vegetables.

Brewing was taken very seriously by households in England. Most brewing was done in the home (Burnett, 1999) and manor houses would have retained the services of a brewer to ensure sufficient supplies. *The English House-Wife*, an influential text about estate management from 1688, reveals the similarity of production processes for grain foods by organizing all use of grain in the same section, starting with malting, moving on to gruel and finishing with brewing and bread-baking, a continuum of the three ways the English consumed their primary and most essential agricultural product (Markham, 1688: 153–75). Markham provides instructions for all aspects of brewing, from construction of brewing facilities to storage of grain, malting and proper brewing techniques. He begins the bread-baking section with a most interesting quote:

When our English House-Wife knows how to preserve health with wholesome Physic, to nourish by good meat, and to clothe the body with warm garments, she must not then by any means be ignorant in the provision of bread and drink; she must know both the proportions and the compositions of the same. *And for as much as drink is in every house more generally spent than bread*, being indeed (but how well I know not), made the very substance of entertainment, I will begin with it.

Markham (1688: 181); italics added

This seems to privilege ale over bread in the diet, but it could also be bias caused by Markham's possible disinterest in bread, preference for ale, or lack of knowledge about bread baking – which could have been a realm of women's industry in which he wasn't competent. Indeed, Eliza Smith's *The Complete Housewife* (Smith, 1757) spends more time on bread and offers no recipe for daily ale or small beer, hinting that the urban housewife could buy her beer from city sources. Regardless of the perceived importance of each type of grain product, ale was part of the food budget for everyone, laborer to aristocrat, and purchased ales or the ingredients for making ale were listed as a food in household budgets in all districts and among all classes (Drummond and Wilbraham 1959: 206–221; Dyer, 1989: 55–71; Dawson, 2009). Household budgets often revealed that as much was spent on ale as on bread, with only meat representing a greater percentage of the food budget (Dyer, 1989: 56). And finally, most country estates grew as much or more barley for brewing than wheat and rye for bread, demonstrating the importance of ale as food *and* drink (Dawson, 2009: 58–60). So perhaps Markham's focus on malting and brewing is not a result of bias or ignorance but an accurate reflection of the economic importance of barley production and beer brewing on rural estates.

Fairly consistent amounts of beer were drunk by the English up until the start of World War One, when grain rationing decreased intake dramatically (Girouard, 1984: 17; Burnett, 1999: 132–133). After the Victorian period the rise of municipal water systems, the popularity of other beverages (such as tea and coffee) and different forms of leisure activities caused beer intake to become less important as a means to nourish the body – and more important as an intoxicating substance. Burnett (1999: 114) reports that in 1684 a levy on beer brewing recorded that 18,582,000 barrels were brewed, enough for 2.3 pints per day (36.8 ounces per day, per person) for every person in England, which would have provided 400–500 calories (KCals) per person. And that represents only the professionally brewed beer available at a time when 65 percent of households brewed their own! For the period 1800–1913, annual per-person purchased beer consumption ranges from a low of 28 to a high of 40.5 gallons (10–14 ounces per day, per person) (Girouard, 1984: 63; Burnett, 1999: 126). But not all of the population would have been drinking purchased ale at this time, since rural farms and manors would have brewed, the middle and upper classes may have substituted wine with meals, and tea was an increasingly popular drink for women and children.

Records from religious and manor houses provide clues about daily intakes of beer by both men and women. A. Lynn Martin has created intake tables for Early Modern Europe and England and lists manifests dating between 1382 and the mid-seventeenth century that provide per-capita household amounts from 137 to 365 gallons per year, with an average of 287 gallons annually. Similarly, for the years between 1300 and 1700, he gives female intake from 91 to 730 gallons annually, with an average of 231 gallons (Martin, 2001: 29; Martin, 2009: 68–69). Overall, allotments of beer per person tend to average around one gallon per day (Singman, 1999: 54). For instance, during the reign of King Henry VIII the queen's maid of honor received "a chete loaf [daily wheat bread], a manchet [fine wheat bread], a gallon of ale and a chine of beef [a large section of beef similar to a rib roast or prime rib] for breakfast" (Marchant, 1888: 53). Burnett, quoting Bickerdyke (1868: 274) from the same court account, adds that the maid also received a further gallon for dinner and supper for a total of three gallons daily from the royal stores (Burnett, 1999: 113). This fed the lady as well as a companion and servant or two, but probably indicated that at least a pint would have been available per person for each meal, possibly providing between half a gallon and a gallon of beer daily. At roughly the same time, the Earl of Northumberland and his wife took two quarts of beer and wine for breakfast, and their two sons were given two quarts – and the children in the nursery were given a quart of beer each to start the day. During this period the Willoughby family produced and consumed between 30 and 42 gallons of beer daily for an establishment that included 40 people, so a rough estimate of a gallon per day may hold true in this example as well (Dawson, 2009: 233). Servants and peasants on estates were accorded set measures of ale or malt to make ale, and Dyer reports that an Emma Del Rood in Bedfordshire was to receive wheat for bread, malt for ale and oats for pottage annually, with an ale allowance of two-and-a-half pints of strong ale a day (Dyer, 1989: 153). These amounts – whether strong ale or small beer (and anything in between) would have provided substantial calories, some protein and respectable amounts of necessary micronutrients such as B vitamins, folate, calcium and magnesium.

Memoirs also provide important clues to the dietary quality of drink. Benjamin Franklin reports that apprentice printers in London drank six pints of strong beer daily, or three-quarters of a gallon (Burnett, 1999: 118). The Earl of Eglington records that in November of 1646 he drank a total of 13 pints of beer throughout the day, with at least one pint with each meal and several in between as well (Martin, 2009: 68), which totals almost 1.75 gallons of beer. That seems excessive, even for an aristocrat (although the descriptive phrase 'drunk as a lord' does come to mind). And then there is Roger Lowe, who drank about two quarts a day at various taverns, and perhaps more with meals. To hypothesize about the possible caloric value of their ale intake requires some estimation of the energy values of past brews; modern bottled beer provides about 150 kcal per 12-ounce bottle, or 12.5 calories per ounce. With that estimation, the Earl would have enjoyed roughly 2800 calories. Roger Lowe would have added at least 800 calories daily and Benjamin Franklin's co-workers could have boosted their caloric intake by 1200 calories. If we use the frequently stated allotment of a gallon per day, the average Englishman could have enjoyed a reasonable estimate of roughly 1200–1600 calories from beer. Given that an active man of that time may have needed about 3000 calories to maintain his weight, these amounts would have safely sustained a fairly active lifestyle – and may have encouraged pudginess.

However, if the beer was small beer, made with already-used barley mash resulting in lower alcohol content, the caloric value would have been less than ordinary beer. The caloric value of small beer is difficult to determine with certainty, but has been estimated using malt weight and alcohol content of beers brewed using old recipes. Drummond and Wilbraham (1959: 114) estimate that small beer provided 150–200 calories per pint (9.375–12.5 per ounce), but do not explain how they came to that figure. In a more recent experiment professional baker and home brewer Jeff Pavlik consulted recipes from historic texts to brew ordinary and small beer. Calculations using original and finished gravity indicate that his small beer provided alcohol of 2.1 percent and about 8.5 calories per ounce. He stated "I could drink a gallon of this ale and still keep productive" (Pavlik, 2011: personal communication), which is probably true when enjoyed in moderation throughout the day. If we speculate that somewhere between these numbers is a reasonable average and hypothesize 9 calories per ounce (and with an alcohol content of 2.5 percent or less), a gallon of small beer would have provided 1150 calories and three pints a day (what might be a child's allotment or an adult's portion if taken only with meals) would represent 432 calories, which would be a respectable amount to augment energy intake in a physically hard-working population, but not enough to cause drunkenness or chubbiness. In other words, if people were drinking the amounts historic texts seem to indicate, beer could have kept the population of England very well nourished indeed. More importantly, reliance on beer as liquid and nourishment would have allowed for an economically efficient use of grain to produce all three dietary staples of bread, gruel and beer. In effect, the Englishman, during those decades when grain was plentiful and the beer flowed fresh and frothy, may very well have been a rather plump person, the ideal padded personification of a Victorian country squire. No wonder that John Bull, the symbol of the British Isles and an icon of the archetypal 'jolly old Englishman' was so often portrayed as possessing a singularly well-developed beer belly.

Conclusion

Here's little Sir John in a nut-brown bowl
And brandy in a glass;
And little Sir John in the nut-brown bowl

Proved the stronger man at last.
And the huntsman he can't hunt the fox
Nor so loudly blow his horn
And the tinker he can't mend kettles or pots
Without a little of Barleycorn.

John Barleycorn, a traditional English folk song

Ale and beer played such an important role in Northern European economy, social life and diet that ale could be argued to be, like wine for the Greeks, a 'total social fact', a substance that embodies multiple elements of cultural and economic life so that an understanding of its uses provides a clear window into social functioning. The use of beer also demonstrates how an economically important crop can become a symbol for a nation through practice, beliefs and myths, and how those myths can change over time to represent different, but equally culturally salient meanings. John Barleycorn, an ancient English folk song, illustrates how central beer production was to the agricultural economy. The song describes each task of the farming cycle that creates beer from barley, and John Barleycorn became a symbol of farming practices in general. The last stanza makes clear that "the huntsman he can't hunt the fox nor so loudly blow his horn, and the tinker he can't mend kettles or pots without a little of Barleycorn" a reminder that both lord and peasant require beer for life. The song also links lord and peasant to each other and to the agricultural practices that create economic prosperity for all. If it were to be suggested that England has always seen itself as an agrarian society, and if that society relies on grain to produce bread and beer, it is easy to understand why beer was respected and considered healthy for all people. But beer also had two sides – it was nurturing when used as a food but disrupting as a drug. As long as the alcohol was low and the beer intake moderate, the likelihood of inebriation was low. But when strong ale (or spirits) was drunk in taverns and men drank without food, intoxication could cause discord and violence. As time has passed, the sixteenth century cultural understanding of John Barleycorn as a symbol of rural life and agricultural production has been transformed into a symbol of the dangers of alcohol; the term 'John Barleycorn' now stands for addiction and the damage alcohol can cause. It has become a code word used by alcoholics everywhere for addiction to alcohol, and was the title of a novel by Jack London about his experiences as an alcoholic.

The transformation of John Barleycorn from a genial sprite in a 'nut-brown' bowl into to a demon who enslaves men mirrors the changes in cultural acceptance of alcohol in Europe and North America. It also reveals the essential dualism of alcohol as food or drug, as a nurturing beverage or dangerous drug. After the start of the nineteenth century the importance of beer declined as other liquid beverages became more popular and mechanized factory work made low levels of inebriation dangerous. Social uplift was only possible among the sober, and ale houses and beer drinking became less respectable; the pub was no longer a third place for all but a refuge for working class men. Regardless, the lure of the third place continues and the pub, although much reduced in number and importance, remains an essential social space. We would not, however, consider the intake that occurs within to be nutritive, as it was for Roger Lowe, and this reveals an important difference in social functioning. The pub is no longer a respectable place to conduct a public social life, but has become a place to spend leisure time in games, courtship activities and intoxication. Nor is it welcoming to all, for most urban and rural drinking places now attract more homogeneous patrons; there is little opportunity for mixing of ages, income levels or class. Alcohol has always had the power to divide – the lord drinks fine wine from a gold goblet, while the peasant drinks ale from a leather *firkin* – but now, those differences are magnified by spatial dichotomies that ensure that the banker drinks Chianti in a yuppie wine bar while the plumber drinks lager at the local.

4

A SHORT HISTORY OF
AMERICAN DRINKING

The Antediluvians were all very sober
For they had no Wine, and they brew'd no October;
All wicked, bad Livers, on Mischief still thinking,
For there can't be good Living where there is not good Drinking. Derry down

'Twas honest old Noah first planted the Vine,
And mended his Morals by drinking its Wine;
He justly the drinking of Water decried;
For he knew that all Mankind, by drinking it, died. Derry down.

From this Piece of History plainly we find
That Water's good neither for Body or Mind;
That Virtue and Safety in Wine-bibbing's found
While all that drink Water deserve to be drowned. Derry down
So For Safety and Honesty put the Glass round.

Drinking song written by Benjamin Franklin

America – the Early Years

The most storied tale of the colonizing of North America brings the Pilgrims to Massachusetts to establish Jerusalem in the New World. In the myth (as understood by schoolchildren) Puritans came to New England to escape religious persecution and ensure personal and religious freedom. The reality is more prosaic, because the real reason for landing at Plymouth was a shortage of beer and near-mutiny among the hired sailors of the *Mayflower*. The Pilgrims meant to land near the Hudson River but landed in Massachusetts because their hired sailors refused to carry them further in fear of running out of beer for the return voyage (Winslow and Bradford, 1986 (1622): 40; Bradford, 1856: 92; Lender and Martin, 1987: 2–3; Barr, 1999: 33). Water becomes rank in barrels during long voyages, and the sailors needed the beer to stay alive during the trip back to England.

Part of the founding myth is a re-imagining of the settlers and their values, an imaginative invention of history that transformed simple religious Separatists into archetypes of moral rectitude who supposedly dressed in black, abjured all physical pleasures (including intoxicants), worshipped free enterprise and lived hard-working lives of piety and faith. The Puritans have become a pre-eminent symbol of the ideal American: personally moral, filled with Christian faith, sober, industrious and staunch supporters of family values. But this set of characteristics was largely a projection by Victorian writers, who sought to support specific social and economic values, including temperance and free-market capitalism. In reality the so-called 'Pilgrims' were creatures of their time and place, and much like any other British or Dutch person of the seventeenth century felt that alcohol was a daily necessity and far healthier than water. Bradford even used the concept of the sweetness (goodness) of wine and beer to explain the taste of the water of the New World: "But at length they found water and refreshed themselves, being the first New-England water they drunke of, and was now in their great thirst as pleasante unto them as wine or beer had been in for-times" (Bradford, 1856: 82). In this extract he is explaining to his audience that the water – a much maligned and often dangerous drink – was as good and healthful as the wine and beer drunk of necessity and for pleasure in the Old World. As a rhetorical metaphor, the new (virgin) world provided a newly healthful (unpolluted) drink. The 'Pilgrims' were soundly of the opinion that alcohol was "a Good Creature of God" (a good substance made by God) as theologians Increase and Cotton Mather both famously stated (Levine, 1978 and 1983; Rorabaugh, 1979: 30–32; Ames, 1985). Their concern was not with alcohol but that men would indulge to intoxication and abuse God's bounty.

Cider and ale were the primary daily liquids of the early colonists, just as they had been for their ancestors in Europe. This highlights another reconstructed myth, that of Johnny Appleseed. While Johnny was indeed a nurseryman who planted apple trees all over the western frontier, he was not strewing seeds for apple pies but planting apple varieties for making hard cider. He even gathered most of his seeds directly from cider pressings, which is the pulp left after the juice has been squeezed from the apple. Apples bred from seeds are usually tart and inedible but perfect for hard cider because the tannins provided good post-fermentation flavor, much as red grape tannins do for wine. Johnny was "bringing the gift of alcohol to the frontier" (Pollan, 2001: 9) while also laying claim to land through speculation in orchards (Means, 2011). Only after his death and during the height of the Victorian fervor for temperance was his story retold to emphasize fruit rather than hooch (Pollan, 2001).

These two examples of the re-imagination of alcohol illustrate how discourse about the past can be appropriated to support modern values and also how embedded the use of alcohol is in the history of the United States. Middle-class

Victorians sanitized the Pilgrims and Johnny Appleseed because their cultural values no longer permitted alcohol to be considered a 'good creature of God'. Between the seventeenth and nineteenth centuries cultural beliefs about alcohol shifted from acceptance and enjoyment of use (in moderation) to an essentialist conflation with evil. Alcohol was no longer a good thing (that could be) abused by people but a bad thing that (always) abused people; sin became a property of the substance rather than an outcome of overuse. During these two centuries alcohol also stopped being a food and became a drug, largely because clean water sources became more available as well as tea, coffee and soft drinks. The rise in popularity (and safety) of other beverages made alcohol less important as a comestible and its capacity as an intoxicant became its primary perceived characteristic. Accompanying changes in cultural perception was a rise in temperance practice and belief; during the Victorian era abjuring alcohol became a means to signal middle-class respectability and a desire to 'better oneself' among the higher working classes and lower middle classes. Temperance beliefs became so normal among many sectors of the population that by World War One the acceptance of nationwide prohibition was almost assured.

But the trajectory of cultural beliefs and practices which turned the once hard-drinking colonies into a nation that outlawed the sale of alcohol illustrates important sociological and anthropological principles. The social importance of taverns and public life gave way to more family-oriented and insular activities at the same time that the tavern was increasingly perceived as a menace to family mores and relationships. Temperance ideology intertwined with social and religious practices to such an extent that to be a drinker was seen by many as admitting to being sinful. During the nineteenth century the conflation of alcohol and immorality was abetted by popular discourses that injected temperance stories and imagery into almost every form of media, further popularizing the normality of condemning alcohol use. Alcohol was blamed for breaking up families, creating poverty, causing illness and leading to crime – from idleness and theft to prostitution and sedition. Consequently, the middle and upper classes began to favor political candidates who promised to support laws to ban alcohol on the local, state and national levels. In effect, if alcohol was a 'total social fact' for the Greeks and Europeans because of economic and nutritional importance, it is a total social fact for Americans because it illustrates cultural norms and values.

Colonial Alcohol Use

If the settlers aboard the *Mayflower* were worried about beer availability, you can imagine that others were as well. Alcohol (beer, wine and distilled spirits) was prominent on most ships sailing to the New World, providing liquids for drinking and nourishment, a means to purify stored water and trade goods to ensure the profitability of the Atlantic crossing. Just ten years after the *Mayflower* arrived in Plymouth, the *Arbella* set sail for Boston carrying three times as much beer as water, 10,000 gallons of wine, rather a lot of gin and another full load of 'Puritans' (Lender and Martin, 1987: 2). This largesse resulted in one of the first recorded New World inter-generational conflicts over youth drinking when church elders complained that youth onboard were "prone to drink hot waters very immoderately" (ibid.: 4). Regardless of dismay over abuse of alcohol, like all people of their time they did not question the general utility of alcohol, merely over-indulgence. The East India Company (the commercial concern that launched many of the Dutch colonists in the New World) specified 50 barrels of beer per 100 men for just the first part of the journey (Rose, 2009: 41). Drinking water was simply not imaginable, coffee and tea were not (yet) widely available, and most of the first settlers came from nations that considered beer to be food and drink and taverns to be important social institutions. Consequently, as soon as possible upon arrival, households and communities set up breweries to ensure a ready supply of necessary liquid for everyday use.

Most beer and ale consumed in the early colonies was made at home, usually by the women of the house. Thomas Paschall, an early settler in Pennsylvania, wrote in 1683 "here is very good Rye … also Barly of 2 sorts, as Winter and Summer, … also Oats, and 3 sorts of Indian Corne, (two of which sorts they can Malt and make good beer as Barley)" (Baron, 1962: 44). These beers tasted unlike modern-day lagers because of additional flavoring agents, as this 1685 diary entry by William Penn makes clear: "Our drink has been Beer and Punch, made of Rum and Water: Our Beer was mostly made of Molasses, which well boyld, with Sassafras or Pine infused into it, makes very tolerable drink" (ibid.: 45). George Washington recorded a similar recipe for small beer using molasses (his original notebook is housed in the New York Public Library):

Take a large Siffer [Sifter] full of Bran Hops to your Taste. — Boil these 3 hours then strain out 30 Gall[ons] into a cooler put in 3 Gall[ons] Molasses while the Beer is Scalding hot or rather draw the Melasses [sic] into the cooler & St[r]ain the Beer on it while boiling Hot. let this stand till it is little more than Blood warm then put in a quart of Yea[s]t if the Weather is very Cold cover it over with a Blank[et] & let it Work in the Cooler 24 hours then put it into the Cask.

Amelia Simmons, who wrote the first cookbook published in the New World, provided a very similar spruce beer recipe in 1798:

Take Four ounces of hops, let them boil half an hour in one gallon of water, strain the hop water then add sixteen gallons of warm water, two gallons of molasses, eight ounces of essence of spruce, dissolved in one quart of water, put it in a clean cask, then shake it well together, add half a pint of emptins [a home-made yeast preparation], then let it stand and work one week, if very warm weather less time will do, when it is drawn off to bottle add one spoonful of molasses to every bottle.

Simmons (1798: 48)

Molasses was still the homebrew calorie source in 1840, when Sarah Josepha Hale called for molasses, hops, fern leaves, ginger and spruce extract to be used in two recipes for beer (Hale, 1996 (1841): 112). The colonial economy was awash in cheap molasses, a by-product of sugar processing. Molasses was used to make rum, which was the primary distilled alcohol of the colonial period. Molasses also was part of the infamous slave trade triangle between Europe, the Americas and Africa that brought sugar and molasses from the Caribbean to the East Coast for rum distillation, which was then shipped to Africa to be traded for slaves, who were shipped to the Caribbean to be sold to the sugar cane plantations for molasses, which was shipped to New England to be made into rum (Coughtry, 1981; Standage, 2005: 101–106; Curtis, 2007). Rum, slaves and molasses – and homebrewed molasses beer – formed a significant part of foundational economy of the United States.

Apples and Grain, Cider and Whiskey

While barley, wheat, corn, rye and molasses formed the backbone of the beer industry, apples provided an important source of calories for cider making. Like beer, hard cider was used by all ages for refreshment and to accompany meals. It provided about twice as much alcohol per unit than small beer and the finished alcohol content of approximately 10 percent allowed storage (Rorabaugh, 1979: 111). It was also cheaper than beer, especially in the apple-growing regions of New England and the Mid-Atlantic (ibid.). During the eighteenth century, after apple orchards came into full production, cider supplanted beer as the primary daily alcoholic beverage (Barr, 1999: 367), with women in the Chesapeake drinking about two pints of cider per day (Meacham, 2009: 2). Cider was relatively easy to make and required little equipment beyond a few trees, an apple press and vessels for fermentation and storage. Fermentation occurs naturally from yeasts available on apple skins – just crush, store, ferment, filter and enjoy.

Estimating exactly how much cider was consumed per capita is difficult because of the lack of reliable industrial (professional) production measurements and because most cider was made in the home. Field (1897: 140) provides numbers of barrels purchased by householders in 1728 ranging from

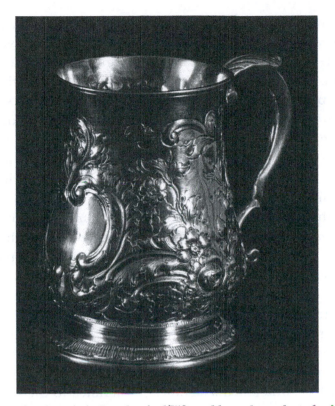

Figure 4.1 **Silver tankard made in London in 1752, and brought to the colonies. This tankard would have been used by a well-off person to drink beer or cider.** (*Source:* Collection of the author, photograph by William Fitts.)

2.5 to 113 with an average of 27, but without knowing more about family composition no approximation of intake is possible. Rorabaugh (1979: 111) estimates that a family could consume a barrel a week during a New England winter. He does not provide his source for this figure, and it is presented as an example of higher usage. To estimate individual intakes from such a figure is difficult because variables such as barrel size, alcohol content and number of household members are unknown. We can hypothesize that with a 31.6 gallon wine barrel (wine casks were used to make and store cider, (William Woys Weaver, 2011), personal communication), a family would have four gallons per day. If the family consisted of three adult males (over age 15) and two adult females (also over 15) on full rations and two younger children on half rations, there would be about 5 pints per day per drinker. Assuming that males may drink more than females, we could speculate a scant gallon per male and half-gallon per female, which is two times Meacham's estimate for the Mid-Atlantic area (Meacham, 2009: 2). Modern hard cider has approximately 12 calories per ounce, so a gallon of cider could provide 1500 calories per day – an amount of energy not unlike that provided by beer in England during the Early Modern

period. While this sounds like a great deal of cider, the amount can be rationalized by usage variables. First, this could be imagined as a possible maximum
amount of cider intake, mentioned in Rorabaugh (1979) because it was a high
figure. Second, cider may have provided most of the fluids for the day, and may
have been sipped slowly and/or intermittently to relieve thirst, which would
lead to less intoxication. Third, caloric needs are higher in cold weather and
cider may have been an important source of energy in the winter, especially if
other carbohydrate food stores (potatoes, corn meal, etc.) ran low. Fourth,
these amounts may reflect winter-time entertaining and visiting shared with
more people than one family.

This hypothetical exercise illustrates two significant facts about early
American use of cider. One, it provided calories which could have been safely
stored without fear of spoilage and, providing that the apple trees stayed
healthy, would have been a predictable dietary resource for farming families at
the mercy of weather, insect predation and food storage losses. Two, it could
have led to a steady state of low-level intoxication that could have been blunted
by heavy farming labor but more likely would have been normalized by drinkers. In other words, people would have become used to feeling a bit buzzed
(much as the English lords who drank large quantities of strong ale would have
been) or may have developed a significant tolerance to the effects of alcohol
(Rorabaugh, 1979: 7). Small amounts sipped regularly throughout the day
would have relaxed drinkers without inducing drunkenness. For much of the
population, especially those who stuck to cider and beer, everyday drinking
could have produced few or no problems with drunkenness or addiction.

Unfortunately, the colonists also drank whiskey, and that tipped them over
into a state of inebriation that was noticeable, problematic and widespread. The
colonies were established at a time when spirits were just becoming popular
and widespread in the Old World, so the colonists brought with them both a
beer- or wine-drinking habit as well as the new practice of drinking distilled
alcohols. From the very start, the New World had to grapple with the problems
associated with distilled spirits. High levels of intake were noticed by fellow
Americans as well as many European travelers; the much-quoted passage from
Anne Royall states it well: "When I was in Virginia, it was too much whiskey – in
Ohio, too much whiskey – in Tennessee, it is too, too much whiskey!" (Royall, 1969
(1830): 93). Just as the production of cider and beer was promoted by the economics of farming, so was the whiskey industry. Many frontier states provided excellent
growing conditions for corn, wheat and rye but had problems getting grain to
the profitable East Coast markets. Grain was hard to store, subject to spoilage,
attractive to vermin and expensive to ship, but could be transformed into whiskey,
which was highly profitable, stable and easily transported. By 1800 whiskey was the
preferred everyday drink, with drams (shots) taken straight and/or watered

throughout the day. No social occasion was complete without a bottle to be shared, and to refuse a drink was considered rude (see Rorabaugh 1979; Lender and Martin, 1987; Thompson, 1999; Meacham, 2009). Whiskey was such an important economic commodity that attempts to tax production caused the first serious uprising against the new state when farmers in Western Pennsylvania refused to pay an excise tax on distilled alcohol, prompting Washington to call up a militia to control the Whiskey Rebellion (Carson, 1983). Because whiskey was made from domestic grains and distilleries were everywhere, the cost of whiskey dropped far below that of other spirits and even below beer and cider (Rorabaugh, 1979: 65–83). Low price combined with the popularity of alcohol at social functions, continued distrust of water safety, and the belief that alcohol was good for health caused the intake of spirits alone (not counting wine, cider or beer) to reach an estimated 5.2 gallons per capita by 1830, or 9.5 gallons for each citizen over the age of 15 (Rorabaugh, 1979: 231–233). Rorabaugh estimates that absolute alcohol intake (raw spirits) from all sources was 7.1 gallons per adult (15+) in 1830 (the high point for the United States); in comparison, the current adult (15+) intake level is roughly 2.2 gallons (WHO, 2011: 277).

Taverns and Pubs in Colonial America

Taverns and bars play an iconic role in the American imagination. Can anyone imagine a Western movie that doesn't include a scene in which the protagonist slams back the shuttered door to a raucous barroom, followed by complete silence while the inhabitants coolly – and with some hostility – assess him? Everyone knows what happens next: he swaggers to the bar, orders a double whiskey, slams it down and starts a bar fight. These scenes provide viewers with an iconic bar scene and an archetypal male gender role, one in which male 'hero' characteristics include being loud, aggressive and a heavy drinker. The typical American bar is a place of male tension and misbehavior, where females enter at their own risk in search, supposedly, of sexual adventure at the bottom of a glass. This idea is not a new one, and fears of this sort encouraged colonial governments to regulate taverns and what they sold. While early colonial leaders were not opposed to drinking in the home and for nourishment, they were very worried about the problems that public intoxication caused and did not wish to transplant drunken behaviors from the Old World to the New. Unfortunately, the tavern was such an essential public space that regulating tavern business was more difficult than anticipated.

Taverns existed in every town and were often one of the first buildings constructed when a colony was founded, frequently located right next to the church or meeting house (Field, 1897: 1; Conroy, 1995: Chapter 1). English and Dutch colonists came from countries where taverns were important community meeting places and provided a 'third place' that allowed people to socialize in a venue where hierarchy was suspended (see Thompson, 1999: 11–15; Salinger, 2002: Chapter 1; Rose, 2009: Chapter 3). In the colonies, these cultural habits continued and taverns were used for trials and political assemblies (Conroy, 1995: 12; Thompson, 1999). Just as Puritans in England had encouraged churches to abandon alcohol-related activities, early colonial leaders worried about the connections between churches, political organizations and taverns. Alcohol itself wasn't the problem, but the abuse of it was a concern, and pubs that encouraged abuse were a problem. This is a distinctly different attitude than held by most people within the Unites States today. In our post-Prohibition world alcohol as a substance is thought of as problematic. Bars and gathering places that provide alcoholic drinks are more likely to be thought of as good places where bad things can happen because of the presence of alcohol. The perceived moral positions of alcohol and drinking establishments have been reversed because how we think about alcohol has changed over the centuries. Early colonists were apprehensive about taverns because they provided an opportunity for sedition (as had been seen in England) and because alcohol use could potentially subvert community control by the upper classes by encouraging riots (Conroy, 1995). The social environment of the tavern – the third place that created internal rules and regulations free from church and state control – was of deep concern to the early Puritan leaders, since they conceived of the ideal state as one which blended religious and political power to create social control. The tavern offered a potential for mob resistance that deeply worried them. On the other hand, taverns provided essential services such as rooms for travelers, food and drink for townspeople, post offices, spaces suitable for political and court meetings and places where community news could be shared with the population (Thompson, 1999: 11).

Because of these worries, taverns were subject to community regulations, including density mandates, tavern-keeper character assessment, liquor controls and price restrictions. For instance, Massachusetts colony leaders lifted bans on sales of spirits in 1639 after regulations failed, and instead mandated that each town maintain a tavern. The catch was that only the morally fit were allowed to run taverns – a law designed to make sure that respectable community members maintained control of alcohol distribution and, presumably, control of the drinking habits of the less moral. In addition, prices and times for selling were regulated, and beer sold outside of meal times was priced higher to discourage intoxication (Salinger, 2002: 103). Tavern keepers were required to ensure moderate intake or their licenses could be revoked. In general, there was much concern over the morals and respectability of tavern keepers as they were seen to be the gatekeepers for public drinking behaviors (Field, 1897: Chapter 2; Conroy, 1995: Chapter 3; Salinger, 2002: Chapter 5; Carmichael, 2009). Regulations like these could be found in every colony and every town, as fledgling governments used the law to shape public behavior in ways they felt would create a better social and political system. To read these regulations now is almost comical; in 1633, for instance, Robert Coles was disenfranchised and required to wear the letter 'D' for a full year in punishment for public drunkenness (Thomann, 1887: 4), and in 1657 Boston residents could be assessed a five shilling fine if they gambled or danced in a tavern (ibid.: 19). Colonial leaders sought to control the public distribution and use of alcohol in order to ensure that the population abstained from intoxication.

The fear of an intoxicated citizenry was tied to fears that precedence and hierarchy would be overturned. The New World followed the socio-political rules of the Old World in starkly delineating the classes and requiring that those of low or middling status defer to their presumed betters. The better classes of the colonial world were the (male) landowners and establishment clergy (and most clergy were landowners) who were also the community leaders and lawmakers. They perceived working class people such as immigrant bondsmen, apprentices and artisans as potentially seditious. Alcohol, because it encouraged a loss of control and feelings of euphoria, could encourage the lower classes to defy the rules and regulations of the colonial governments and to, in effect, defy their betters (Conroy, 1995: 172–174). Levine (1978 and 1983) argues that the Puritans of the time considered human nature to be inherently sinful and that laws were necessary to contain and control baser instincts. In this context, the extensive, widespread and often-unenforceable laws, excise duties and taxes governing production, distribution and use of alcohol within the public sphere are understandable (see Thomann, 1887, Volumes I and II for a full list of colonial liquor laws). Colonial leaders sought to preserve the political status quo and to improve the characters and lives of the governed. In the colonial era those who needed to be governed were the working classes (especially apprentices and contracted laborers), African slaves, Native Americans and the poor. Many colonies and municipalities supported laws that made selling liquor to them illegal or forbid taverns from issuing credit to ensure that the indigent could not drink. But early Americans were not so worried about the drinking habits of the wealthy and respected; it was assumed that the 'better people' could handle intoxicants and had the right to drink, even to drunkenness, on occasion (Rorabaugh, 1979: Chapter 2; Levine, 1978 and 1984). Taverns were dangerous because they were public and used primarily by the lower classes. The upper classes drank at home or in clubs and so their drunkenness was private – and less visible. As a result, taverns, unlicensed alcohol (especially spirits) and sales to the wrong sorts of people or at the wrong time were the focus of most laws in colonial and early America. These fears did not go away during the nineteenth century, and bars, taverns and saloons were to remain a primary focus of the Prohibition and Temperance movements.

Temperance and Prohibition in the United States: The Great Experiment

A more serious consequence of spirits drinking in the young United States was widespread public drunkenness: distilled alcohol is intoxicating rather than nourishing, and regular drinking of too much high-proof booze can cause personal and social problems (Nicholls, 2008). During the century before 1830 the use of alcohol shifted from being largely nutritive with some drunkenness to more drunken in character, in part due to a change in use from beer and cider to whiskey (Makala, 1983). Between 1790 and 1830 intakes of alcohol climbed steadily among all population groups, with most problems occurring in a subset of male drinkers (see Rorabaugh, 1979; Lender and Martin, 1987; Gately, 2008: Chapters 17–19; Smith, 2008). The American Temperance Society estimated that half of the adult male population was drinking two-thirds of all spirits, with one-eighth of all men drinking the most, at 24 ounces per day (Rorabaugh, 1979: 11). These figures are not surprising, considering that even today addiction researchers (and on-campus alcohol counselors) estimate that 15 percent of drinkers cause 90 percent of all alcohol-related problems. Rorabaugh argues that during this time the population shifted from being 'sipping drunks' (people who take small swallows throughout the day) to binge drinkers who ingested large quantities quickly (ibid.: 149–150). The fear of social danger from alcohol contributed to a shift in beliefs about alcohol use that presaged widespread and popular temperance movements during the Victorian era (Levine, 1993).

While political and religious leaders primarily feared drink-related incivility among the lower classes, during the eighteenth century doctors began to question the value of alcohol to the body (Levine, 1984). The rise in spirits drinking led to higher rates of public intoxication, higher rates of habitual use and higher rates of illness due to alcohol intake. The concept of addiction was not prevalent at the time; instead people believed that drinkers became 'habituated' to the good feelings caused by intoxication (Levine, 1978; Ames, 1985). Benjamin Rush, an Edinburgh-educated physician (and Declaration of Independence signer) published one of the first widely read tracts against intemperance. Since heavy use of spirits quickly led to visible intoxication, Rush argued against distilled spirits in favor of 'temperance'. 'Temperance' meant moderation rather than avoidance (Reckner and Brighton, 1999), and Rush's unique barometer placed fermented drinks in a different category than distilled ones. His 'Moral and Physical Thermometer' published in *An Inquiry into the Effects of Spirituous Liquors on the Human Body and the Mind* (Rush, 1790) rewrote how people thought about alcohol and helped to start the Temperance Movement of the nineteenth century. In his thermometer the drinking of hard alcohol is listed as an intemperate behavior, and it is explicitly linked to specific types of physical and moral degeneracy (see Figure 4.2). By questioning the value of hard alcohol, he altered how people understood the action of alcohol in the body. No longer was it merely a good creature that could be abused by a sinful person but rather a damaging substance that could hurt a good person. This shift in conceptualizing how alcohol affects the body, mind and spirit encouraged the inclusion of temperance ideals into the religious and political platforms of the following century and set the stage for teetotalism and Prohibition.

While the medical establishment and the clergy read Rush's manifesto, the drinking public did not. The rates of alcohol intake climbed alarmingly during the early part of the nineteenth century and the young country appeared to have gone on a communal binge (Rorabaugh, 1979). With overall per-capita

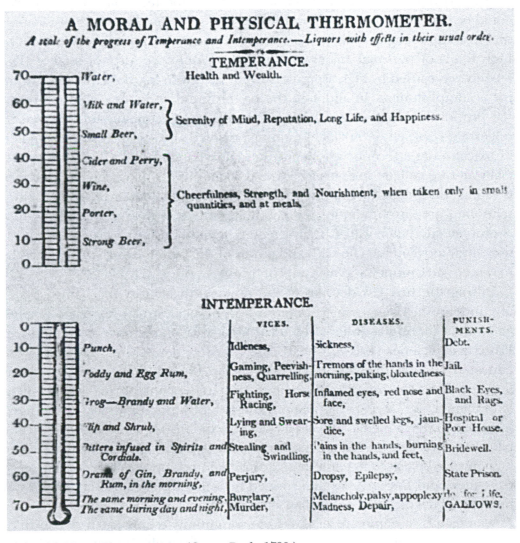

Figure 4.2 **Moral Thermometer.** (*Source*: Rush, 1790.)

intakes roughly three times the average of today, levels of intoxication were high and visible to most citizens. The shift to what Rorabaugh calls "communal binges" was marked by changes in social behavior and in the meaning of alcohol. First, shifting to whiskey increased the likelihood of drunkenness. Second, while Western Europeans and colonials had always accepted low-level public intoxication (what might be called 'mild pixilation'), during this period they began to accept more extreme behavior and consequences. Third, increasing numbers of social occasions were marked by whiskey drinking, and the sharing of a bottle was a way to demonstrate good-fellowship, solidarity and a lack of hierarchy. Fourth, whiskey played an important economic role because it was made of corn, which was essential to the American economy – corn fed people directly as pone, mush and bread, indirectly as hog feed and the remainder could be converted to whiskey for drinking and sale (Rorabaugh, 1979: Chapter 4). Fifth, Rorabaugh argues that between 1790 and 1830 the nation was beset by high levels of personal anxiety, which led to increased alcohol intakes. The anxiety was caused by high aspirations combined with low skills and motivation for accomplishment. In addition, the political and social power structures of the previous century were changing and individual economic futures seemed uncertain (Eriksen, 1990). The resulting personal and social tension promoted intoxication as a form of self-medication (Rorabaugh, 1979: Chapter 5), especially among college students who found themselves with an educational/professional mismatch in training and job availability (ibid.: 138–140). Their schooling prepared them for the life of a gentleman clergyman, but the new century needed men with skills in engineering and business to run the nascent industrial movement. The skills and power of the old elite were pre-empted by new men, new money and new ways of living.

During the first few decades of the nineteenth century the United States was undergoing changes in economic function, social structure, religious belief and moral identity – shifts often associated with temperance movements in Protestant societies (Eriksen, 1990). Most of these temperance advocates were educated male clergy who sought to improve the lot of their fellow citizens using moral persuasion and religious faith to encourage self-advancement (Rorabaugh, 1979: 191–194). Some temperance organizations encouraged members to sign a pledge to avoid all alcohol, and thus became known as 'teetotalers' for agreeing to give up alcohol 'total abstinent' (Fuller, 1996: 84). The men involved pledged to help eliminate drunkenness by actively recruiting more teetotalers and the societies they formed became popular social institutions in many small towns. Their focus then shifted from personal recruitment to political campaigns to eliminate alcohol from community events (such as Fourth of July parties) as well as towns and counties – what Gusfield describes as a change from assimilative to coercive reform (Gusfield, 1986: 6). Teetotalers shifted from moral persuasion to legal restriction, reasoning that if men wouldn't stop drinking on their own they would be forced to do so for their own good.

Alcohol became a convenient scapegoat and perceived cause of community problems. Magical thinking encouraged the belief that the elimination of poverty, violence, immorality and other social ills could be achieved by making access to alcohol illegal (Levine, 1984), a regulatory process known as 'prohibition', and that it was the duty of community leaders to do so for the good of the citizenry. Power to change society was seen to reside in citizens' rights to use laws to deny other citizens the opportunity to engage in activities deemed immoral. Reckner and Brighton argue that "coercive methods arise when reformers perceive that their ideology has been rejected, and the unreformed group poses a threat to the reformer" (1999: 81). Not only did this perspective alter how citizen groups understood political and social class interactions, it also altered the drinking habits of much of the aspiring middle class, because drinking became associated with lower-class status. This was particularly apparent in the industrial towns of the Northeast, where an influx of immigrants who worked in factories were perceived as threats to the established Protestant order. The perceived breakdown of cultural rules and social constraints in urban environments was caused by a deep distrust between the working and middle classes who no longer worked or lived near each other; this fueled a temperance movement designed to protect the deserving from the immoral (Johnson, 2004). In no other country has temperance fever taken so quick and so strong a hold, or rooted so deeply in national consciousness and self-identity.

Scholars provide a number of reasons for the rapid rise in acceptance of abstinence. First, the religious revival known as the Second Great Awakening (of the early- to mid-nineteenth century) altered the ideology of Protestant religious practice from predestination to personal salvation through faith and self-improvement. Acceptance of Jesus Christ could then be signaled to peers through right living – orthodoxy witnessed as orthopraxis (Ames, 1985; Wurst, 1991; Fuller, 1996: Chapter 4; Reckner and Brighton, 1999). The Lutherans, Methodists, Presbyterians and Quakers all viewed temperance (and abstinence) with favor; some religious denominations even defined temperance and abolitionist activities as faith practices. As evangelical fervor spread, many groups explicitly banned drinking as sinful (Levine, 1993) and to this day abstinence is most common among the Evangelical Protestant lower-middle classes (Gusfield, 1986: 48). Second, temperance – and later abstinence – was tied to desire for economic advancement through industriousness, self-control and middle-class morality (Wurst, 1991; Levine, 1993; Johnson, 2004). The mark of an 'up and coming man' was his abstinence from alcohol and tobacco (Reckner and Brighton, 1999), and so alcohol use became associated with economic stagnation, personal failure, working class culture and often-despised immigrant and minority groups. According to Levine (1978: 14),

> The Prohibition campaign of the early 20th century focused on other evil effects of alcohol: liquor's role in industrial and train accidents; its effects on business and worker efficiency; its cost to workers and their families; the power and wealth of the "liquor trust"; and especially the role of the saloon as a breeding place for crime, immorality, labor unrest and corrupt politics. In a sense, "demon rum" became less the enemy than the "liquor trust" and the saloon.

Liquor use was seen by the aspirant middle classes as something that corrupted and enslaved the working and lower classes, restricting movement into 'proper' American culture and prosperity.

Class struggle is part of the third reason for the rise of temperance ideology. Gusfield (1986) argues that the economic and social changes of the early nineteenth century excluded the old power elite of clergy and Protestant/Puritan landowners. Their response to losing political and economic power was to attempt to retain social and religious power through temperance societies that reinforced their social position (see also Hofstadter, 1955: 287–292; and Johnson, 2004). In effect, being temperate (and later abstinent) became a status symbol because it was associated with elite values and social practices (Gusfield, 1986: Chapter 1) and was attractive to those who wished to better themselves or who wished to appear to be 'of good character'. Gusfield quotes Copeland to illustrate the appeal of adopting non-drinking as a status marker to differentiate the aspiring self from those below: "wherever the groups and classes are set in sharp juxtaposition, the values and mores of each are juxtaposed. Out of group opposition there arises an intense opposition of values, which comes to be projected through the social order and serves to solidify social stratification" (Copeland, 1939, quoted in Gusfield, 1986: 27). That quote mirrors one from Mary Douglas: "the more that alcohol is used for signifying selection and exclusion the more might we expect its abuse to appear among the ranks of the excluded" (Douglas, 1987a: 9). Since most working-class drinking is done in public, and middle-class and above in private, perhaps we should amend Douglas's statement to read "we expect *the perception of* its abuse ...".

Gusfield argues that abstinence was popular because it enhanced social status through adoption of practices that signal personal morality, while Levine maintains that abstinence was used to signal industriousness and economic worth. These reasons are really two sides of the same coin, since all temperance actions and beliefs validate abstinence practices. The stereotypes that create the 'drinking other' as a less moral entity continued throughout the nineteenth century and fostered anti-saloon nativism that made the passage of the 18th Amendment politically rational (Clark, 1976; Duis, 1983: Chapter 9). Drinking, immorality, poverty, immigrant or minority status and lower-class culture became conflated in the discourse of temperance; Clark (1976: 58) states that saloon drunkenness was seen to encourage "sexuality, brutality and violence" and that temperance and abstinence achieved real popularity because they supported bourgeois family values. He argues that during the nineteenth century the nuclear family became the ideal form of family structure for most Americans. The Victorian nuclear family ideal presumes that the father is working while the mother stays within the home to raise children and manage the household. The outside (economic) world was considered dangerous and potentially immoral, while the family home was reconceptualized as the moral center of the community. This is part of the compartmentalization of American life that became more prevalent during the nineteenth century, in which different spheres of activity such as work and home were meant to be kept separate – as were women, men, children and the classes (Rorabaugh, 1979: 168). The nuclear family as economic unit was relatively new in the nineteenth century because farming communities found the extended family a more efficient structure for management of economic and community life. The newer time-based industrial economy favored the worker as individual and shifted the economic unit from a multi-worker family to the single worker, who must then somehow provide for a family (Epstein, 1981: Chapter 3). This model works for the middle-class and above but factory work rarely paid enough for the working classes to keep their women at home. Among the professional classes female paid work was not considered respectable, so if the husband drank and couldn't work the family was left destitute. Anything that removed income from the nuclear consumption unit became problematic, and so alcohol was explicitly linked to family-destroying behaviors such as prostitution, gambling, bar-hopping, wasting time, missing work and abandoning family responsibilities (Epstein, 1981: 102). Alcohol became the pre-eminent symbol of sinful behavior of all kinds, not just intoxication.

Two broader ideologies supported the link between temperance and family values. First, the cult of domesticity or 'angel of the house' conception of the female role placed women outside of the economic sphere as the moral guardian of the family and defined her proper place as within the home, taking care of husband and children (Epstein, 1981). Second, the adoption of "bourgeois interior" values (Clark, 1976: 12) of "self-confidence, character and conscious … developing consciousness of individual, rather than communal, dignity, this turning inward for new sources of individual direction, destiny and discipline …." In short, the presumed ideal social structure for the development of the family and nation became the nuclear family led by a self-made Protestant patriarch. The political assumption was that the American experiment was only possible through protection of the nuclear family unit, which meant temperance and legal prohibition against alcohol. Clark sums these beliefs nicely:

> The purpose of Prohibition was to protect the values sheltered by the American nuclear family. The origins lay in the slow articulation of deep anxieties: that the new world of industrialization, opportunity, and social turmoil was a moral frontier, that it demanded new patterns of interpersonal relationships, and that these new relationships were threatened by the unrestricted use of distilled spirits
>
> Clark (1976: 13)

The various reasons for the popularity of temperance are not mutually exclusive and work together neatly to form a dichotomized and dualistic mapping of American values and behaviors. On one side was a set of metaphorical 'bad' things such as drinking, sexuality, working class values, immigrants and minorities, non-Protestant status, urban life, bachelor culture, lack of time scheduling, unrefined leisure, lack of personal control, lack of cleanliness, lack of gumption to 'better oneself', loss of status and so on. On the 'good' side were those accomplishments and characteristics that were admired by the middle class: thrift and savings, White Protestant Christianity, well-ordered family life, business success, social status, small-town life, hidden or restrained sexuality, time control, self-control, work, patriarchal control of family life, modest women and silent, obedient children. These linkages were so apparent that adoption of a temperance lifestyle was de rigueur among strivers who wished to better themselves or to appear respectable to the public. Alcohol became so potent a symbol of evil that when Carrie Nation used an ax to destroy saloons in the early twentieth century (all while quoting from the Gospel at high volume), a clear crime against property and industry, many people professed admiration for her ideals and methods. Support was so widespread that many Christian-identified citizens took to wearing pins in the shape of her ax (see Figure 4.3) to symbolize approval of her mission as a 'home defender' (see also Epstein, 1981: Chapter 4). While her actions were little less than vandalism and her mental state thoroughly imbalanced, her widespread popularity illustrates how much alcohol was feared.

Today alcoholism is viewed as an individual problem that causes emotional problems for spouses and families, but at the turn of the last century it was a family problem that caused financial turmoil. Women had far fewer opportunities for employment or for divorce, and families were dependent on male wages. Alcoholism demonstrated the cracks in the Victorian economic system that defined men as economic and women as domestic, and female involvement in the temperance movement was motivated by need as well as opportunity. Female leadership in anti-alcohol organizations provided many middle-class women with an opportunity to use their stifled brains, organizational skills and professional capacities respectably. Christian-affiliated temperance clubs were

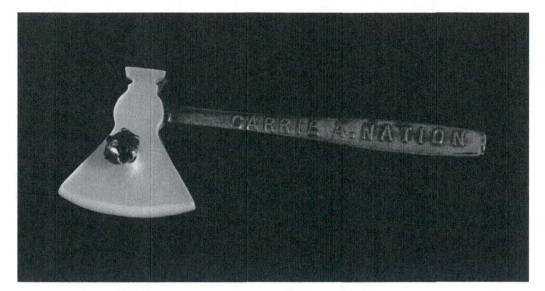

Figure 4.3 **Carrie Nation pin.** (*Source:* Collection of the author, photograph by William Fitts.)

outside of the economic sphere and posed no threat to male status or workplace activities, and allowed many intelligent women to develop public speaking and organizational skills. These skills later set the stage for first-wave feminism and female suffrage (Mattingly, 1998; Martin, 2002; Parsons, 2003).

Temperance Literature

Another reason that middle-class women were such enthusiastic abstainers of alcohol and supporters of temperance/prohibition was the preponderance of literature that described the dangers of alcohol. Between the 1820s and the 1920s hundreds of tracts, poems, plays, songs, stories, how-to books, novels and medical texts were explicitly pro-temperance, and there was a robust market in what Warner labels 'temperance weepies'. These were highly emotional tales of degradation, redemption and salvation that reached female audiences through public lectures, magazines, church bulletins and moralistic novels (Mattingly, 1998; Crowley, 1999; Parsons, 2003; Warner, 2008: 55). The classic tale is one of initial moral compromise (the first drink!), sliding into drunkenness, failure, hitting bottom, acceptance of the ministrations of God, a loving wife and/or a temperance advocate, and the eventual and slow return to health, wealth and happiness. It is essentially the same narrative trajectory of the typical Alcoholics Anonymous story today, although the weepies were more frequently told from the perspective of a wronged woman or child. The trope of a dying child, especially a sweet and virginal daughter, was particularly potent as was that of an innocent and nubile girl fallen into sin and degradation after a single glass of wine offered by a handsome stranger at a dance, who is (of course) a white slaver.

One of the most famous of the temperance tales is *Ten Nights in a Barroom,* written by T. S. Arthur in 1854. The story follows the downfall and eventual salvation of the drinking protagonist, whose daughter is killed by a flying bottle when she comes into the bar to beg him to return home to his loving family. On her deathbed she entreats him, in excruciatingly bad dialog, to lay off the hooch. He agrees. This story was made into a play, a book, a movie and even a musical and was the second most popular book of the Victorian era, after *Uncle Tom's Cabin.* The plot mirrors other crusader messages, such as the song *Come Home Father* that tells the sad tale of a young girl trying to get her father to leave a saloon because the baby is dying at home. Alcohol proves stronger than

"Thank you; no wine for me," replied Amy.—*Page 391.*

Figure 4.4 **Scene from the novel *Strong Drink* (Arthur, 1877). A young lady turns down a glass of wine at a party.**

family and in the last stanza the baby has "gone with the angels of light" still begging for a kiss from papa (Epstein, 1981: 106).

Other messages were more subtle. Many poetry books contained anti-drink sections, such as the poem about Johnny Rich in *Farm Ballads* (Carleton, 1873: 35–41). The poem opens on a dark and stormy night with a charming home scene of a successful farmer surrounded by his industrious family. A drunken Johnny Rich knocks on the door, seeking respite from the cold. The farmer admits him, and devotes many stanzas to listing his crimes while drunk: theft, aggression, bad behavior towards women, etc. The poem ends in Christian charity, with the farmer swearing to keep him warm and safe in the hopes that he will yet reform. Another set of stories, taken from *Strong Drink* (Arthur, 1877), are little more than abstinence sermons repackaged as a novel. Alexander Granger is a successful man who falls into evil ways and lands in the gutter (literally) but is ultimately redeemed by Christian faith, his loving daughter and a temperance friend; he regains financial success and takes his proper place among the financial elite. The message is clear: sobriety equals success, intemperance creates failure, and women and God must guide men away from immorality.

Many temperance texts provided highly disingenuous 'scientific' information about alcohol production and use. The Reverend J. T. Crane explains fermentation as a form of rot rather than a biological process caused by yeast: "crush an apple, and its myriads of cells are ruptured and its juices begin at once to decompose. The cider-mill does this work of destruction on a large scale, and the process of decay proceeds with equal pace ... when the process of decay began, the atoms which composed the sugar entered into a new combination and formed alcohol ... thus bland and pleasant food, touched by the fatal hand of decay, becomes a weapon of death" (Crane, 1871: 124–125). Standard home medical texts often wrote of alcohol as a poison and carried warnings like this one: "*Drink Makes Idiots* – one of the best proven and most disastrous examples of this is seen in children who have been conceived at a time when the father was partially intoxicated. There is no doubt whatever that under such circumstances the child is pretty sure either to be idiotic, or to have epileptic fits, or to be of feeble mind." The next entry is 'Alcoholism in France', where after describing the grave problems of alcoholism in that country the authors assert French medical advice states "alcoholics become insane easily and are liable to very painful forms of paralysis. We often treat working men who have been very robust but have become rapidly consumptive because they have regularly taken before each meal their aperitifs. The children of alcoholic parents are almost always badly formed, weak minded, insane, scrofulous or epileptic. They die often in convulsions" (Truitt, 1912: 212). The only four entries about alcohol in Truitt's book are 'Alcoholic Heredity', 'Crime', 'Drink Makes Idiots' and 'Alcoholism in France', which neatly defines the prevalent discourse of the time.

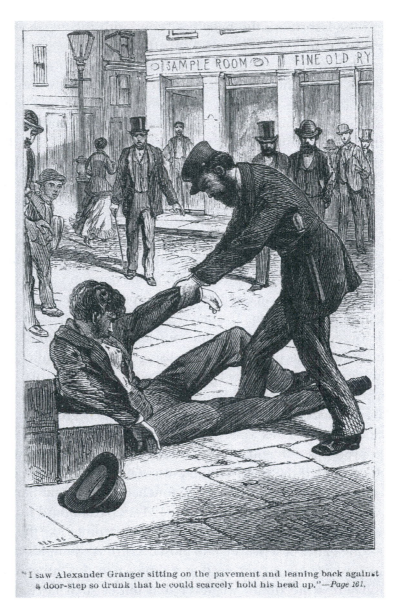

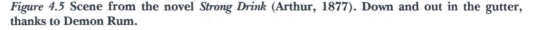

"I saw Alexander Granger sitting on the pavement and leaning back against a door-step so drunk that he could scarcely hold his head up."—*Page 161.*

Figure 4.5 Scene from the novel *Strong Drink* (Arthur, 1877). **Down and out in the gutter, thanks to Demon Rum.**

The final example of temperance literature comes from a book published in 1920 titled *Father Penn and John Barleycorn*, which purports to use history to explain why the 18th Amendment was finally passed in 1919 (Chalfont, 1920). The author, while correctly instructing that William Penn built a brew-house for his estate, assures us that he "deplored the excessive use of strong liquor, but drank it in moderation" and that "is not to be construed as reflecting in any way upon his lofty character" (ibid.: 15). He also implies that Penn abjured alcohol in the frontispiece of the book, which shows Father Penn with a cudgel labeled '18th Amendment' chasing John Barleycorn through the woods. Perhaps this could be interpreted as metaphorical, except that the remainder of the text cherry-picks liquor laws to suggest that early Pennsylvanians were at heart temperance advocates and abstainers. The book assures that the founders of the country meant us to be dry.

Conclusion

The 18th Amendment was passed in 1919, with 'Prohibition', or the legal restriction of alcohol trade, beginning in 1920. The law was repealed in 1933 because it had been an unambiguous failure. Abstinence proponents had argued that banning alcohol would rid the nation of almost all social ills, from poverty and

Figure 4.6 **Father Penn and John Barleycorn.** (*Source:* Chalfont, 1920.)

ill health to prostitution and vagrancy. Instead, the years of Prohibition were some of the most lawless on record, with the Mafia and other organized crime groups controlling liquor distribution, illegal bars (speakeasies) popping up everywhere and widespread violence caused by gang warfare. As a result, by 1933 the desire to repeal the 18th Amendment was almost universal (Cashman, 1981; Peck, 2009; Okrent, 2010). Making alcohol illegal effectively convinced most on-the-fence drinkers that booze was a very good thing indeed and that laws that inhibited use were unenforceable, undemocratic and un-American. Throughout the 1920s the cult of the cocktail made imbibing almost as popular as it had been during the country's early years, although per-capita amounts never rose to the level they had been earlier. Regardless, the ideology of temperance remains powerful in the United States and conflict over intoxication continues to inform social patterns and political action to this day, especially in the debates about the appropriate legal drinking age and legalization of other drugs, such as marijuana.

5

IT'S HAPPY HOUR! MODERN AMERICAN DRINKING

[I]f people have been brought up to believe that one is "not really oneself" when drunk, then it becomes possible for them to construe their drunken changes-for-the-worse as purely episodic happenings rather than as intended acts issuing from their moral character. So construed, not only can the drinker explain away his drunken misbehavior to himself ("I never would have done it if I had been sober"), those around him can decide, or be made to see, that his drunken transgressions ought not – or at least, need not – be taken in full seriousness ("After all, he was drunk"). We are arguing, then, that the option of drunken Time Out affords people the opportunity to "get it out of their systems" with a minimum of adverse consequences.

MacAndrew and Edgerton (1969: 169)

I once did research in the American South, deep in what is known as the 'Low Country' of South Carolina. It is a beautiful area with deep cultural traditions and a strong belief in Christianity. The region is also rich in bars, saloons, private drinking clubs and weekend honky-tonks – there seem to be as many bars as churches. Alcohol was available everywhere – in teacups at afternoon parties given by church ladies, in bottles shared while fishing from the dock and in red cups at every BBQ. One day while shopping in the liquor store for a bottle of scotch, I recognized someone I had met earlier in the week and said "Hi." I was cut dead, ignored completely and my greeting unacknowledged. The next time a bottle was needed the same thing happened, and then a third time. Baffled (and with hurt feelings), I consulted a local friend who started laughing and responded "you sure are not from here! Don't you know you *never* say hello to Baptists in the liquor store?" Since the Southern Baptist church frowns upon drinking, the polite act while encountering a Baptist caught red-handed with booze was to pretend ignorance. Not knowing that buying alcohol was so culturally weighted, I inadvertently 'outed' several secret drinkers. Of course, after that I only said hello to Episcopalians in the liquor store, because they drank without shame. As witnessed by a joke told by Baptists in South Carolina: "whenever you have four Episcopalians, you have a fifth."

In this particular South Carolina town, social life was divided between work time, social time, sacred time and party time. A Venn diagram would show overlap between work, social and party time, but sacred time was separate, with different clothing, language, activities and levels of sobriety. However, the Saturday Night Party Time often bled into Sunday Morning Sacred Time, as evidenced by the occasional smell of stale bourbon at the nine o'clock morning service. The culture of the United States, and particularly that of the South and Midwest, carries many traces of Prohibition to this day. The United States has higher rates of self-reported total abstinence than other non-Muslim alcohol-drinking nations, with roughly one-third avoiding alcohol (in contrast, only about 9 percent of Swedes and 11 percent of Norwegians abstain). Abstention is highest in working-class women and lowest among upper-class white men, a pattern with a deep history among Americans (see Dollard, 1945: 99–100; Peck, 2009). I was offered the Southern staple 'sweet tea' while visiting with working-class South Carolinians, but offered alcohol when spending time with the wealthy. The latter were far more likely to be Episcopalians as well (a denomination often called 'Whiskeypalians' in the South).

This illustrates the contentious nature of alcohol intake in the United States in the post-Prohibition era. Even though media celebrate and glorify alcohol drinking, a surprisingly large section of the population avoids all alcohol. Even among those who do drink, intake is bounded by rituals and rationalizations that indicate a deep-seated belief that alcohol intake might be wrong. The United States remains a nation of 'all or nothing' drinkers (Warner, 2008), with nervous tension defining the behaviors that separate wet from dry. Many Americans also have a tendency for compartmentalized or dichotomized drinking, as demonstrated by the Southern Saturday night whiskey-soaked honky-tonk followed by sober Sunday morning church attendance, each marked by opposites of behavioral and moral norms. Yet to the practitioners of this style of drinking the bounded articulations between the worlds of drunkenness and sobriety are normalized by cultural beliefs that segregate behaviors by time, place and behavior – what MacAndrew and Edgerton (1969) label 'time-out drinking'. In time-out drinking many rules for daily social behavior are relaxed and drinkers are permitted to 'get away with' violent or sexual behaviors that would otherwise be forbidden (Redmon, 2002 and 2003). It is no mystery that one of the most successful and iconic Texas rock and roll bands, ZZ Top, had a mega-hit with the song *Beer Drinkers and Hellraisers*, or that the song has become a modern anthem for the partying crowd. That beer drinkin' would precede hellraisin' makes perfect sense in a culture that celebrates time-out drinking and sanctions consequences.

This chapter examines alcohol intake through time use, semiotics and history, and argues that dichotomized drinking patterns are a result of historic trajectories that tie the nineteenth century to the modern day through belief systems rooted in temperance practice and sharply delineated patterns of work and leisure. These compartmentalized fields of social action use alcohol as a semiotic sign that signals or frames leisure (Gusfield, 1987) and as an instrument ensuring identity shifts caused by intoxication. Dualism is reinforced by patterns of work in corporate culture and by American concepts about control of the self. In addition, dichotomizing beliefs about alcohol use are articulated across time and space, from person to person and between micro-cultures within America in such a way that broad cultural themes can be stacked together to create rational belief systems about intoxicants. Boundaries between time and social space are recognized as areas of liminality (limbo) where alcohol use and drug-taking behaviors may have special and specific signaling and behavioral relevance. However, it is important to point out that this chapter examines cultural elements that have influenced how Americans think about alcohol use, but those elements do not determine how they actually drink. Most Americans do not drink in an 'all or nothing' manner; most people are moderate drinkers. In other words, even if belief systems suggest that the primary way to drink is to intoxication, almost all drinkers learn to regulate intake to ensure good health and few consequences.

Morality and Time in American History

How, precisely, does an item such as alcohol turn so definitely from a 'good creature' (Levine, 1978) into a symbol of moral danger and decay? As described in the previous chapter, changes in economics and social life during the nineteenth century demonstrated how religious belief, economic practice and self-identity favored sobriety over drunkenness, and total abstinence over moderation. Alcohol and awareness of time use became a symbol – a short-cut for public presentation of self – used to signal morality and industriousness (Gusfield, 1986 (1963): 12; Levine, 1997: 9–19; Peck, 2009: Chapter 8). Over time abstinence and support for prohibition became a central and core identity of the 'good self' among the middle class in the same way that certain sets of beliefs are core to particular religious or political groups. Personal avoidance of alcohol and support for Prohibition became an unambiguous good with the expectation that when alcohol was abolished most social ills would disappear. When Prohibition failed (because it didn't eliminate expected social problems) temperance proponents did not renounce their beliefs in favor of moderation. Instead, the American population bifurcated into drinkers and non-drinkers, roughly along lines of income, religion and region. The East and West Coast educated middle classes tend to be drinkers, while working-class Midwesterners and Southerners often eschew alcohol, especially those from evangelical churches.

Cultural ideas about bodily practices such as intoxicant use tend to get linked to morality, so that adoption and transmission of such beliefs and behaviors become natural and normal. In a semiotic sense, morality is signaled in a one-to-many manner, since usually there are many different types of behaviors that are considered to be a part of – and essential to – a moral life. By adoption and display of one of the 'many' behaviors the social actor is assumed to be upholding the 'one' (morality) and a natural and corollary assumption by others upon witnessing (or reading) that particular behavior is that the person is abiding by the rest of the 'many' behavioral expectations. In other words, one type of behavior indicates other behaviors, all of which tend to get stacked together (the 'many') to indicate the character trait (the 'one', in this case being a moral person). In this manner a behavior can become a semiotic signal (a 'sign') indicating good character in a social actor, and can be read as a shortcut to determine if the person is moral. Avoidance of liquor among religious abstainers may be read as acceptance of religious doctrine as well as other moral perquisites such as avoidance of promiscuity, theft, lying, etc. Adoption of such signaling behavior is used to appear respectable to others, and transmission of the beliefs and behaviors becomes imperative. In order to be considered 'good parents', mothers and fathers must teach children to respect those values and to model them in public and within family life. Children grow up assuming that being a good person equates with behaviors indicated important for morality by parents and peers. This creates a coherent system of beliefs about individual practice and character that fosters a sense of identity and dictates proper presentation of the self.

To return to the example of the South Carolina town, if being a 'good Baptist' means avoiding alcohol, by avoiding alcohol one is identified as being a 'good Baptist' and therefore a good person. Other values important to maintenance of 'good Baptist' status, whether they relate to behavior (sexuality, financial probity, integrity, etc.) or belief (acceptance of Church doctrines) are assumed by the public practice of avoiding alcohol. In this case, alcohol use is a shortcut that points to the possible expression of other vices (because no vice exists in isolation), a conflation demonstrated in the thinking of many Prohibition groups of the nineteenth century (Warner, 2008: 89–90). For me to acknowledge the very human act of drinking alcohol in that place and time and among those people was a sign that I was questioning their morality. I didn't know that cultural language, and couldn't read the signs appropriately. Because drinking alcohol is such a socially awkward act an entire set of behaviors has arisen to make cultural sense of buying alcohol: it was ignored or compartmentalized by all participants. The very fact that accommodation was made illustrates that the tabooed drinkers were considered moral in the eyes of their temporarily blind neighbors, for if they had not been, the natural response would have been to acknowledge the drinker's actions, to acknowledge the drinker, and thus to publically question his morality. And I, in my Episcopalian unawareness of the finer points of Southern politeness, had done precisely that. No wonder I was cut dead!

To provide a non-alcohol example of how some behaviors can operate as semiotic signs, think about how cigarette smoking is used to illustrate character in contemporary movies. Given that smoking has become an unacceptable vice indicative of lack of control of the self (Stearns, 1999) it is no wonder that in current films only the bad guys smoke. And when they smoke, they often do so in a manner that indicates a troubled character – they drag deeply, with agitated motions of head and lips. They grimace, they gesticulate with the cigarette, they chain smoke without enjoyment. Sometimes women smoke seductively, using the cigarette as a phallic symbol to indicate that they are sexually rapacious. Financiers smoke large cigars when discussing how they will cheat or steal from a rival businessman. Mobsters smoke Cohiba Cubans to show that they are outside of society and proud of it. If and when a main character smokes it can be a device to demonstrate severe anguish, high eccentricity or to suggest that the character needs mental treatment; the plot of the movie then revolves around the character getting help. The role of the Dr. Grace Augustine character in the movie *Avatar* is a complex but good example – she smokes in the lab to demonstrate her unhappiness with research priorities and to signal resistance and tension. Once she is among the aliens, where she feels comfortable and happy, she no longer needs to smoke. Smoking is so verboten in United States culture that the smoking scene was a primary criticism of the movie (trumping a hackneyed story and overall bad acting) in the columns of many film critics. It was shocking precisely because in movies the good guys usually don't smoke, and Dr. Augustine was a main character and a 'good guy'. The use of a cigarette was designed specifically to alert the viewer that something was wrong with the situation. The viewer read the semiotic evidence and understood that the plot of the movie would resolve the problems so that Dr. Augustine wouldn't feel a need to smoke any more.

Dualism and Time Use

In the previous chapter the rise of Prohibition was attributed to adoption of an industrial economy, religious revivals beginning in the 1830s and the rise of middle-class beliefs about home life and women's roles. Alcohol was considered a danger because it posed an economic and social threat to work and home life. As a result, adoption of abstinence became a means to demonstrate good character, industriousness and family values. In addition, structures of production shifted from small businesses with task-oriented schedules to factory work that regulated workers' bodies by clock and process. Clock and industrial time led to an acceptance of daily and weekly schedules that sharply delineated work and leisure and emphasized a dichotomized lifestyle that positions work as a sober activity, alcohol intake as a leisure activity and free time as potentially (and perhaps ideally) intoxicated. The rise of the timed work week completely altered how cultural actors viewed their interactions in time and space, which in turn became linked to ideas about bodily and mental control of the self. Time use (as a product of *Homo economicus*) and self-control also became linked to ideas about morality, capacity and character. The specifics of how perception of self-control and use of time changed are important to understand, however, in order to explore modern drinking habits and the meaning of alcohol use today. After all, most Americans understand that "Miller Time!" means far more than cold beer – it signals Friday nights and weekends, relaxation, parties, friends and free will. Most specifically it signals the end of the work day or work week. It is a symbol of a dualistic time map (work/play, employer time/my time, sober/drunk) that channels cultural expectations about how individuals might utilize alcohol.

Levine (1997), Zerubavel (1985) and Lefebvre (2004) have explored how time use is determined by cultural beliefs and habits. Zerubavel understands time perception to be determined by four cognitive constructs. The first is sequential, which is the awareness of 'before and after' that determine a proper structure of action (Zerubavel, 1985: 20). In the case of alcohol use, sequence illustrates cultural rules such as '21 before drinking' or 'work before play'. Since the normative defines the abnormal, in the case of alcohol use that explains why drinking at a forbidden time (before 5pm, before a party, during instead of after work, etc.) can be considered problematic. A second structure of time is duration, or the normative periods applied to linear sections of time. This socially constructed experience of time provides the 60-minute hour, the two-hour 'happy hour' or the four-year college education. The third structure is the standard temporal locations of social events (ibid.: 7) such as dinner time, rest time and even 'drinking time', when most people are doing roughly the same thing at the same time. Finally, there are 'uniform rates of recurrence' or rhythmicity, that determine how and when social events are constructed within linear time frameworks. These include daily, weekly, monthly and annual patterns of social life, such as holidays, religious events and secular festivities such as the Fourth of July. All of these temporal structures together create the cognitive concept of the routine, which places social events into linear time and determines proper times for human actions. Personal and collective routines silently determine identity by, as Zerubavel describes, "supporting life-cycle calendars for role enactment" (ibid.: 139). In contrast to the routine is spontaneity, the 'anti-schedule' (ibid.: 44), which influences alcohol intake because intoxication is an acceptable activity for periods of personal spontaneity such as vacations and weekends. Zerubavel maintains that temporal symmetry contributes to social cohesion: "a temporal order that is communally shared by a social group is unique to it to the extent that it distinguishes and separates group members from 'outsiders', contributes to the establishment of intergroup boundaries and constitutes a powerful basis for mechanical solidarity within the group" (ibid.: 67). For example, the time and duration of the midday meal alters depending on culture since some groups prefer a short, solitary lunch while others consider the midday meal to be family time and might spend several hours at table. Not surprisingly, the former tend to avoid alcohol at this meal while the latter might enjoy several courses, often with wine (de Certeau, 1998: 85–100). Zerubavel's frames allow for models that construct the social meanings of time as well as time articulated in space, as shown by the calendar, sacred and profane time, and private and public time. Each of these categories contributes to understanding alcohol intake because each culture has beliefs, practices and rituals that mark these times as appropriate or inappropriate for drinking.

According to Zerubavel, the Benedictines were the first to define the day and week with religious, work and social events planned for particular hours. Every moment of a brother's day was accounted for with absolute regularity (a routine), which became the model for the current industrial and post-industrial schedule (ibid.: 35, referencing Mumford 1963: 14). Each human activity and event had a proper place and time, a way of socially constructing life into cognitively ordered (and orderly) sections. This allows for compartmentalization of tasks, which contributes to a compartmentalization of roles determined by task, time and place. For instance, between 9am and 5pm one might be a worker, perhaps an architect, who wears a certain kind of clothes, talks in a professional register, and personifies an identity that is particular to that role at those times. Outside of those times the role may shift to that of a mother, daughter, wife, community volunteer or friend. Each role has expectations about presentation of self (clothing, language register, behavior, etc.) that are read by others as appropriate or not. Acceptable performance of identity requires that roles aren't confused – so while being an architect one shouldn't use the clothes, language register or actions of the 'free-time' person (Goffman, 1959: Chapter 1). Work and leisure are also usually defined by time and identity patterns that conflate with other cultural categories. For example, time and economic output are linked cognitively so that 'time is money' and time itself is a commodity to be 'spent', 'invested', 'allocated', etc. (Zerubavel, 1985: 56; Levine, 1997: 18). Work is not leisure and leisure is not work for modern routines, and our clothing, language and beliefs demonstrate these dichotomies.

Similarly, the sacred and profane or personal and work time are subject to temporal division and compartmentalization of roles. As described earlier with the example of Saturday night in relation to Sunday morning, sacred time is sober while profane time is not. Each of these scheduled time slots dictates a different type of time use that is connected to a different self-identity and social performance. This explains the stark differences between behaviors during Carnival and Lent in early modern Europe, as well as the drinking on the 'down low' of the Southern Baptists in the liquor store. Zerubavel quotes Durkheim to explain these divisions: "it is necessary to assign determined days or periods to the [religious life], from which all profane occupations are excluded, there is no religion, and, consequently, no society which has not known and practiced this division of time into two distinct parts, alternating with one another" (ibid.: 104). Temporal segregation is also essential to mark work vs. private time, or private/public times as well as private and public roles (ibid.: 139–141). Private time is anti-schedule and anti-routine while public time is usually filled with work or civic activities dominated by precise expectations of professionalism. Routines and strict schedules are essential to public/work time: time does not belong to the person, instead, the body of the person is regulated by the schedules of work and community responsibility. Zerubavel points out that these temporal discontinuities cause a dualistic experience, a "'pendulum view of time' … that temporality is essentially a discontinuity of repeated contrasts, a 'succession of alternations' between the sacred and the profane, with festivals marking the temporary transition from one opposite to another" (ibid.: 112). As a consequence the modern world contains the work week and the weekend, work-time and vacation, work-time and holidays. Each is starkly contrasted by role, identity, time use, habitus and appropriateness of drinking/drug-taking behaviors. The cognitive structuring of time with the cultural building blocks of sequence, duration, temporal location and uniform recurrence explains why "it's Miller Time!" makes sense, and why holiday office parties can provide alcohol without anyone questioning the presence of cocktails in the work-space.

Henri Lefebvre (2004) adds to our understanding of time through analysis of everyday life patterns. He focuses on the rhythms of everyday (day, week, calendar year, life) as constructed through cyclical and linear perceptions of time. Cyclical time is organic, repetitive and predictable, and based on natural (biological) rhythms. Linear time is quantitative, resulting from social actions and human schedules and the "monotony of actions and movements, of imposed structures" (Lefebvre, 2004: 8). Lefebvre examines the shape of the day and its shared rhythms, what Zerubavel calls the social cohesion of temporal symmetry (Zerubavel, 1985: 64; see also Schatzki, 2009 and Shove, 2009). He argues that cyclical and linear time is grafted onto – and becomes meaningful through – spatial coordinates of action in time that cause the quantitative to become qualitative and to have human (social) meanings and values. Lefebvre maintains that the pattern is knowable and predictable, that we can read our social environment through the language of space in time, and that these shared expectations of lived rhythms form a semiotics of the everyday (Lefebvre, 2004: 30; see also de Certeau, 1984).

These rhythms are culturally derived, determined and perpetuated through education. Children are taught to move in space and time according to a schedule agreed upon by all; doing the proper thing at the proper time in the proper place makes one an in-control person fulfilling a proper cultural role. Cultural time is marked by a three-part rhythm of control (work), rest, reward (Lefebvre, 2004: 41). This triad is analogous to the more accessible categories of work, free time and rewards given to keep the cultural actor on track, to appease the system. 'Miller Time', in effect, is explained by the rewards category, and Lefebvre's schema suggests that the dichotomization of the times for control and complete stop may survive because of the rewards system. But that is obvious, since otherwise the phrase 'Miller Time' would have no cultural meaning. Without the punctuated equilibrium of work and leisure there is no recognition of the difference and no need for the reward of the beer. The beer rewards the worker and justifies his work.

If Zerubavel examines how time-use is culturally constructed through specific temporal components, Lefebvre explores how cultural time interacts with lived space. And it is in that analysis that the third 'diversion' time between the two other categories becomes culturally important – the 'pause that refreshes', to borrow an advertising slogan used by Coca-Cola. While the dualism of work and leisure is obvious, Lefebvre suggests that we have ignored the lacuna that divides them and ignored the mechanism that allows cultural actors to shift identities from one to the other. 'Miller Time' suggests not just day and hour and physical intake of alcohol, it also cues us to shift identities from work to leisure (or vacation) and cues our audiences to the shift (Gusfield, 1987). But it also works on multiple levels beyond the semiotic since alcohol intoxication allows for the adoption of new identities and social roles as the effects blur the boundaries of the self within the social. As Lefebvre himself points out, "at the end of the week, in place of the traditional weekly day of rest and piety, 'Saturday Night Fever' bursts out" (Lefebvre, 2004: 74).

If time is measured in two ways (cyclical and linear), then the clock is the literal metronome and cultural rhythm that divides the two. Doing the right thing at the right (clock) time marks one as belonging, as Zerubavel has pointed out. Lefebvre introduces the idea of cultural syncopation, with that slight second 'behind the beat' at the switch between dichotomous time periods. In effect, he argues not just for a semiotic triad that sets the beat of social movement (one, two, three … work, rest, reward …) but also that they do not meet or blend; they are fully disassociated because the third only points to the shift between the others. There is thesis and antithesis, but no synthesis, only the pause that indicates the swing to the other dichotomy. Lefebvre makes clear that this use of time is imposed by culture and not authentic to humanity – that linear time squashes natural biologic and social cyclical time, and that the tension between the two is always present. Linear time causes the enculturated person to conform by subsuming cyclical and natural time to clock-time, to social schedules and to the routine. Natural man is spontaneous, cultural man regulated.

Clock-Time and American Work

Clock-time regulation is a recent development. While linear time has always existed, the measurement of time by clocks rather than natural or social/religious events (dawn, noon, Matins, etc.) is only a few centuries old. The regulation of work schedules by clock-time is newer still, dating to the nineteenth century; the punchable time clock debuted in the 1880s and was the start of the empire that later became IBM (Levine, 1997: 68). Clock-mandated synchronization altered work life in the United States during the nineteenth century and made possible the industrial schedule (Thompson, 1967; Levine, 1997). Eighteenth-century work was marked by task and natural time (sun-up to sundown) or by the bells of local churches rather than by the precise measurement of a clock (Hensley, 1992). Apprentices and masters worked together without the rigid start and stop time that came later, as demonstrated in Benjamin Franklin's autobiography and in the diary of Roger Lowe (Martin, 2006) in which workers made time for pints of beer throughout the day. This is not to suggest that the workday was easy or short (it was not), simply that it wasn't measured by the clock in the way that it is for most industrial workers today. There was no 'Miller Time' because there was no precise 'end of work at 5pm'.

Without accurate and synchronized clocks speed of work could not be measured, and Taylorism and efficiency studies only became possible after the regularization of factory time (Levine, 1997: 70). Once output per hour could be measured, the value of time became intrinsic to profitability for the capitalist factory owner as well as the industrious or entrepreneurial artisan striving to 'get ahead'. In an achievement culture, time is money (ibid.: 18) and industriousness marked by speed of accomplishment against a measurement of linear time. The 'up and coming man' carried a watch (ibid.: 69), and used it to demonstrate his seriousness of purpose and his industry: he did not waste time but got ahead through hard and fast work. Indeed, Van Bueren (2002) used archeological garbage studies to demonstrate that levels of alcohol intake were lower in the households of early twentieth century aqueduct laborers who owned a clock. Lefebvre (2004: 41) might argue that this demonstrates education in appropriate acculturation – the 'dressage' of work schedules.

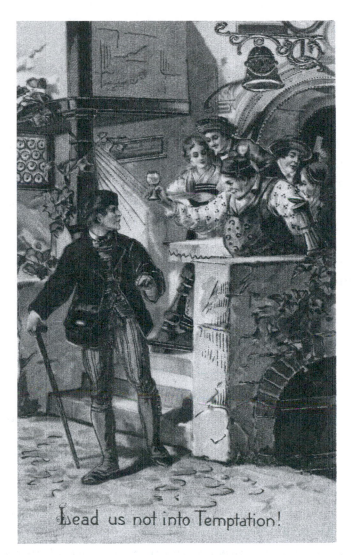

Figure 5.1 **Temperance postcard from 1880.** (*Source:* Collection of the author.)

The good, middle-class American (and aspiring working class man) was a man who didn't waste time drinking because keeping busy was a cultural ideal (Gusfield, 1986: 46–47). Busy-ness also conflated with morality: "the moral gate-keepers of the new industrial society were equally convinced of the virtues of clock-time and were more than willing to add their own voices to its promotion. The latecomer was characterized as a social inferior and, in some cases, a moral incompetent" and "the trait of punctuality came to be associated with achieve-ment and success. Living on clock-time became a defining characteristic of a new class of people on the move" (ibid.: 69–70).

More recently, Goldman and Papson have argued that movement and speed have become central and essential elements of the depiction of effective business, and that in advertisements for many modern companies the semiotics of visual speed represent efficiency and salability. In such depictions, referents to actual linear time as well as space (geographic and social) drop out completely because only the symbols of speed are necessary to carry the message of 'good business' (Goldman and Papson, 2011: 4). Examples of speed imagery used to sell alcohol (as an antidote to speed) can be seen in the 'Rush Hour' ads from a 2003 Jamieson Irish whiskey campaign archived in the marketing section of the website of the Center on Alcohol Marketing and Youth (http://www.camy.org/).[1] These ads are situated in specific (and hip) cities, and provide a photo of four attractive young professionals having a cocktail at an outdoor bar while the world speeds around them. The ads, regardless of city, contrast the ease of the drinking couples by representing the environment around them as a blur. The takeaway is that having a whiskey cocktail will stop the stress and bustle of work, and that a drink (of their brand's whiskey) will allow people to connect meaningfully.

Living on clock-time and expecting time to regulate action in relation to task rather than the task regulating use of time irrevocably alters the human experience of time. Even if the stopwatch of Taylorism isn't directly measuring outputs, the worker internalizes the efficiency model and accepts it as normal. Anyone who has ever spent time in a culture that follows cyclical or task time rather than clock-time registers this cognitive difference. It is met with irritation when trying to accomplish something (the 'mañana, mañana' culture) and with delight when on vacation, when being 'off the clock' is exactly what we desire (Levine, 1997: 89–95). The focus on speed also fuels the desire for a vacation, since clock-time and efficiency create stress. Levine describes the work of psychologists Diane Ulmer and Leonard Schwatzburd on 'hurry sickness', a complex of behaviors that includes privileging economic goals over social experiences, rapid thinking that negates analysis and a preoccupation or worry with future events (Levine, 1997: 21–22). In public health, the psychological and biological cost of timed tasks in which the pace is set by someone other than the worker is well known; Syme, Marmot and colleagues have demonstrated that stress caused by hurried work schedules contributes to health problems (Levine, 1997: 154; Syme, 2004; Marmot et al, 2006). While most industrial work schedules are timed, even professionals learn to abide by clock-time through scheduled meetings, conference calls, appointments and even rushing to catch the morning train (Wilk, 2009).

---

[1]   Unfortunately none of the brands mentioned in this book would allow reproduction of their advertisements. In order to see examples of alcohol ads, the reader is encouraged to visit the website of the Center on Alcohol Marketing and Youth, a program supported by the Johns Hopkins Bloomberg School of Public Health: http://www.camy.org. CAMY offers a comprehensive gallery of alcohol advertisements that can be searched by brand: http://www.camy.org/gallery.

Stearns (1999: 311) notes that the concept of 'stress' is a rather new one, used since about 1920 and only with some regularity after World War Two, and almost always in relation to time regulation (see also Southerton, 2009). He suggests that the normalization of time stress combined with the need to model good working behavior has created a peculiar form of addiction to stress in Americans, who now equate the anxious feelings of rushing through the day in order to manage a (multi-tasking) schedule with the proper identity of a good worker. In turn, this stress fuels the need for release in the form of a time-out or vacation period of the sort Lefebvre describes.

Being too busy (or thinking we are too busy) has become normal, how we expect to work, and how we model good working habits to others. It is an 'all or nothing' approach to economic production in which you keep up and are successful or fall behind and lose. Indeed, much of the self-help literature is devoted to time management to become even more busy, which has become a primary nexus of control of the self and one in which productivity is always linked to effective and efficient use of time. Most Americans view self-control as more important than skills or intelligence in 'getting ahead' (Stearns, 1999: 156). Americans view self-improvement *as* self-control, with success and riches promised if only the self can be mastered – particularly in use of time (Stearns, 1999: 77). This has its roots in the Victorian era, during which self-control became associated with good morals, being a good worker and supporting family values. Self-control over time was also a key component of a temperance lifestyle, since control over alcohol, tobacco and other 'sins' was presumed to occur naturally through the maintenance of a well-regulated life (Gusfield, 1986: 31; Clark, 1976: 26; Smith, 2008: 75). Put succinctly, "the Protestant Ethic provided the psychological justification for the organizational spirit of rational capitalism; a drive towards systematic control of the inner self eventuated in a drive toward systematic mastery of the outer world" (Lears, 1994: 46). Stearns maintains that the Victorian symbols of self-control are not exactly those of today but that significant areas of overlap exist, particularly in the avoidance of wasting time and belief in developing strong work habits. A more pertinent difference is that the Victorians expected that people would need help with self-control and thus created many social structures designed to scaffold morality, such as clear rules for behavior as well as chaperoned activities for young men and women designed to limit sexual temptations. In the modern world we have removed most of that scaffolding and expect people to maintain control on their own, often in the presence of great temptation. This also contributes to feelings of stress and additional loss of control, since having to make decisions rather than follow an internalized cultural script creates tension about capacity to meet expectations in accordance with morality and values. And, as recent research has demonstrated, the frequent need to resist temptation often decreases willpower, which increases stress and ultimately induces a loss of self-control in which 'resistance is futile' (Baumeister and Tierney, 2011).

Work, Stress and Alcohol

Feelings of stress contribute to increased alcohol intakes in individuals and groups, according to many historians, anthropologists and psychologists. While most early Western analyses traditionally linked excessive alcohol intakes (drunkenness) to individual characteristics (Rush, 1790; MacNish, 1827), anthropologists and sociologists have examined cultural patterns of stress and anxiety in relation to higher rates of intake. One of the first cross-cultural and comprehensive reviews of alcohol-related behavior explicitly linked drunkenness to higher levels of social stress (Horton, 1947). Horton argued that societies with increased anxiety tended to have higher rates of inebriation as well as moral strictures against drunken behaviors. The anxiety and rule-breaking create a dualistic cycle of tension, alleviation via inebriation and more tension due to fears of immorality – all of which leads to compartmentalized drinking patterns. This is similar to the time-out American drinking behaviors described by Rorabaugh, who reasoned that the stressful economic situation of the early Republic, augmented by a belief system that equated alcohol intake with personal and social freedom, encouraged solitary binging or 'spree' drinking (Rorabaugh, 1979: 163–169). The spree then led to deep feelings of anxiety and a resumption of good behavior, reinforcing dichotomized and compartmentalized drinking behaviors.

Csikszentmihalyi (1968) analyzed structures of group drinking across Europe and the Unites States and argues that American drinkers tend to be isolated rather than communal drinkers, and that the architectural layout of most American bars discourages social interaction in favor of drinking alone. Solitary drinking is precisely the kind of alcohol use that tends to be a response to anxiety and stress. In other words, he intimates that Americans tend not to use the pub as a 'third place' but as a destination for drunkenness rather than sociality. This is interesting since the idea of a 'third place' mimics that punctuated third beat that Lefebvre describes as a place neither home nor work, where the rules are loosened or defined by immediate social groups rather than by institutional or governmental regulations. The third place brings people together (as Csikszentmihalyi describes for many European bars), while American beliefs about alcohol use (which affect bar design) encourage drinking for effect rather than social solidarity – the bar becomes a destination (a time-out place) rather than a pause between roles or time periods.

Field (1962), in re-examining Horton's cross-cultural data, argues that anxiety alone doesn't explain cultural drinking, that high levels of individualism combined with low social cohesion lead to higher levels of tension and increased drinking. Societies with greater communal organization (stable kin groups, collective ownership of property, patrilocal residence patterns, respect-based hierarchies, etc.) tend to have controlled, friendly and informal collective drinking habits and little overt drunkenness. These societies also tend to control aggression in children while those with less cohesion and more anxiety permit disobedience and self-assertion in youth. Certainly the very individualistic, property-oriented culture of the United States fits into the pattern of societies that exhibit anxiety-based time-out/dichotomized drinking cycles, as does the American habit of encouraging aggression in children in order to raise the individualized, 'take charge' and assertive adult considered an ideal cultural actor. It is possible that multiple elements of American culture, including a preference for personal independence, high levels of time and work stress, widespread access to temptations, as well as the structural and cultural spaces of drinking establishments interact to create acceptance of time-out or dichotomized intake habits.

Leisure, Compartmentalization and Alcohol Use

Leisure becomes a place of temptation in a world in which work and leisure are clearly demarcated and antithetical and where work-time is tightly scripted. Stearns (1999) points out that even though Americans view work and time control as essential to demonstration of appropriate self-identity, they also recognize the importance of anti-work, or leisure. Just as Lefebvre (2004) and Zerubavel (1985) suggest, the natural reaction to work is leisure time or personal time, and one cannot exist without the other. Stearns calls this "compensatory leisure mode" and argues that in the twentieth century leisure has come to be defined by release from work, by abandon and by a reversal of all that is respected and expected during work time (Szala-Meneok, 1994; Stearns, 1999: 153-158; Redmon 2002, 2003a and b; Haywood and Hobbs, 2007). This is exactly the kind of behavior pattern that Rorabaugh chronicles in early America and which MacAndrew and Edgerton (1969) describe as a 'time-out'. In contrast, middle-class Victorians expected that leisure would mimic the control of the workday, and would be spent in improving activities such as sport, family time or civic duties (Levine, 1997: 41; Stearns, 1999: 153; Warner, 2008: 27–28). In the modern day and for many people, leisure has become the obverse of work and deeply carnavalesque, with workday expectations inverted. The advertising slogan: "what happens in Vegas stays in Vegas" is a good example of the activities expected on vacation. The triad of Lefebvre's analysis here meets the public time/private time dualism of Zerubavel, neatly reinforcing the need for reversals of behaviors, identities and roles. Linear time gives way to anti-time, when the clock is abandoned in favor of the moment. Individual control and time scheduling melt into social and event time and the natural/cultural rhythms of the cyclical calendar re-emerge. Alcohol facilitates this transformation because it is anti-linear time, encourages submersion in the moment, the social group and the event. Time is lost as intoxication and sociality take over. The cultural actor ignores the clock and loses control. The sober worker unbound becomes free, spontaneous and 'authentic' – characteristics released and promoted by alcohol use. Alcohol becomes a symbol and sign of leisure, of free time, authenticity of self and of social life.

Such dualism creates compartmentalized behaviors and roles, as described earlier. The worker is not the same person as the one on vacation because leisure-time is a time-out period and roles and behaviors must reflect the difference. Rorabaugh was one of the first historians to point out that American drinking patterns were compartmentalized, and perhaps more so than in other cultures (Rorabaugh, 1979: 168; Gusfield, 1986: 76). Ruth Engs has argued that episodic and dichotomized intakes (or binge drinking habits) characterize Northern European Protestant cultures (Engs, 1995; Room and Makela, 2000) that use beer and spirits rather than wine. Given that the colonies were initially settled by people from Northern Europe it makes sense that those drinking habits would be replicated in the New World. Today compartmentalization is often used to indicate a psychological state in which roles and activities are sharply divided in time and space, especially in relation to behaviors that are regulated by morality. At times these discontinuities cause dualistic personality development so that the person literally becomes a different character in each locale, a process that occurs due to anxieties caused by immoral behaviors. What develops is a 'good' role and time slot as well as a 'bad' role and time slot, often with the 'bad' role unacknowledged or 'on the down-low'. This behavioral splitting can occur during time-out periods (vacations, weekends, etc.), which is why the phrase 'what happens in Vegas stays in Vegas' makes sense. However, these are exactly the conditions described earlier in relation to the perception of time described by Zerubavel and Lefebvre in which public/private periods are delineated, or where work is separate from leisure.

An excellent example of compartmentalization and use of alcohol is the Amish Rumspringa, which is a period in which Amish youth may step outside of their communities to live a mainstream life (Schachtman, 2006). During this time alcohol/drug use and sexual experimentation are condoned and young Amish dress like modern youth, listen to contemporary music, drive cars and adopt many of the attitudes of the larger culture. At the end of this period they must decide whether or not to return to the Amish community and if they return they must formally join the church and put Rumspringa and its behaviors behind them completely. Rumspringa, like many 'time-out' periods, allows for exploration outside of normal moral codes and a sowing of wild oats at a time when youth are questioning the beliefs of their home culture.

Because Rumspringa ends and reintegrates youth back into the community it ultimately supports the normative Amish codes of behavior. The wild years of Rumspringa, when left behind, create a stronger Amish community because the boundaries are so clearly marked and respected. Many college students also perceive the university years as a 'time-out' because they are bracketed by childhood family time and adult time and end with the ideal of an individualized, employed professional. Since escapades during college often rebel against childhood rules and expectations (parents frown upon Beer Pong) but can (in theory) be left behind at graduation, college is perceived as a period in which students can experiment with drugs and alcohol safely, just as Amish youth might.

The time-sites or locations of leisure such as weekends, vacation and evenings have a 'time out' reputation, especially in a capitalist culture in which work and consumption might define the self. And as time-outs they encourage the use of the most popular legal drug, alcohol. The appeal of a television show like *Jersey Shore* rests on these lifecycle dichotomies because the antics of the players are only permissible as a time-out from regular life, and the drunken antics shown are amusing for precisely and only that reason. Similarly, vacation periods such as college spring break and its adult version (Las Vegas and other casino towns, New Orleans, Club Med, cruises, etc.) also highlight bars, drinking and nightlife. Many advertisements for Las Vegas vacations, cruise lines and regional tourist attractions include photos of cocktails or mention that the trip is 'all-inclusive' (meaning 'all-you-can-drink') to emphasize the fun the vacation will offer. For these advertisements to be effective they must play upon already-accepted cultural tropes. In other words, they are not suggesting to anyone that they should drink on vacation – it is not a new idea. They are merely reminding the viewer that their proper vacation will include the intoxication necessary to make it a good time.

In effect, leisure is only 'real' if temptation is presented, accepted and enjoyed. Conventional morality must be overturned and restraint ignored. Americans are often 'all or nothing' vacationers as well as 'all or nothing' drinkers, and vacations and drinking belong together. This is classic 'time-out' drinking, especially if the transgressions are removed from everyday life and space, occurring elsewhere (Vegas, Ibiza or Daytona Beach) where 'what happens there stays there'. Time-out vacations function both as the rest period and the rewarding pause (Lefebvre, 2004: 41) as well as compensatory leisure that rewards the self-control of the work week (Stearns, 1999: 153–154; Hayward and Hobbs, 2007). As private time, it is in stark contrast to public time (Zerubavel, 1985: Chapter 5). It functions as a cultural time-out that condones loss of control and disinhibition (MacAndrew and Edgerton, 1969: Chapter 5; Marshall, 1983; Redmon, 2002 and 2003) because conventional society pretends it doesn't really happen, just as my neighbors in South Carolina pretended they didn't see Baptists in the liquor store. It is also a neat way to contain and explain deviant behavior through a peculiar form of regulation of negative consequences that restricts use by age, role, social place and time (Lemert, 1962), especially in a culture in which self-control is valued and drunken behavior considered sinful. For instance, the Saturday morning campus 'walk of shame' can be explained away by the loud exclamation, "OMG, I cannot *believe* how drunk I got last night!", which is believed to indemnify the consequences of sexual transgression. It seems that intoxication creates a cultural time-out that makes transgressions disappear from social memory. But do such transgressions really disappear? With Facebook, cell phone cameras, texting and email, pictures and descriptions of behaviors can go viral in seconds. Sometimes, what happens in Vegas (or college) doesn't stay there, as many have learned to their sorrow.

Liminal Times and Spaces

The flow of linear time reveals work and play dichotomies, and alcohol can function as a cue or bridge between periods. In addition to the dichotomized time periods that segment events, there are also boundaries that divide sections of linear time and events across days, years and even lifetimes. This section explores the idea of time boundaries as liminal periods that affect the drinking habits of Americans. Having dispensed with work and leisure periods, we will focus on the boundary time between that marks the shift from work to leisure. Earlier we examined the 'third place' as a liminal space marked as in-between work and home, and that it may function to encourage drinking and social behaviors. Gusfield (1987) has provided a superb theory of why alcohol fits into these cultural interstices so neatly, and his theory can be expanded to examine liminality in time as well as space, with a particular focus on college life.

Liminality was initially used by Arnold van Gennep (1960 [1909]) to indicate a time in a person's life when they move from one cultural status to another, usually with the aid of a ritual that has a beginning, a middle period of transition and an ending. Upon completion, the person is re-integrated into the community with a new status. Victor Turner (1967: 93–111) later focused on the middle period of the ritual process, describing it as a time of limbo or of being between identities. During these times, rules may be overturned, daily schedules altered and spatial relationships remade through isolation or forced relocation. Cultural roles and gender status can be ambiguous and it may be a time when people are tested to prove their right to move into the new role or status. A good example of a liminal period is Rumspringa, which tests a youth's commitment to the Amish culture. During Rumspringa he or she is neither fully mainstream nor Amish, and at the end is welcomed back into the Amish community. Other periods of liminality are mourning, age-rituals such as confirmation or Bar/Bat

Mitzvah, or even an engagement to marry. Periods within a life can be liminal including the 'tween' and 'teen' years. When examining the course of a life, the sequencing of events is defined by cultural norms, so that events that occur outside of the regular structure are often considered abnormal, such as marriage and/or bearing children before college rather than after. In this respect, the liminal period can be understood as a sequencing measure (Zerubavel, 1985: 2–9). For many middle-class youth college has become a liminal period, since it occurs between childhood and economic adulthood. Status during college is off-kilter because while students can vote, marry and join the army at 18 years of age, they cannot legally buy a beer until they are 21. This logical inconsistency fuels the social belief that the legal age is a joke and creates a special kind of liminality vis-a-vis intoxicant use. If a young person can decide who should be president or use a gun it is assuredly silly to say the same youth can't buy a beer.

Liminality can also be marked as cultural or physical time within a person's life or a state that defines a role. Some persons may inhabit a state of liminality throughout their lives either because of a failed ritual or because their status is ambiguous within a culture. For instance, a few cultures have a gender category that is neither male nor female, and people so designated may perform male or female roles within the culture throughout their entire adult lives. People on the edge of respectability may also be liminal in that social rules and mores may not apply, such as a rock star whose drug use is silently condoned, if not fully accepted. Similar drug use by someone at the center of society and in a position of respectability (such as a political or religious leader) would most likely end a career immediately. Most cultural insiders can easily map a spectrum of roles of responsibility and respectability, often with religious, teaching or political leaders located in spaces in which drug and alcohol use can damage careers. A liminal role is one in which identity is fluid and negotiated, and where social rules are ambiguous. People whose lives are on the fringes of society, such as musicians and artists, are often permitted far more freedom with intoxicants, sexuality and manners.

The centrality or liminality of role within a culture may also affect how insiders 'read' alcohol or drug use in others. In the class I teach I pose a thought exercise that has the same terribly predictable results every semester. Here it is: it is 2pm and you are walking through a city square in the center of town, a popular and trendy area. In the middle of the square you see a man drinking from a bottle nestled inside a paper bag. He is sitting on a park bench, and looks somewhat unkempt. As you leave the square you encounter a popular and expensive café with sidewalk dining. You see a man sitting at a table with a bottle of wine. He is well-dressed, with a suit and tie; his briefcase is next to his chair. Then I ask the class to tell me a story about what is going on in the square, and the tales are completely predictable, with almost no variation from year to year. They tell me that the man on the bench is an alcoholic and an 'out of work' bum since he is drinking alone and in the middle of the day. And the man at the café is "waiting for a girlfriend or a business partner, he's just closed a big deal and is celebrating." These elements are added to the very bare description of the scene and the students flesh out the situation using standard cultural scripts. However, their accounts make several assumptions that reveal cultural biases: that the man on the bench is out of work and a 'bum', and that (naturally) that means he is an alcoholic. That he is drinking alone (what if a friend just got up?). None of these elements were present in my description – they are added because that is how the students interpreted the semiotics of his clothing and behaviors. On the other hand, the nicely dressed man has a friend added (so he is not drinking alone!), and the presumption that he is waiting for a woman or a business partner also references success (because he's either getting lucky or getting rich). Often the students will add a second wine glass to the description when they tell their story about the scene. But I never mention any wine glasses when I pose the problem. He is also given a rationale for drinking that negates the possibility of an alcohol problem – he is celebrating a 'big business deal', so drinking during the day is made acceptable because it is festive. In short, the poverty of the first man dictates that he is an alcoholic, while the prosperity of the second insulates him from the cultural taboos against drinking alone in the middle of the day.

After they finish their revisionist fantasies I administer the *coup de grace* – I tell them that both men are doing exactly the same thing: drinking alone, outside, at a time of day when cultural rules dictate that drinking is not acceptable. The men are exactly alike, except for clothing. But! but! but! the students say, the man at the café bought an expensive bottle of wine and the bum is drinking cheap crap beer or thunderbird! I reply that they don't know that the man at the café bought an 'expensive bottle' and he probably hasn't even paid for it yet – he may be planning to walk out on the tab. And the guy on the bench could be an eccentric multi-millionaire enjoying a first-growth Bordeaux and it's only in the bag because drinking in the park is illegal. But the clothes! But the briefcase! Wrong, I say, it means nothing – the two men are doing exactly the same thing at exactly the same time. We simply read their situations as different – or wish to read them as different – because of cultural tropes that validate the clothing and appearance of the one but not the other. Just as drinking alcohol indicates a totalizing semiotic text to a Baptist (who perhaps also smokes, fornicates and ignores the Scriptures) so does nice clothing signify that the man is successful, therefore not an alcoholic. That is because his appearance is central and mainstream and because he looks respectable. If he were dressed in Goth clothing or shorts and a t-shirt a different story would be told, and it might allow for the possibility of problematic drinking because such clothing is closer to the fringes or liminal. In fact, the appearance of certain kinds of clothing or self-adornment (rock-star-type clothes or visible tattoos) can cause people to assume drug and alcohol abuse because they place their wearers outside of the center of the 'respectability' diagram. That is why no-one is surprised when rock stars asphyxiate in their own vomit, and why they are *very* surprised when a rocker is an abstainer. It's outside of the cultural script for that role.

Liminality and Daily Schedules

Points of liminality or limbo within a life can be mapped through examination of linear and event time. Times of day, the week and the year all have structures of action determined by cultural expectations – professional, personal or religious. For instance, think about a college student's weekly schedule, starting with Sunday. What does the student do each day? Is the Sunday schedule open? Does it resemble Monday's schedule? Why or why not? If a student's week is mapped using standard activities and appointments, there may be periods of time that are empty or mark transitions from one time/place/role to the next. Thursday may start with a 9am wake-up followed by coffee and checking email/Facebook. A quick shower, then he runs to make a 10am class. Class is out at 11:20 but it takes 10 minutes to leave, then a walk back to the dorm for lunch at noon. Fifteen minutes are spent in the dorm room and lunch takes 45 minutes. Back to the room for a quick nap, at 2pm run to a class that ends at 3:30. At 4pm the student has a two-hour lab section. The student then goes to the gym and works out for an hour, arriving back at the dorm at 7:30 in time to catch the end of dinner. At 8:30 he walks to the library, intending to work on a paper due Monday. At the library he runs into some friends who tell him about a party later that night and they make plans to meet up in an apartment to pre-game at 10:30. The student leaves the library at 9:45 to go back to his dorm and dress for the party. At 10:15 he walks to the friend's apartment, arriving at 10:30. The pre-game begins with a power hour and at 12 midnight the participants stumble out to find the party. He leaves the party at 3am and walks back to his dorm room. Questions: where are the liminal time periods located? Do they lead to a loss of time or of focus? Where does he shift social roles or identity? How much time does he spend studying? How much studying does the student really have time for? When, aside from the pre-game and party time, would student cultural rules permit alcohol intake? In other words, is there any time during the day in which the student could have a drink besides the pre-game and party? Why or why not would those times be acceptable?

Now, mentally contrast the college schedule with that of a man in his thirties. He gets up at 6am, showers, has coffee/breakfast and makes the kids' lunches until 7am, commutes an hour to the office, and arrives at 8:15. Work until noon, take a client to lunch until 1:30, back to the office until 5:30, commute, return home at 6:45. Prepare and eat dinner until 8pm, then help two children with math homework until 9pm. Oversee children's bedtimes until 9:30, chat with spouse until 10pm. Watch the evening news and a sitcom, fall asleep at 11pm. When are there periods of liminality or time limbo in this schedule? Is this time lost or can it be recovered? When might this adult take a drink, according to cultural rules of normal alcohol intake? When would taking a drink indicate a problem?

In each of these days there are significant portions where the person is 'in betwixt and between', to use Turner's description of liminality. There are far fewer times for the working adult than for the college student, who has limbo times before and between classes, before and after dinner, and then has a relatively free schedule after dinner that is nominally supposed to be spent studying. There are also specific transitions between blocks of time such as before and after work (or after the lab, for the student) and before and after meals. Each has free/private/personal time starting around 10pm during which the external scheduling ends. And, according to the day of the week the schedule may shift as well, since Thursday has become a 'party night' for students while Sunday and Monday are most certainly not. Similarly, the working man may have a Friday or Saturday night with dinner out, meetings with friends or a family event. The critical question for alcohol use, especially in relation to the ideas of Zerubavel and Lefebvre, is when and where is alcohol use acceptable within these schedules, and when is it not? And how does alcohol use function (besides as an intoxicant) within the daily or weekly schedule?

For instance, students at the university where I teach believe that drinking alone is a sign of alcoholism. That means that the only time a student can drink is in class, at lunch or dinner, in the library (if studying with friends) or at the pre-game or party. However, drinking alcohol is not acceptable in classes or the library, nor is drinking allowed in the dorms – so drinking at lunch and dinner couldn't occur without subterfuge. So the only time the student can drink is between classes or at the pre-game and party. But between classes he is alone, so he can't drink. Culturally, the only time the student can drink is with friends, ideally at a party or bar. On the other hand, the working adult can drink anytime except at work, because adult mores accept drinking alone but abjure drinking during work periods. However, he couldn't drink during his morning commute (especially if driving), and probably wouldn't drink while helping his children do their homework (although if helping with calculus might require a martini afterwards). He might have a drink at lunch or with dinner. He could go to a pub (third place) between work and home, and as long as he still got home in time (and able) to do his evening tasks he'd be fine. He might have a 'nightcap' while watching the news before bed. As long as he refrained from overt drunkenness none of these occasions would be marked as problematic. However, if he drank before or during work or had too much at dinner or opted to go out to a bar every night he might be considered to have a problem. The critical analysis, using the time theories discussed earlier, is how work/leisure/reward and the structures of time (sequence, duration, temporal location and recurrence, and their cultural manifestations of sacred/profane and public/private) channel acceptable drinking times. Liminal periods can either encourage or discourage alcohol use depending on their sequence in the larger cultural schedule.

Similarly, the need to shift the pendulum from work to leisure (or from sacred to profane, public to private) creates a brief pause that can be used to signal the next period in the sequential structure. Zerubavel quotes Edmund Leach to describe how this liminal period can signal a transition:

> Leach has proposed a "pendulum view of time", claiming that temporality is essentially a discontinuity of repeated contrasts, a "succession of alternations" between the sacred and profane, with festivals marking the temporary transition from one to another. The fundamental difference between sacred time and profane time results from the fact that, from a cultural standpoint, they are essentially considered to "belong" to two entirely different planes – and are even represented by two entirely different modalities – of temporality.
>
> Zerubavel (1985: 112)

This quote could be amended by the phrases public and private time sequences and make just as much sense. The point is that there is a changeover liminal time slot that signals the next time sequence and cultural actors can read and use this switch to convey what they are doing. Garfield (1987) analyzes this in relation to alcohol use and theorizes that alcohol functions as a framing device to alert others to 'what is coming next' as well as what kind of time sequence one currently inhabits. "The relation between alcohol and the passage from one realm to another is to be studied as text, that is as a statement or language through which a message is being communicated" (ibid.: 77). In particular, alcohol signals the passage from work to play, since the two realms of time are mutually exclusive in time use and personal identity. Thus having a beer or cocktail in one's hand is a semiotic text that states 'leisure', 'vacation' or 'play' rather than work. It is a keying device that not only operates as a text but also as a vehicle for the event (leisure) that it announces. It is a marker for 'private time', 'profane time' and for 'my time' in the same way that a coffee cup signifies 'work time' and 'time to concentrate'. It also signifies sociality and festivity (ibid.: 79). Alcohol, additionally, can frame a 'time-out' period for behavior since it is believed that alcohol disinhibits (MacAndrew and Edgerton, 1969; Levine, 1978) so consequences are to be ignored. Alcohol keys, frames and makes possible the reading and participation in leisure time by signaling the end of work and preparing the drinker psychologically to 'have fun'. Alcohol use thus initiates the liminal period, cues the shift to the time-out period, makes possible the performance of leisure, play and sociality and, eventually, excuses the behaviors that arise from intoxication. For all of these reasons "it's Miller Time!" and "TGIF" can be read by almost all adult Americans as "5pm, Friday" and "time to have fun."

Alcohol as cueing and framing text also functions in annual rituals and in the celebrations that mark lifecycles. Most cultures that use alcohol include it as a transformative element in sacred and profane celebrations, from weddings and wakes to Fourth of July and Labor Day BBQs. The rite of communion uses alcohol to literally transform (according to Catholic theology) the wine to the blood of Christ – which symbolically transforms the participant to a member of Christ's Church. And can anyone imagine a Christmas party without ample 'cheer' in the form of champagne, cocktails or a 'wassail' bowl? The ultimate ritual of liminal time change – New Years' Eve – is a perfect example of how alcohol is used to create awareness of temporal transformation and to create a mood of festivity to baptize the New Year. Rituals of change that mark transitions in a life are also celebrated with alcohol, and indeed, often require it to make the ritual official. The toast given at a wedding is not just an excuse to drink a glass of champagne, it is also an ancient ritual that acknowledges the new status of the couple – recall that the word 'bridal' arises out of the old Celtic tradition of the 'Bride Ale' that makes the wedding official. Even the toasts that accompany the 'bottoms up' are a form of deep verbal tradition (an incantation) that welcomes the bride and groom into each other's families and circle of friends. Celebrations that mark the transition from childhood to adulthood, such as twenty-first birthday and graduation parties, almost always include toasts and alcohol. Alcohol marks these occasions as meaningful because it signifies the liminal periods indicating status change that are deeply embedded in Western cultural history. Alcohol is a form of psychotropic onomatopoeia that signals change at the same time that it creates an altered state of being. Rituals with alcohol are collective, subjective and join people in a sacred, shamanic journey from sober state to intoxication and transformation and eventually to reintegration into community. It metaphysically ushers individuals and societies through the three stages of liminality (separation, transition and reincorporation) and in so doing creates new social roles and statuses that allow the stages of life to progress along a normative sequence.

Conclusions

Alcohol has many meanings in the United States as well as a more contentious history than in most Western alcohol-using nations. Analysis of the history of

Table 5.1 **Alcohol dichotomies**

Sobriety	*Drunkenness*
Schedules and routines	Spontaneity
Making money	Spending money
Saving/making time	Killing/wasting time
Compartmentalization of activity/roles	Authenticity of self/role-playing opportunities
Compartmentalization of priorities	Doing what you will
Sacred time	Profane time
Work	Leisure
Work-week	Weekend
Work schedule	Vacation
Public	Private
Solitude	Sociality
Accomplishment	Slacking
Self-control	Losing control
'Work Hard'	'Play Hard'
Work/home time-space	Liminal/time-out space

alcohol in the Unites States reveals a deeply dualistic understanding of its use, and one that would probably shock the original settlers from England and Europe who welcomed alcohol as a 'good creature' and as an important element of the diet. The cultural dichotomies are stark and probably contributed to the rise of Prohibition as well as the continuation of temperance ideals among a significant portion of the population. Dualism has also encouraged a culture of 'all or nothing' drinking that allows for time-out intoxication and behaviors. However, while many Americans seem to regard alcohol mostly as an intoxicant, many do not drink in a time-out manner, nor do they use alcohol as a drug. Additionally, most students do not abuse alcohol even if they may experiment with intoxication during their college years. Many Americans are able to have a drink or two alone or with friends without causing problems for themselves or others. This analysis of time use and culture is not meant to indicate that Americans are necessarily more prone to alcohol abuse than are people in other countries, merely that there are elements of our culture and history that encourage categorizing alcohol as a drug rather than as a food. This means that there is a persistent belief among Americans that use has a presumed goal of intoxication – which cognitively eliminates the possibility of moderate use. The result is an America deeply divided about alcohol use and also ripe for time-delimited overuse. A mapping of alcohol dichotomies illustrates these belief systems, and challenges us to think about how such divisions contribute to acceptance of intoxication (Table 5.1).

6

ALCOHOL ADVERTISING

You are walking down the street and in the bus stop you see an advertisement for Three Olives brand vodka. It shows a woman in a tight-fitting skimpy black dress crouching in a martini glass. She is wearing stiletto-heeled sandals, her hair is long and flowing, and she has a come-hither look in her eye. The ad asks "What's in your Martini?"[1]

A few hours later you are getting ready to go out with your friends. It's Thursday night, the bridge crowd will be at home, so it's a good night to hit the hot bars. You decide that a little black dress (LBD) is in order, maybe you'll meet an older guy with some class. You look for your strappy sandals, and blow-dry your hair off your face. Your girlfriends join you while you put on makeup and you all decide to have a few shots to pre-game. Your roommate pulls out a bottle of Southern Comfort and you wrinkle your nose and tell her that you're really in the mood for some vodka shots. "Yuck!" everyone says, too harsh. OK, "how about we make some martinis?" you suggest, but everyone rolls their eyes and measures out the SoCo.

Later, at the bar, a guy friend of your roommate's decides everyone needs some tequila shots to "get the night going." He walks up to the bar and bangs his fist down to get the bartender's attention and loudly yells "we need six shots of Patron right away!"

The next day, while visiting your friend, you leaf through a Maxim magazine and see several Patron ads. You notice them because unlike the other ads in the men's magazine they don't have scantily clad women; they seem tasteful. They all show a picture of the bottle against a white background with octagonal blocks containing words. One ad says "Rock Star" and "Movie Star" in the boxes, with

---

1 Unfortunately, none of the brands mentioned in this book would allow reproduction of their advertisements. In order to see examples of the ads described, the reader is encouraged to visit the website of the Center on Alcohol Marketing and Youth, a program supported by the Johns Hopkins Bloomberg School of Public Health: http://www.camy.org. CAMY offers a comprehensive gallery of alcohol advertisements that can be searched by brand: http://www.camy.org/gallery. Most of the images described in this chapter can be found filed under the brand name at the CAMY website.

the legend "Some Perfection is Debatable." Next to the photo of the bottle are the words "Some is Not." You figure the tequila must be a fancy kind because they are advertising it as a rock star brand. The next page has another Patron ad, but this time the boxes over the bottle state "Size 2," "Size 0" and "Size –2." "Jeez," you think, "is there even a size –2? I must be fat if I don't know about it."

Alcohol Advertising

Alcohol ads are everywhere. Once you start looking you see them in the oddest places. They are in bus stops and on the sides of buses, on billboards, inside metro stations, plastered on the sides of cars and even in the toilets at popular restaurants. Turn on the TV and you will see more ads – for beer, wine and spirits. Radio, newspapers and magazines carry at least a few and some magazines carry dozens. Maybe as a child you saw the Budweiser frog ads and thought them cute, without really noticing what they sold. Now, you see an ad like the one from Three Olives vodka and you want the dress, you want the look, you want the fun and excitement of being that woman at that time, in control, popular, at hip cocktail parties, successful, strong and ... in a glass? Hmmm, isn't that kind of like being in a see-through prison? Can she get out of the glass? And what's she doing there anyway? Why would a girl in a glass be a good way to advertise liquor? What does it all mean, and why do you notice it? And, ahem, might the 'glass as prison' be a kind of subversive metaphor for the pain of addiction, or is it meant to mean something else? Is she really strong and in control (because of her beauty) or does the glass mean that she's a kind of prisoner or slave? After all, she's on her knees, which isn't a very strong position. But if she's not powerful, why does she look so strong and sexy? Does the martini make her sexy? Hmmm, you probably need to think this one through a bit more, eh?

Alcohol ads are everywhere, and their messages are often rather simple. They tend to emphasize fun, companionship (either of friends or sex partners), status or connoisseurship (how to choose and enjoy 'fine' wines and liquors). Most themes or rationales (beyond connoisseurship) are indirect and suggest purchase by referencing something other than the alcohol itself. In effect, alcohol use becomes linked to specific forms of valued social or personal characteristics (fun, sociality and success) rather than to the effects of intake. Alcohol is rarely advertised as something that will intoxicate and only among specialty brands are flavors emphasized. While advertising in general relies on semiotics (the use of signs and symbols to convey a message) to point to reasons for purchase, alcohol advertising uses symbols and signs that point away from the substance more than most product categories. After all, it's not very convincing to baldly state "drink this booze, it's really strong and will mess you up" since intoxication is culturally problematic. It's far better to rely on symbols that imply that "if you buy this booze you will have a good time with friends" which the ad viewer can then safely translate to mean "this booze will mess me up and make sure I have a good time with friends."

Advertising Shows the World 'As It Is'

Emphasizing fun, status and companionship works for advertisers because human beings are an affiliative species and these themes resonate deeply with people in every culture. Most cultures that use alcohol understand its ability to foster connections and to demonstrate social and economic hierarchies. According to Mary Douglas (1987a) alcohol performs three important social tasks. Alcohol use (how it is shared and with whom) constructs the world 'as it is'. As demonstrated with the cultural construction of time, alcohol use charts how people interact with each other and reveals unwritten rules about conduct and social life. Alcohol use also defines identities and social groupings because those who are culturally allowed to drink together often have connections in other social realms, such as marriage and/or business. Drinking together indicates a connected social world and connections between people. In most cultures, a man and a woman drink together (alone) only during courtship, because the disinhibitive effects of alcohol might lead to sexual activity ("candy is dandy but liquor is quicker"). Until recently most respectable drinking was accomplished in same-sex (homosocial) groupings rather than in mixed groups because males and females were not supposed to mix socially unless properly supervised. Nowadays mixed-group drinking can occur, but hook-ups often result, which demonstrates how alcohol use mirrors larger changes in social mores. As a second example of the world 'as it is', the rules surrounding hospitality are important in most cultures with behavioral expectations of host and guest made clear as a part of good manners. It would be a grave social error to charge for drinks at a wedding, since it is defined as a ritual party given by the parents of the married couple for the community of friends and family. The parents are hosts and must give hospitality rather than sell it. They, in turn, derive social power and hierarchy through being hosts; their social status rises because they give away food and drink (and hopefully, a good time) to their community members. These rules are often demonstrated in advertising images, since advertisements mirror the world 'as it is', so analysis of ad themes both illustrates and reveals cultural norms of behavior.

Advertising Provides a Model for Social Relationships

Second, drinking constructs an ideal world by defining relations between people and giving cultural structure to the connections between gods and men. Most cultures with alcohol integrate it into religious rituals – the sacrament of communion is a good example. In this ritual the wine becomes not only the symbol of the blood of God (and thus a symbol of the connection between God and man) but, depending on the beliefs of the church, may be transformed into the actual blood of Christ. His sacrifice for mankind is rendered tangible as worshippers drink the blood of God as evidence of their inclusion in the community of Christians. To an anthropologist the communion could be described as a representation of the covenant between God and mankind; the wine stands for the commitment between the two parties, just as the community toast at a wedding represents the social acknowledgment of the commitment the new couple bears to each other. An otherwise social union – marriage – is made holy by shared drinking as surely as communion represents being within the community of Christ. On more humble planes, who drinks with whom, where and when often maps culturally normative relationships between age and gender cohorts. One unwritten rule prevalent among Americans is that people of different generations shouldn't drink together; it's considered odd, for instance, for generations up or down to join a drinking party between same-age friends. Among college students, the idea of 'going out for drinks' with older people is frankly shocking, probably because students haven't yet entered into cross-generation work or community relationships that foster such gatherings. These cultural rules are mirrored by advertising that rarely shows different age cohorts drinking together. The 'normal' way for alcohol advertisements to demonstrate social behavior is by providing an image of same-age friends or potential sexual partners interacting. Because alcohol plays such an established cultural role in courtship, few brands would want to create confusion for the target audience by mixing age cohorts to imply a May-December romance.

Advertising Reflects the Economics of Alcohol Use

Mary Douglas's third function is economic; every society that uses alcohol creates economic structures for production, distribution and consumption, and alcohol usually provides significant revenue to producers and the state. Advertising is part of the economic power of alcohol because it generates revenue for agencies and media, promotes purchase and provides templates for appropriate use. Alcohol ads demonstrate how to enjoy the product and, through linkages to semiotic themes designed to encourage purchase, provide models for lifestyle identities. If it can be said that 'you are what you eat' it certainly follows equally that you are also 'what you drink', and brand identities work for a reason. Alcohol functions economically in four ways. It employs millions of people in direct production (making wine, etc.) and advertising, distribution and service jobs. It demonstrates economic control and power through taxation, rights to produce and distribute, monopolies and ownership of the means of production as well as the 'earned' right to drink through hard work (work hard, play hard), ability to buy, or accomplishment ("it's been a hard week, I need to party!"). Since it is a high-status item in most cultures, ownership of alcohol production and distribution capacities is often a mark of economic distinction; a good example is desire among the wealthy to own vineyards in Napa, Tuscany or the South of France. Third, because centralized political power is often linked to alcohol production monopolies, many cultures develop alternate economies of production and distribution as resistance to mainstream power and control (Gamburd, 2008). Such black markets have immense social power and meaning even if not official. Good examples include the alternate economy created by the making of moonshine in the American South and the elaborate distribution networks at universities to ensure that underage students have access to alcohol. The social networking necessary to get an undergrad male into a fraternity party – and better yet, to be served beer – represents the articulation of high levels of social capital, planning and wiliness. The status allotted to fraternity members because they are able to distribute alcohol to underage students grants them social power on campus and among their peers – women as well as men.

Consumption of branded alcohol provides a means to demonstrate selfhood, status and identity through displays of choice and purchasing power. This refers to connoisseurship as well as distribution in the gift economy. The wine aficionado is a good example of status through connoisseurship, and the fraternity house that throws the biggest and best party on campus an example of status through distribution. The latter mirrors the power the Celtic war band leader gained from providing a drinking party in the mead hall, proving the enduring popularity of demonstrating hierarchy by providing alcohol. Most important for advertising, however, is the opportunity that alcohol presents for demonstrating both knowledge and economic capacity through choosing the right kind of alcohol in social situations. It is this kind of status identity that advertisers induce by encouraging buyers to create a richer, more powerful or sexier 'self' through purchase of their particular brand of hooch. As Berger has stated, "publicity proposes to each of us that we transform ourselves, or our lives, by buying something" (Berger, 1972: 131), and alcohol ads use references to status to imply that purchase makes the buyer a more successful person in the eyes of his peers.

Advertising works to encourage desire for the product by emphasizing what the product can do for the buyer, or what kind of person the buyer will become when a purchase is made. Advertising, especially for alcohol, creates lifestyle identification: "I am this kind of person (or I wish to be this kind of person) so I should buy this kind of scotch." Lifestyle branding is usually the favored form of advertising message since appeals for effect are culturally problematic. Most societies that use alcohol tend to have cultural rules that forbid solitary drinking, making most alcohol intake public and a very good medium for status display. Showing alcohol as a prestigious consumption item in close association with other markers of power, wealth and status implies that the brand is used by those who are higher up the social scale. Even in less wealthy nations the lure of showing off with alcohol is a strong motivator for purchase. Among middle-class Africans in Nairobi, Johnny Walker scotch is the favored drink and is demonstrating impressive growth in sales each year. *The Economist* (October 1, 2011: 72) states: "premium whisky tastes good, gets you drunk and may impress your peers. What's not to like?". And because alcohol is a consumable – it is drunk and is gone – it is an ideal focus for continual advertising to trigger repeat sales. Unlike other consumerist forms of showing off (such as diamonds or fancy cars) it is used up, which makes it especially profligate and demonstrates the economic grandiosity of its user.

Branding almost always relies on a desire for status or identity construction to sell a product that is pretty darn similar to other products of the same type. Most popular light beers taste much the same, as do the heavily advertised vodka brands. Often the major difference between products is the meanings that social actors project onto the brands, and those meanings are carefully constructed by advertising messages used to promote the brand. The 'Discerning Taste' advertisements for Grey Goose vodka are a perfect example – the strategy links the brand to images of social and financial success such as posh apartments, yachts, opulent dinner parties and 'VIP' entertainment venues. The Grey Goose website offers a link to examples of both print and film advertisements, and while the campaigns change each year they all emphasize high-end and glamorous lifestyles. Grey Goose was relatively unknown in America until advertisements were placed in aspirational magazines such as *Vogue*, and the first messages were about flavor with testimonials and recipes. After brand introduction the message switched to status and most ads now show the vodka used by glamorous people in exclusive settings. Grey Goose has carefully managed its media presence to link the brand to highly desirable examples of success to encourage the aspirational buyer to purchase in order to have 'the good life' shown in the ads. To quote the company's own PR announcement: "creative elements of the campaign capture particular moments, people, places, and events in the lives of GREY GOOSE consumers revealing their unyielding lifestyle of discerning taste" (Grey Goose, 2007).

Mary Douglas's three roles for alcohol mirror how alcohol is advertised and demonstrate how deeply alcohol use is dictated by social expectations and cultural values. Alcohol is usually advertised as something that fulfills social desires such as status display and companionship. Even clear functions such as taste are rarely advertised without reference to social activities or status, since a brand would not want buyers to limit use to a specific taste experience. It's far safer to link alcohol buying to social desires in order to encourage everyday use and repeat purchase. In order to convey the necessity to purchase a non-essential good such as alcohol, advertisers must link the brand to a function beyond the utilitarian, and that is usually a lifestyle identity that promises to transform the buyer. In effect, most alcohol ads rely on what Berger (1972: 149) calls the "dreamt future": "the interminable present of meaningless working hours is 'balanced' by a dreamt future in which imaginary activity replaces the passivity of the moment. In his or her day-dreams the passive worker becomes the active consumer. The working self envies the consuming self" (see also Williamson, 2005: 161). Cashman argues that Americans are "aspirational consumers, buying not just to subsist, but to make statements about our progress in the world" (Cashman, 2006: 175) but that "advertising coaxes consumers into vainly pursuing a lifestyle that's tantalizing within reach yet forever beyond their grasp" (ibid.: 184). And because alcohol is relatively inexpensive, it's an easy indulgence to make the consumer feel glamorous, successful, or one of the beautiful people. As one student in a sociological study of drinking explained: "alcohol allows people to be the kind of person they 'are in their head'" (Vander Ven, 2011: 167), and alcohol advertising to young people (teens through the twenties) almost always relies on lifestyle messages that promise glamour, pleasure, fun and sexual success (Gunter, Hansen and Touri, 2010: 31). This fantasy creature – the ideal – is one that inhabits the dichotomized world of leisure, autonomy, and of the authentic self discussed in the previous chapter. It is also a creature of the time-out; the perfect self – autonomous, high-status, sexually attractive and authentic. Alcohol is the medium of the dreams for the ideal leisured self (certainly as demonstrated in advertising messages) but also the disinhibiting instrument for attainment of that self. Alcohol advertising contributes to the dualistic or dichotomized world that separates work and play, sobriety and intoxication, and the everyday self and the 'authentic' ideal self. Indeed, alcohol advertising is dependent on that dichotomy, since without it there would be no message to advertise.

How Alcohol Advertising Works

Alcohol ads are designed to make you notice the brand, to want to purchase the brand, to properly enjoy the brand, and then to buy the brand again. Please note the excessive use of the word 'brand', since advertising isn't designed to make you buy alcohol, but to buy and use a specific kind of alcohol and to become a believer in what the brand represents. Brands have social meanings created by advertising and by the community of users; successful advertising reflects community use as well as the core message (O'Guinn and Munoz, 2005). After all, if you are buying for effect (and most alcohol is purchased for effect) any kind of alcohol will do because they all intoxicate. The only alcohols advertised are the ones that make enough product to be able to afford widespread print and TV/radio/internet ads to create a set of 'sticky' symbols that adhere to the brand (Williamson, 2005: 24). It costs an enormous amount of money to support an advertising campaign that successfully links intangible ideas like fun, companionship and success to specific brands, so most ads are for mass-produced alcohols with few individual characteristics in taste or production. These 'brands' must create a connection with specific social and cultural ideas in order to sell, since they are often indistinguishable in flavor. And why would a company put that much effort into selling something that is essentially easily reproducible and anonymous? Simple: alcohol can be very, very profitable because the raw materials and processing cost a pittance in relation to the price the product commands at market. Many alcohols are so cheap to produce in relation to the selling price that manufacturers can afford to spend a great deal on advertising in order to link a story to their product. According to the Campaign for a Commercial-Free Childhood, alcohol brands spend $2 billion every year in the United States alone to advertise their products. Alcohol advertising is ubiquitous, meaningful and deeply important to alcohol companies' profits.

Semiotics

Advertisements use stories to convince the viewer/buyer that the item being sold will enhance life in specific ways, and these stories (myths) are designed to connect ideas about identity and character to the use of the brand's products (Holt, 2005). These myths connect a favored concept (such as freedom, success or admiration) to the brand in a process that Williamson defines as ideology, or the "representation of imaginary relationships between real things" (Williamson 2005: 74). There is no real reason for financial success to be connected to a brand of vodka, for instance, but that is exactly what Grey Goose does in advertisements by portraying well-dressed people in high-cost settings. For advertising to be successful and for the brand to be purchased, the users must accept the stories and want to live the myth by using the product. Williamson (2005: iv) sums up this idea neatly: "advertisements' role is to attach meanings to products, to create identities for the goods (and service providers) they promote: a process today described as branding." Advertising encourages purchase using symbols to connect a narrative to the goods and services to be purchased. The story has several elements: the originating myth, the actual use-value (what the good will do), the perceived-value (what the use-value will do for or mean to the buyer) and what use means within the culture (the messages that using the good conveys to other people). The advertising story is usually about 'lifestyle' which could be broadly described as "stuff you buy that expresses something about yourself or who you wish to appear to be." Lifestyle consists of attitudes, habits and possessions that are associated with a particular person or group

(American Heritage Dictionary, 2009) and is performative because it can be used to communicate about the self to others. As an aside, it is important not to confuse 'lifestyle' and 'life': the former is what you buy and the latter who you are – but in a consumer society sometimes the difference becomes blurred.

The goods we buy provide symbolic messages about us to others (our 'style') and are semiotic, communicative and culturally negotiated (Veblen, 1899; Baudrillard, 1985; Dyer, 1988: 116; Ewen, 1990; Tomlinson, 1990; Foster, 2005; Williamson, 2005: 35; Manning and Uplisashvili, 2007). Advertisers use these systems of story-telling to raise brand awareness, encourage purchase, and educate to use and enjoy the product so that the buyer has a positive experience and comes back for more. The need to create repeat purchases is particularly keen with alcohol since use destroys the product. It is perhaps because use cancels the perception-value of booze that many drinkers display their bottles openly on liquor trays, specially made serving tables or (the ne plus ultra of the mid-century American house) a home wet-bar with open shelves for bottles and glasses. The college student version is the display of empty high-end spirits and microbrew bottles in the kitchens and living rooms of bachelor apartments. These displays exist because they say something about the person who lives there, and they provide that message through semiotics.

Semiotics is the study of signs as a part of social life, or the study of the connection of concepts to things and to the symbols that represent those ideas and things. "A sign is quite simply a thing – whether object, word, or picture – which has a particular meaning to a person or group of people. It is neither the thing nor the meaning alone, but the two together. The sign consists of the Signifier, the material object, and the Signified, which is its meaning. These are only divided for analytical purposes: in practice a sign is always thing-plus-meaning" (Williamson, 2005: 17). Ferdinand de Saussure defined the sign as the signifier (sounds and images) and the signified (concepts and things) connected by an arbitrary relationship. It is arbitrary because it is culturally constructed and can shift; the culture using the sign decides its connection and meaning, although the process that came to link the sound to the idea or thing may be obscure to the people who use it. It is the process that attaches meanings to the sign that is of most interest to anthropologists. Charles Peirce defined the sign as tripartite (rather than dyad) using the terms 'Representamen', 'Interpretant' and 'Object'. A Representamen is the form of the sign (a sound, image, or symbol), 'Interpretant' what it signifies (what the sign means to the viewer) and the 'Object' is what the sign references. Peirce further divides the sign into three types: icon, index and symbol. An icon looks like the object, the index demonstrates cause and effect in relation to the object and a symbol is arbitrary: for example, the word/sound 'blue' means a specific color in English that is symbolized by the word 'azul' in Spanish. But signs go well beyond simple words and sounds that convey the idea of a thing to include gestures and sequences of communicative action that allow cultural actors to perform for each other.

As an example, when someone smiles it usually indicates happiness or delight, and the nuances of the smile (ironic, playful, heartfelt or suggestive) can be read by people within the culture. A smile used in an advertisement is indexical because it indicates happiness with the thing advertised and implies that the buyer will be happy as well should he purchase and use the product. The smile might be doubly indexical by being, for instance, a suggestive smile given by a sexually attractive person, thereby indicating that the buying is linked to happiness with the product as well as with the possibility of having sex with the model or someone like the model. Then smile/product/sex is a singular linked (Peirce) sign that corresponds to representamen/object/interpretant. Should the viewer read the sign in this manner, the advertisement will have succeeded in creating a potent myth or story (or ideology, according to Williamson) that connects sex and the emotions or desires that surround sex with the brand. It is ideology because sex and the brand/product may have nothing to do with each other in reality, and it is only through semiotics that the ideology makes sense and has the power to compel purchase. A semiotic analysis of an advertisement reveals multiple layers of messages from direct signs and symbols (Rozik, 1997; Berger, 2007: 137-151) to a looser examination of the sociology of the symbolism (Goffman, 1976), so close appraisal reveals metaphors, stories and connections of real complexity.

SKYY vodka used the actress Jessica Simpson in one of the more infamous alcohol advertisements of the last decade. The ad (which can be viewed in the SKYY Vodka section of the print marketing section of the CAMY website http://www.camy.org) shows a man and a woman near a pool; she is in the water, he is on the tiles next to the pool, relaxing on a chaise longue. She is in the water on a blow-up float, wet and wearing a see-through white dress, slip or nightgown with strappy high-heeled silver pumps, while he is fully dressed in a dark suit and tie, shoes and sunglasses. Both are wearing what appears to be expensive clothing. He is armored against the gaze of the viewer in this pose, and fully covered, made invulnerable by the power accessories of tie, suit and sunglasses. She is vulnerable and slightly ridiculous in wet dress and wet 'fuck me' sandals. Between them, and hard against the softer textures of float, dress and water, is the object being sold: a bottle of bright-blue vodka. He is pouring her a drink from the bottle; they both have glasses with ice and lime but his is either not yet filled or recently emptied and held loosely upright near his crotch, while her fingers encircle a glass held near her breasts. He is holding the thick and rigid bottle while the liquid flows into her glass. The tip of the vodka bottle aims toward the fabric 'V' barely covering her bra-less, almost bare breasts.

His body is fully facing the viewer, although his head is turned, and he wears a self-satisfied smile. His eyes can't be seen because they are covered by sunglasses. Her body leans toward him receptively, with her arm raised to further 'open' her body to him, although her face and her seductive smile are aimed at the viewer. He is watching her; she is watching the viewer, or perhaps watching the viewer watching her/them.

In this example, words (symbols) have been used to describe (not analyze) the pictorial signs (icons) used in the advertisement, but the meanings of the images and the words are reasonably similar and tell a story to the viewer. What are the symbolic elements (tropes) of that story? How is gender depicted? What does it mean that he is fully clothed and she is not, that he is on solid ground but again, she is not? That he is dry and she is wet? What does it say that he is on a rectangular chaise on top of hard, clean white tiles while she is bathed in the blue of the swimming pool water? Is there a relationship between the blue of the pool water and the blue of the vodka bottle, and what does that imply? What does it mean that both the woman and the product are 'wet'? What is the symbolism of the bottle and the glasses? Are bottles to men as glasses are to women, as one anthropologist has asserted, because the hetero-sexual sexual act 'fills up' a woman with liquid the way a bottle 'fills up' a glass (Guthrie, 2000: 20-21)? Does the bottle mimic the penis in placement and angle? Does the 'V' of her bodice represent the 'V' of the female genitalia? How does the ad depict the relative power of male and female, and does this imagery reproduce or contradict standard cultural metaphors about males and females? Is she subordinate to him, and if so why and how, and what are the elements of the images that indicate this relationship (Goffman, 1976: 40-67)? What elements of the image are odd or anomalous and what does that mean to the story being told? How do you interpret the nonsensical in the ad? What is the story that 'sells' the product in this ad? Is this ad designed to attract and compel a male or a female audience? Why or why not? Above all, how does the ad make you *feel?*

As you can see by just this small list of possible questions about the symbolism of the advertisement, there is a great deal happening in the image. As you visually and mentally peel back the layers of possible meaning you are participating in the story of the advertisement just as surely as the couple depicted, and the work you do to interpret the ad causes you to buy in to the story, to justify the advertising message and to make it rational. You accept the story even if it is a bit nonsensical. Somehow your mind links the vodka with the messages within the image, and perhaps you have an emotional reaction to the story. Perhaps somewhere deep inside you wonder if that vodka makes a man successful in business and sex, or if you are a woman, you wonder if the vodka makes a woman beautiful and sexually alluring. Perhaps you end up thinking that SKYY vodka is young, high-end, hip and sexy, and the prefect drink for young, hip, sexy, well-off people. You want to be young, hip, rich and sexy, and the ad is successful if you are induced to pick up a bottle of the vodka the next time you are shopping for booze.

Alcohol Advertising Myths and Tropes

Understanding the semiotics of an advertisement is particularly important for understanding alcohol promotion because signs in ads always link to something other than the primary effect, which is intoxication. Alcohol brands *must* use ideology to sell because they cannot, except in the example of taste or texture, indicate direct use-outcomes, since showing intoxication in an advertisement would be counterproductive to selling. An iconic or indexical set of signs, such as a photo of someone who is drunk or representations of the effects of drunkenness (a pile of vomit, overturned furniture, broken glassware and bottles, a walk of shame) would not induce purchase nor would it be considered culturally acceptable except when used ironically. Alcohol must point away from itself to induce purchase using semiotic linkages to acceptable social functions and outcomes. It must convince the viewer that purchase results in achievement of positive goals rather than negative outcomes such as inebriation and addiction. Because ads function to raise brand awareness as well as induce purchase, many are aimed at younger drinkers and some seem to be targeted at future drinkers (otherwise known as children). Ads that remove all referents to intoxication while using symbols that appeal to children (such as the animated Budweiser frogs) are often vilified by parent groups for creating positive feelings about a brand in those who are too young to understand intoxication. Alcohol ads with scenes of people in their early twenties often portray drinking as the ticket to mature, fun, inhibition-free lives filled with parties and popularity (Linn, 2004: 158). Children who see these ads link alcohol to fun and personal social success but have no understanding that alcohol can also be dangerous. Other forms of media attractive to youth portray alcohol use as something that successful and popular people do frequently and without consequences (Smith and Donnerstein, 2003). Most ads that appeal to younger people utilize glamorous, attractive, slim and well-dressed people doing exciting leisure activities; leisure is depicted as the 'good life' and occurs with drink in hand. Drinking becomes part of a consumptive entertainment and leisure lifestyle that conveys a 'brand personality' about the self to others. Advertisers may even use symbols of drug use (emotional exuberance, club or rave backgrounds, drug paraphernalia) to convey an 'extreme' life or ultimate fun (Duff, 2003; Nahoum-Grappe, 2008). But consequences are not depicted. Indeed, alcohol advertisers want youth to believe that alcohol is a risk-free magic potion that everyone uses to solve problems and bring out the best in themselves (Strasburger, 2002).

Stripping consequences from use has a long history in the selling of products considered sinful such as tobacco, alcohol, gambling, guns and prostitution. It is also common to link several 'sinful' activities together to provide a promise of pleasure, as does a humorous beer handbill from around 1900 (see Figures 6.1 and 6.2). The handbill demonstrates the importance of careful ad placement for sin products. Closed, it's rather naughty because it appears to portray a naked woman in an embrace with a man, but open reveals a more respectable scene. It would have been given out in male-only settings such as clubs, bars and sporting events rather than made available to a wider (female) audience. Similarly, today's ads for alcohol products are carefully placed in the appropriate media, so that risqué print advertisements designed to attract young male drinkers are (supposedly) not seen by children – or matrons. Ads linking sexual gratification to alcohol using attractive near-naked females are found in *Maxim* or *Sports Illustrated*, while the Grey Goose ads discussed earlier were in *Vogue* magazine, a publication that appeals to aspirational women. To reverse their placement would cause viewers to visually register the anomaly and to recognize that the product advertised is out of place and potentially sinful. To link alcohol use to sexual access and success in *Maxim* reflects the normative use of alcohol in courtship. Linking the glamour (and fashionable attire) of the dinner party with the use of Grey Goose reinforces its message of success, refinement and exclusivity while downplaying the power to intoxicate. "Through abundant use of lifestyle symbols, advertisers focus on selling not merely the product, but a total lifestyle that promises pleasure, sexual attractiveness, adventure and sophistication, among other desirable attributes" (Pennock, 2007: 9), and pleasure, sex and adventure are the primary tropes used to advertise alcohol to college-age drinkers (Saffer, 2002; Duff, 2003). Because the advertising images are bracketed by media messages that support that lifestyle the product is presented as a rational consumption choice.

Sin ads pay careful attention to target markets (who, why, where, what), media outlet (TV, radio, print, internet, direct product placement) and message (fun, status/class, sex, potency/power). This process is called 'ROI' by advertising copywriters, and stands for the planning that identifies appropriate (meaningful) Relevance, Originality and Impact messages and outlets. From ROI arises a strategic model that designs every element of an ad campaign: awareness, acceptance, preference, search, selection, use and satisfaction (Thorson, 1995). Introduction of a brand will begin with messages designed to increase awareness, proceed to messages about selection and use, and then will move into lifestyle imagery. Often the arc of the brand campaign can be recognized through analysis of signs and stories from particular ads. Introduction may focus on 'Tomb style' images with clear pictures of the bottle to encourage recognition, continue with pictures of the bottle plus recipes, and then

Figures 6.1 and 6.2 **Advertisements for Indianapolis Brewing Company** *Progress* **Brand beer, circa 1908.** (*Source:* Images used by permission of William Woys Weaver and the Roughwood Collection.)

adopt lifestyle messages about what the brand will do for the buyer. Sometimes the two styles of print ads are combined, to present the bottle and provide a story about what kind of person buys the product. In a recent Ultimat Vodka ad, the bottle is foregrounded in deep blue, with a background that shows iconic buildings from a number of nations: the Eiffel Tower, the Leaning Tower of Pisa, the Capital Buildings of Washington DC, a shrine in Kyoto, the Sydney Opera House, the Statue of Liberty and many more. And next to the bottle a beautiful blond woman gazes at the viewer. In this ad the customer is encouraged to think of the self as a sophisticated world traveler familiar with glamorous cities, and who either travels with a beautiful blond woman or is a beautiful blond woman. The relatively asexual ad allows both men and women to place themselves into the story as a powerful, wealthy and sexually attractive buyer, deserving of the ultimate in vodka – Ultimat.

Advertisers must also control the symbols and meanings they convey to each target market group and the promotional tools used to raise brand awareness and use (Davidson, 2003). It is for that reason that so many advertisers of youth-oriented alcohols such as beer, alcopops and sweetened spirits use product spokespeople to provide attractive giveaways in college bars (Kuo et al, 2003). Just as the naughty beer handbill discussed above would have been distributed in male-only settings, beach balls touting Corona Beer are given out in sports bars near campuses – they wouldn't be attractive in a downtown cocktail lounge.

Bringing the campaign directly to the user through individual contact, blogs and viral internet markets is one of the most effective ways to reach a target audience, especially one that must be tightly controlled (Springer, 2007: Chapter 9). Many advertisers recognize that employing popular students as 'brand reps' is an easy and relatively cheap way to ensure appropriate product placement, while guaranteeing that the marketing reaches its target audience effectively and efficiently. Such tightly controlled campaigns are essential when selling socially unacceptable products.

Alcohol ads, like all ads, are highly scripted, culturally dense and can require serious analytical unpacking. As print media they can endure as much scrutiny as a Late Renaissance painting, full of metaphors and allegory designed to convey cultural messages. As Lotman explains (quoted in Berger, 2007: 137),

> Since it can concentrate a tremendous amount of information into the "area" of a very small text... an artistic text manifests yet another feature: it transmits different information to different readers in proportion to each one's comprehension; it provides the reader with a language in which each successive portion of information may be assimilated with repeated reading. It behaves as a kind of living organism which has a feedback channel to the reader and thereby instructs him.

> Lotman (1977: 23)

Berger paraphrases this passage to mean that everything in an advertisement is important and that the more you know, the more you can see in a text. And by reading the text, especially one with complex emotional indexing (happiness, satisfaction, pride), we engage in a transaction that places us into the message and which places the self in the action of the text. We imagine ourselves in the 'dreamt future' and "having initially derived its meaning from correlation with things or people ... which have a place in external systems or groups, a product is then made to give back meaning to us, and create a new system of groups" (Williamson, 2005: 45). We read the emotion and promise, correctly link to the lifestyle and product shown and mentally place ourselves in the ad to recreate our sense of self to reflect the myth of the advertisement. In the subjectivity of reading the text, in our involvement with it, we ultimately objectify the self by creating an image of 'what we could be' as defined by the advertisement.

Williamson argues that ultimately it is we who are the product: "we are thus created not only as subjects, but as particular kinds of subjects, by products in advertisements" (ibid.: 45) and that "we are both product and consumer: we consume, buy the product, yet we *are* the product. Thus our lives become our own creations, through buying; an identikit of different images of ourselves, created by different products" (ibid.: 70). Our lives are transformed by our agency as consumers: "it proposes to each of us that we transform ourselves, or our lives, by buying something more (Berger, 1972: 131). Similarly, Dyer (1988: 116) writes "advertisements do not simply manipulate us, inoculate us or reduce us to the status of objects; they create structures of meaning which sell commodities not for themselves as useful objects but in terms of ourselves as social beings in our different social relationships. Products are given 'exchange value': ads translate statements about objects into statements about types of human and social relationships". Our reading of the text of the ad is active, as is our use of the product and our management of use in relation to social approval; we are agents in our consumption and we make sense of ourselves as we make sense of the ads (Williamson, 2005: 170). As one of the creators of the Absolut brand has stated: "basically, my profession is about invading peoples' integrity ... I get them interested in things they are not interested in, and I get them to long for things that they didn't know existed. That's why it is fundamentally meaningless to ask people what they want" (Hamilton, 1994: 102). Consumption remains a performance, and the script is written by the advertising message – we are interpreters only.

Alcohol Stories Have Emotional Meanings

It is critical to understand the stories used to sell alcohol and how they present lifestyle themes while also reflecting, as Mary Douglas maintains, an economic product that provides an identity for the user. Advertisements promise access to the story, but the buyer must place the self within the narrative and must be able to see himself in that situation. Berger (2007: 16-21) lists six primary tropes and myths used in advertising; they are heroes and heroines, sexuality, humor, fun, success and reward. Different types of consumer goods use each trope differently, of course, with some inapplicable for some goods – sexuality would not be used to sell diapers nor would humor sell mortuary services. Alcohol ads can and do use all of these tropes successfully, and thus create in the mind of the public the idea that the product is linked to those myths. More importantly, how we use alcohol and how it functions within the culture support all of those tropes, from the warrior/hero (the Celtic Chieftain) to the reward ("it's Miller Time!"). These stories and more are also listed by John Berger (1972: Chapter 7) as myths or culturally sacred stories that are used in advertising and include religious metaphors (Adam and Eve), historical experience (French Revolution, Puritans coming to America, Sam Adams beer), elite culture (Anglophilia, Francophilia, opera, Europe, status goods, etc.), pop culture (Sci-fi, Westerns, Rap) and everyday life (family scenes, work scenes, etc.). Holt describes primary American myths used in advertising as the frontier, the self-made man (which links to rugged individualism and success), and the melting pot (assimilation and success in America), all of which are "constructed around ideals of individual success and manhood – what it takes to be a man" (Holt 2005: 285). Breed and Defoe (1981) identified favored lifestyle themes such as wealth and success, social approval, hedonistic pleasure, sex and exotic locales. The most frequent alcohol themes listed by Atkin and Block (1981) were social connection, gender identity (masculinity/femininity) and escape. Using a weighed frequency model, Strickland et al. (1982 a and b) determined the most popular themes were (in order): quality, tradition, information, foreign settings, special occasions, sexual connotations, individuality, success, conformity, close friendship and humor.

More recently, Strasberger (2002) identified rock music, young and attractive people, adventure and humor as popular themes used in alcohol advertising aimed at youth. Duff (2003) has argued that primary themes for alcohol ads aimed at youth are leisure, consumption, sex, extreme sports and other forms of drug cultures that contribute to a lifestyle of leisure activities. He maintains that earlier advertising tropes of reward for accomplishment or work have been eclipsed by messages that promote leisure consumption of alcohol divorced from work and cultural responsibilities, or as a separate 'time-out' of intoxication unrelated to larger life goals. These myths can be understood to be overarching cultural stories about how to live appropriately while the themes or tropes are the individual thematic elements that function as implied goals within the advertisement.

In addition to myths and tropes, advertisers use emotional appeals and natural human drives to compel purchase. Desire is a potent element in publicity, since desire arouses envy, and envy can drive consumerism. As Berger (1972: 132) argues,

> Publicity persuades us of such a transformation by showing us people who have apparently been transformed and are, as a result, enviable. The state of being envied is what constitutes glamour. And publicity is the process of manufacturing glamour ... Publicity is always about the future buyer. It offers him an image of himself made glamorous by the product ... The image then makes him envious of himself as he might be. Yet what makes this self-which-he-might-be enviable? The envy of others. Publicity is about social relations, not objects ... The happiness of being envied is glamour.

According to Jack Solomon, the 'American Dream' is one of having more possessions than the next person and of being envied for success. To be worthy of envy is to be sexier and of higher status, to have the right things (Solomon, 1988); fear is triggered by not having the right things, by not fitting in materially, which induces guilt that the self is not living up to the promises of self-realization and perfectibility. Jib Fowles (1998/1976) has enumerated these potent desires even more clearly, by listing 15 emotional appeals that advertisers use to encourage purchase. They are the need for sex, social affiliation, nurturance, guidance, aggression, achievement, domination, prominence, attention, autonomy, escape, to have aesthetic sensations, satisfy curiosity and to fulfill physiologic needs such as eating and sleep. Of course, there are more emotions that can be used, but these are the ones that Fowles identifies as most prevalent in advertising. Solomon might argue that desires and fears can be attached to each of these emotional needs, which can then be represented through the use of signs that point to specific tropes and stories. Several of the tropes and emotional needs overlap, including the obvious (sex and the need or desire for it) and the more subtle, such as success and the need to dominate. Stories and myths may lend themselves to particular tropes and emotions, such as elite culture, success and the need for prominence, or adventure, masculinity and the need to achieve. Ideology allows you to design a campaign that links the product to the story, trope and emotion; to link things together that are not naturally related.

You can now combine the columns in Table 6.1 to create an advertising campaign. First, decide on an alcohol product, the demographic to be targeted and define a media aperture (print, radio, tv, internet popup, etc.). From there, you will use the Relevance, Originality and Impact method to define your message. You want it to attract the right person, at the right time, to create the right effect. Then choose the advertising stage (awareness, acceptance, preference, search, selection, use and satisfaction) to target. Using the table it's quite easy to pick the signs and emotions necessary to create an advertisement: simply pick one from each column and story-board the campaign. So, for instance, if your product is beer, your audience is twenty-something males, the stage is selection, and the media aperture is *Maxim*-type magazines in February and March, just before college spring break. You've already done the awareness stage with a 'Tombstone' ad that shows the product, so now you can move on to lifestyle connections (Thorson, 1995) that would cause someone to buy your beer rather than a different one. You want to identify your beer as the one that will meet a need in the viewer, and your job is to match the emotion to the stage. So, your product is beer, your story is 'exotic locations' and your trope is escape. You decide a good emotion to trigger for selection might be 'the need to escape', 'the need to satisfy curiosity' or 'the need for aesthetic connections'. The copywriting team has a few of the beers and brainstorms the emotions, the locales and the drives. What story line, text and images do you decide upon?

Myths, Tropes and Emotions: Examples

In the 1990s Corona Beer altered its message in order to regain market share. The beer first became profitable in the United States during the 1980s when it

Table 6.1 **Alcohol advertising campaign design table**

Stories/Myths	Tropes	Emotions/Drives/Desires
Religious metaphors	Wealth/status/class	Envy
Historical experience	Success	Fear
Elite culture	Hedonistic pleasure	Guilt
Everyday life	Freedom	Fear of not belonging/desire to belong
Adventure	Consumption	The need for sex
Heritage	Sex	The need for social affiliation
Production process	Fun	The need to nurture
Sports/extreme sports	Companionship/camaraderie	The need for guidance
Exotic locations	Gender identity (femininity/masculinity)	The need to be aggressive
Heroes/heroines	Humor	The need to achieve
Good times	Potency/power	The need to dominate
The frontier	Uniqueness/individuality	The need for prominence
The self-made man	Choice	The need for attention
The melting pot and successful assimilation	Social approval	The need for autonomy
Time out	Escape	The need for escape
Rock music	Conformity	The need to feel safe
Celebrity	Quality	The need for aesthetic sensations
	Tradition	The need for satisfy curiosity Physiological needs

was a relatively cheap beer popular among college students as a symbol of Spring Break excess. The message could be identified as exotic locales/good times, companionship and the need to escape. The ideology of the advertisements linked the beer with "having a wild party with friends, like we did in Cabo." But after market share fell in the 1990s the company changed the message, keeping exotic locales and the need to escape, but shifting away from the party linkage to embrace a 'getting away from it all' trope addressed to young working men and women. The linkage shifted from partying in a group to escaping/time out/getting away from work with close friends or a partner. The primary message was relaxation. And sales of Corona roared back as it became popular with young, overworked yuppies (Holt, 2005) whose 'dreamt future' resembled Corona's tropical beaches, good times and complete ease. The myth of 'getting away from it all' is perfect for alcohol sales because it resonates deeply with the American consciousness of time use and the 'work hard/play hard' ideology. It reproduces the cultural dualisms discussed in the previous chapter and reifies the use of alcohol as a mechanism for 'time out' drinking and escape from everyday life. A beer in hand is necessary on vacation, for that is what being away from work is all about – a complete reversal of the daily grind of professional life. The sobriety of the work week succumbs to the intoxication of freedom and of the vacation. And Corona can help you get there!

The themes and myths used to sell alcohol are deeply familiar to most Americans because they need to have cognitive relevance and cultural meaning to be effective selling messages. But they also have to resonate with the viewer – they have to grab attention, hold it and cause a reaction – preferably an emotional one. For a sin product like alcohol the stories and tropes used to be noticed are often risqué, offensive or ironic because they can be; other product categories would refuse to be identified with culturally suggestive images because it might hurt sales. With alcohol, notoriety can raise awareness and increase interest in the product, especially among young men and women who might perceive the product as edgy or cool. The mildly offensive advertisement for Canadian Club that states "Your mom wasn't your dad's first" (available in the marketing gallery of the CAMY site: http:// www.camy.org/ under the brand 'Canadian Club') skates on the thin edge of decency because it calls attention to parental sexuality. With that line, the other text and photos provide a message about masculinity that implies that a real man has multiple sex partners, goes out 'on the hunt' and, of course, drinks whiskey cocktails. It finishes with the line used throughout the campaign: "Damn right your dad drank it." The other prominently placed ad in this campaign shows a man with fishing poles about to enter a boat filled with other men; here, the line reads "Your dad was not a Metrosexual." These ads use vintage-style, washed-out photos of middle- or working-class homes and activities, seemingly from the 1960s and 1970s – exactly the kind of picture a twenty-something might find in family albums – to portray 'dear old Dad' in scenes from his (wild and crazy and very masculine) youth. The visual images, words and tag lines are vaguely shocking and out of place, and are likely to be noticed as a contrast to the slick, brightly colored and hard-edged images of club scenes or high-end locales other alcohol brands currently favor. More than merely sensational, they also encourage an emotional response because they ask the viewer (presumably male) to think about a father's sexuality and masculinity, an action not normally encouraged in American culture. The ads are also subtly ironic, since Canadian Club is considered an old man's brand, and may represent an attempt by that company to raise its profile with a new generation of drinkers.

This kind of ironic, vaguely shocking message is exactly what is used to gain the attention of youth. Youth are the primary target of many brand campaigns for consumable non-necessary items because they are highly invested in impressing peers, are creating a self-identity, tend to purchase more things than older people and can remain valued customers for many years. This is especially true for alcohol advertising, since the highest per-capita drinking is usually accomplished during the twenties. As a result, a relatively high percentage of ads for alcohol are aimed at the prized demographic of males between 15 and 35 years of age.

Themes such as sexuality, success and wealth, adventure and rude humor are popular with this age group, as demonstrated by what O'Reilly and Tennant (2009: 94) label the "fart index." Advertisers often employ shocking or offensive messages to win the attention of young people (O'Reilly and Tennant, 2009: 92–95). According to Kalle Lasn, there is so much marketing noise, jolts and shock (marketing 'clutter') in the environment that we unconsciously block out much of it, so marketers simply turn up the volume to get noticed (Solomon, 1988; Lasn, 1999: 13–18; O'Reilly and Tennant, 2009: Chapter 2). And then the public ratchets up the shields, and the ads ratchet up the noise. Lasn argues that this overload of consumerist messaging leads to cultural dystopia marked by mood disorders, hype, unreality and 'infotoxins' (disinformation), info-overload and erosion of empathy. Lasn maintains that constant bombardment of marketing and publicity urging us to buy stuff not only corrupts our values by advocating consumption as a means to establish identity but deadens us to the surrounding social and natural world. As we become more thing-oriented and less aware of the people and world around us, advertisements become louder, more strident, more shocking and more emotional in order to get our attention.

Advertising and the College Student

Alcohol advertisers consider college students and young adults a primary target for their products. Many of the themes used to promote alcohol are myths and stories that can be used to create a sense of self through metaphors that provide examples of how to live. The myths can be adopted as self-identity or as a means to brand the individual. If someone thinks of himself as rugged, strong and a real go-getter, and Brand X sells itself as a drink for rugged go-getters, he may think it a good idea to buy Brand X because it's a signal he can send to others that he is a rugged go-getter. At that point he is invested in that brand and all that it represents, and uses it as a semiotic sign to convey something about himself to others. He becomes a sign for the brand just as the brand is a sign he uses to communicate. The stories used to create a brand are about a lifestyle that the buyer aspires to, and he will buy as a means to signal his acceptance of the lifestyle. To buy Grey Goose vodka announces that one sees the self as the sort of person who has sophisticated dinner parties, lives in a sleek loft and owns a large sailboat. That vodka really has nothing to do with these material possessions or class attainments is unimportant once the buyer accepts the ideology of the advertisement.

But do advertisements represent the world as it is, or do they create a new cultural reality based on the myths they tell? Do they follow culture, or lead, or a mixture of both? What kinds of metaphors do they sell as normal, and is it possible to read advertisements as examples of lived culture much as an anthropologist might read the daily existence of a tribal society he or she visits? What do advertisements tell us about ourselves, and does it have any validity?

The primary myths and tropes used in advertising are deeply embedded in our normative culture because if they weren't, the advertisements would have no meaning and would not be able to sell. They represent cultural realities. One of the better examples of how ads reflect cultural themes is the time/work dualism of American life patterns. Because alcohol can be used as a semiotic short cut to indicate leisure, vacation, not-work, etc., advertisements can use leisure, vacation, etc., to reference alcohol. When alcohol ads reference work they do so to portray the alcohol as a reward for work done or as an antidote to work, either by referencing work or by presenting the evidence of not-work such as a beach scene or a nightlife scene. After all, if "Weekends are for Michelob" as the old television ad assured us, then Michelob must mean weekends. Some advertisements rely entirely on the observer knowing and accepting the work/play dualism in order to make sense, as does a series of advertisements for Bacardi.

In a group of ads that contrast night and day, Bacardi lists mundane jobs as day activities while Bacardi defines the night. "Veterinarian by Day – Bacardi by Night," "Fundraiser by Day – Bacardi by Night" and "Asset Manager by Day – Bacardi by Night" are three examples (all of these ads can be seen at http://www.camy.org/gallery in the 'Bacardi Superior Rum' file). Bacardi implies that the break between night and day is stark and definite, leading to a change in clothing, activities and identity. Bacardi is the vehicle to a different, exciting and wilder life. The person becomes the drink, and the drink transforms the person into a nightlife superstar, sexy and available and wild. We know it's wild because the woman in the "Veterinarian by Day – Bacardi by Night" ad is wearing animal-print underwear and it appears that she is taking off her clothes in preparation for a sexual adventure (sex equals night, just as work equals day). By (barely) dressing her in animal prints the ad references her supposed profession of veterinarian but the choice of intimate wear also suggests that her underlying and authentic personality is wild and crazy and sexually available. There is an implied shift in personality between day and night personae, but the underwear suggests that regardless of daytime profession, she's still a wild and crazy gal up for anything … with a little help from Bacardi. Bacardi provided other interesting examples such as "Librarian by day – Bacardi by Night," showing a woman holding a drink dressed in little beyond a gold bra and sarong, thus playing upon the cultural mythologies about repressed but sex-crazed and available working women (what Berger (1972: 138) labels 'free-wheeling'). Another implies a threesome by showing a laughing, very happy man holding two women (a blond and a brunette, naturally) with the message "Double-Clicks by Day – Bacardi by Night." Bacardi becomes the referent for uninhibited threesome sex as the mind automatically fills in the unsaid story, "Double-Fun by Night." Perhaps the best example of the series was "Vegetarian by Day," which provided a fetching scene of a laughing, long-haired woman in low-slung jeans and a black bra who appears to be kneeling on the top of a bar (there are bottles behind her) pouring a drink into the mouth of a man who is licking the drink up from her navel. Her pelvis thrusts forward, and should the man be just a few inches lower the act would probably be illegal in most Southern States. The message is unmistakable: "Drink Bacardi and Get Laid." You can buy the woman as easily as you can buy the beverage – if you drink Bacardi.

These ads were placed in magazines such as *Maxim* and *Rolling Stone* that are attractive to college students on the cusp of adulthood. Their dreamt future is one of a successful professional job (such as veterinarian or computer mogul), but also, it seems, of continuation of the care-free and intoxicated habits often excusable during the college years. This tension between responsibilities and fun mirrors the tension between the 'work hard, play hard' mantra of many students, and is one that replicates the work/play dualism of American life. More disturbingly, these ads portray alcohol use as intoxicated abandonment and seem to promote drunkenness rather than moderation. Cameron Duff (2003) argues that alcohol advertising aimed at the youth market differs from older forms of advertising that emphasized alcohol as a reward for labor. He maintains that ads for youth represent alcohol as essential to leisure and consumption (rather than as a balanced part of work/leisure), and that the form of usage is of the 'time-off', or 'time-out' variety because ads contain codes for extreme intoxication. He is particularly concerned that all references to responsibility and social obligation are absent, in contrast to earlier ads for 'work reward' alcohol. For instance, most ads show leisure activities, either of sports (extreme sports such as snowboarding) or club scenes, and many people are shown with ecstatic looks on their faces suggesting extreme intoxication. Most show young and very attractive people who appear to be enjoying expensive forms of leisure, as demonstrated by pictures of fashionably dressed, maniacally grinning beautiful young women exiting limousines while holding bottles of up-market champagne. Some ads even use drug metaphors to sell alcohol, as does one for a caffeine/alcohol blend that shows a woman snorting up a spilled drink through a roll of paper, much as someone might snort cocaine. The ad text reads "The Next High." Duff contrasts these scenes with beer and liquor ads aimed at an older demographic that emphasize having 'a cold one' after a hard day's work or enjoying a beverage while doing something that requires some sobriety, such as playing golf or talking with friends. He concludes that alcohol advertisers are positioning their product to be considered an essential part of leisure activities and that doing so promotes a 'time-out' style of drinking. Certainly the message of abandonment, time-out behaviors and the out-of-control self can be read into the manic smiles on the faces of many drinkers in advertisements.

There are ads that reference work to sell a reward drink but they tend to be aimed at specific markets and specific demographics. For instance, Ultimat vodka has been running a series of ads that suggests that high-rolling Manhattan hedge fund managers drink their brand. The sapphire-blue-colored ads are carried in the *New York Times* and are Tombstones with text. One reads "Your boss is the most powerful man in finance. You're his protégé. His 10th in the last 6 months." Another one states "You work for the best firm in the city. You make seven figures. You spend less time outside than prisoners on Rikers Island." And yet another states "Congratulations. You're part of the 1%. Which also happens to represent your free time." And finally, the last one, which is most revealing of values gone awry: "Your kids love their Christmas gifts. Your wife adores the diamond earrings. They called your office to tell you." This campaign carries the theme "Find Balance. Find Ultimat," which replaces the theme used in earlier ads for the brand, "Live ultimately." The advertisers perceive their target demographic to be "college graduates who are superambitious and want to climb up the corporate ladder very quickly," a group that "works hard and plays hard afterwards," and that Ultimat is "giving them balance at the end of the work day" (Elliott, 2011). Ultimat is suggesting that in order to relax one must consume the brand, that it is both the reward and the means of release. It is the perfect time-out consumption habit for the modern 'stressed-out' yuppie who makes too much money but has too little time to enjoy the fruits of (presumably his) labor. So the solution is easy, just jump-start the relaxation process with a branded intoxicant and you will achieve instant emotional nirvana. As well as a status boost when your friends see you drinking a 'premium vodka'.

Conclusion

Advertising campaigns as disparate as Bacardi and Ultimat may seem to have little in common, but when examined in light of time-out drinking paradigms they reveal similar themes and stories. Both advertising strategies promise release from stress if the product is consumed; Bacardi from sexual frustration and Ultimat from overwork. Both assume that consumers will rely on purchased consumption for leisure instead of doing something active to relax such as exercise, meditation, reading or spending time with family. Both assume that the work hard/play hard metaphor is accepted and deeply meaningful to the viewer and that he accepts that a proper life is extreme in work and extreme in play. Both ad campaigns create a dualistic universe in which cultural actors assume differing identities in each role. Both place the viewer at the center of cultural action, as an agent with supreme power over self; social relationships drop out or are used for self-gratification only. The only person of importance is the buyer, who is a supremely self-actualized and self-created individual, a 'master of the universe' who can demonstrate his originality by buying ... A mass-produced intoxicant advertised to supremely self-actualized and self-created individuals who are 'masters of the universe' who can demonstrate originality by buying ... A mass-produced intoxicant advertised to supremely self-actualized and self-created individuals who are 'masters of the universe' who can demonstrate originality by buying ...

7

WHY DO STUDENTS DRINK?

Gin Sling
In the good old colony times
When we lived under the king
Each Saturday night, we used to get tight
A-pouring down gin-sling

And Senior and Junior and Soph,
And Freshman and Tutor and Prof,
When once they began, they never left off
A-pouring down gin-sling

Harvard drinking song (Hayes, 1866: 84)

How Much Do College Students Drink?

Do college students really drink a lot and if so, why? There is anecdotal evidence of high-end college-age drinking stretching back to the start of the university system (Strauss and Bacon, 1953; Engs, 1977; Giles, 1991; Banks, 1997; Nuwer, 1999; Engs, 2002; Vicary and Karshin, 2002; Dowdall, 2009; Syrett, 2009) but little research on campus intakes and consequences until the 1950s when Strauss and Bacon (1953) published *Drinking in College*, a survey of 27 colleges conducted between 1949 and 1951. In the 1970s and 1980s concern about alcohol intake in general prompted increased examination of student drinking, and Students Against Drunk Driving (SADD), Boost Alcohol Consciousness Concerning the Health of University Students (BACCHUS) and the Inter-Association Task Force on Alcohol and Other Substances Issues (IATF) were established. These organizations problematized student drinking by focusing on negative consequences rather than reasons for intake. The discourse of negativity was cemented in the 1990s with the publication of reports from the Harvard School of Public Health College Alcohol Study, a survey of over 140 schools and many thousands of students (Wechsler et al., 1994, 1995, 1998; Wechsler and Wuethrich, 2002).

The Harvard study examined correlates of binge drinking behaviors after defining a binge as four drinks in one sitting for a woman and five for a man (Wechsler and Austin, 1998). The investigators found that negative outcomes such as missing class, driving drunk, doing something later regretted and having unplanned (and unprotected) sex were much higher in prevalence among frequent binge drinkers – who were defined as the roughly 20 percent of students who reported being drunk three or more times per month (Wechsler et al., 2000; Dowdall, 2009: 48-53; Scott-Sheldon et al., 2010). More importantly, reporting a cluster of five or more of these problems was 20–25 times more prevalent among frequent bingers than among other students (Dowdall, 2009: 50). In other words, regular and heavy episodic drinking was linked to serious consequences that affected student functioning and academic outcomes. While this could be said to be something of a 'no-duh' finding, the Harvard Study provided important and solid evidence of increased academic and personal problems linked to high-end drinking.

The Harvard Study also demonstrated that significant numbers of college students were binge drinking on a regular basis. Because of the widespread media coverage of the study, the phrase 'binge drinking' became synonymous with college intake. Unfortunately, the definition for 'binge' used by the study differed from the popular understanding of the term and implied that students were becoming profoundly intoxicated on a regular basis. The traditional meaning of the phrase connotes a several-days-long period of drunkenness, often involving loss of memory, episodic disappearances and addiction (Chrzan, 2010). The Harvard Study defined a binge as five drinks per sitting for a male and four for a woman (Wechsler et al, 1994; Wechsler and Austin, 1998; NIAAA, 2004), an amount that may or may not cause intoxication depending on the length of time drinking, type of drink, and stomach contents of the drinker. Regardless, this metric morphed into the definitive definition for binge drinking without losing the earlier connotation of being out of control drunk; it was partly this collision of meanings that propelled popular interest and public health fears about college drinking. These fears were cemented with the publication of an article that proclaimed that 1400 college students were dying annually due to alcohol intake, mostly from car crashes (Hingson et al, 2002). Three years later, the same authors asserted that the number had increased to 1700 deaths per year (Hingson et al., 2005). However, these were not actual measurements but estimates based on a scaling up of a small sample. This was considerably more deaths than had previously been measured: while one report quantified 620 alcohol-related deaths of college students over a four-year period (Dowdall, 2009: 53), Hingson et al. estimated far more, many occurring during summer breaks and off campus. The larger number was eagerly picked up by national media and has since been reported as fact by the popular press and in some academic texts (DeSantis, 2007: 168–169; Neighbors et al., 2005; Smith, 2011: 112).

The reality that the articles were an estimated statistics test has been forgotten in the general panic of being told that the US is losing upwards of 1700 college students annually.

Regardless, the Harvard College Alcohol Study did establish that roughly 48 percent of male and 40 percent of female students drank more than five drinks at any one time within the previous two weeks and that 30 percent of male students drank at least ten times per month (Wechsler et al., 2000), findings broadly replicated by the Core Institute's annual surveys of college behavior (Core Institute, 2010), by Martens et al. (2008) and in Smith's study of emerging adults (Smith, 2011: 111). Almost one-third of all male students were drunk three or more times during a month, and 50 percent of students drink to get drunk (Dowdall, 2009: 26–27). These figures held steady over the period 1993–2001, and in 2002 the National Advisory Council on Alcohol Abuse and Alcoholism issued a widely influential report titled *A Call to Action: Changing the Culture of Dinking at U.S. Colleges* (NIAAA, 2002) that encouraged college administrators to reassess campus alcohol policies and to expand alcohol interventions. This report also listed the mortality numbers from the first article by Hingson et al. (2002) as concrete fact, further inflaming a desire to decrease campus drinking and its consequences.

It is absolutely true that many college students drink, sometimes drink heavily, and that drinking causes serious academic, social and health consequences to students (Aertgeerts and Buntinx, 2002; Vicary and Karshin, 2002; Wechsler and Wuethrich, 2002; Turrisi et al., 2006; Smith and Berger, 2010; Heather et al., 2011; Smith, 2011: 110–147). Among college personnel who work with campus drug and alcohol infractions, it's pretty much an accepted rubric that roughly 15 percent of students cause most of the campus alcohol- and drug-related problems – a figure that approximates the number of high-end drinkers in Strauss and Bacon (1953: 105) and in the studies discussed by Engs (1977). While these high-end drinkers are often linked to a greater number of adverse consequences that cause them to be singled out by administrators, the fact remains that between 40 and 50 percent of students are still drinking more than the 5/4 binge category on a fairly regular basis. This amount is usually enough to cause intoxication, or a blood alcohol content (BAC) of greater than 0.08 (NIAAA, 2004), and so can be considered to be an appropriate metric for the measurement of drunkenness, if not of the traditional sense of the word 'binge'.

The 5/4 binge metric provides an independent variable that allows investigators to test a range of associated dependent variables from psychological and socio-demographic characteristics to consequences. Intake levels coupled with frequency measurements can be tested against the probability of particular individual and communal consequences (Fielder and Carey, 2010; Scott-Sheldon et al., 2010) and college-age drinkers can be assessed for a variety of psychological, social and structural traits that may be correlated with higher rates of intake (Weitzman, Nelson and Wechsler, 2003; Furnham, 2004; Borsari and Carey, 2006; Huang et al., 2008; Kitsantas et al., 2008; Martens et al., 2008; DeSimone, 2009; Theall et al., 2009; Zamboanga et al., 2009; Atwell et al., 2011; Nemeth et al., 2011). Since Strauss and Bacon's early report there have been a multitude of studies about drinking on campus, with variables of intake and outcome studied and analyzed from every conceivable theoretical perspective. The research on campus alcohol abuse is comprehensive and has definitively proved that high-end drinkers experience and cause more consequences (missing classes, lowered grades, interpersonal problems, accidents and violence) than do moderate and non-drinkers. As a result, the focus of most research has been on identifying students at highest risk for abusive drinking, measuring the negative consequences of student intake and the testing of programs designed to decrease high-end intake among students. But the vast majority of students do not experience lasting consequences such as course failure, imprisonment or bodily injury, nor do they develop abusive drinking habits. They more typically endure minor or fleeting consequences such as hangovers, social and sexual embarrassment (the 'walk of shame') and grade reduction rather than failure. For many students these consequences are more than enough to encourage moderation, but others relish their misadventures and continue to over-indulge at a rate higher than is healthy for them or for the campus community. For that reason alone it is essential to find ways to decrease alcohol abuse among students, but in order to be able to teach moderation we need to understand why students drink to excess. What does intoxication do for students and why is drinking such an established part of college life?

Why Do Students Drink? What Does Drinking Accomplish?

To start with, students drink for many of the same reasons that adults do: for fun, intoxication, to be social, display status and to ease interactions with potential romantic partners. They tend not to use alcohol explicitly for food (beer and cornflakes for breakfast is something of an urban myth), but it could be argued that in accordance with Mary Douglas (1987) students also use alcohol for rituals, since drinking plays a central role in many Greek initiation rites and other events such as sports activities, birthday celebrations and end-of-finals parties (Leemon, 1972; Triese, Wolburg and Otnes, 1999; Sande, 2002; Neighbors et al., 2005; Glassman et al., 2010). Alcohol intake is a rite of passage activity for students and young people in all cultures that use alcohol (Butler, 1993; Room, 2004; Crawford and Novak, 2006; Shachtman, 2006). Above all, students drink because they can: their lives are often free of the rigid time schedules that mark adult life.

A number of studies have examined reasons for drinking (not drunkenness or binging) among students and have uncovered predictable results, including social lubrication, 'liquid courage', facilitation of bonding and connections, event and memory creation, out-of-self experience, relief from boredom and tension, affirmation of freedom and increased probability of desired sexual encounters (Keeling, 2000). The Core Institute study found many of those reasons, plus a few more: alcohol gives people something to talk about and facilitates friendship, makes people seem sexier and makes the drinker feel sexier (Presley et al., 1998). Drinking is a primary leisure activity for many youth and promotes feelings of freedom, is fun, and is perceived to help cope with problems (Leigh and Lee, 2008; Hunt Maloney and Evans, 2010: 17–26; Aldridge, Measham and Williams, 2011 Chapter 3). Recent studies have examined motivations in a more ethnographic manner and found that students utilize drinking episodes instrumentally to create a drunken, fun-loving social image (the 'Drunken Self') that upholds a 'work hard, play hard' ethic, to dampen critical self-dialog, to demonstrate friendship through caretaking and to create stories that can be shared with others to project an identity that is fun, socially competent and popular (Vander Ven, 2011). The importance of drinking locations and activities to establishing and creating identity is also highlighted by Grazian (2008) and DeSantis (2007), both of whom focus on the gender performance opportunities of display and play at bars, clubs and Greek events.

Ethnographic party observations and diaries from nine years of a medical anthropology course on alcohol add to these categories.[1] In reports and observations students use alcohol to strategically manage identity through public display of social, economic and sexual status, negotiate friendships, accomplish risk management and create rites of passage that mark the transition from adolescent to adult. Above all, college students use alcohol to facilitate sexual relations and to negotiate and explore gender identities. While drinking alcohol may seem like a transgressive activity, ethnographic studies of drinking events demonstrate how essential alcohol intake (and its avoidance) is to social identity in college. Drinking accomplishes important social and developmental tasks and makes possible experimentation with potential adult roles, including gender performance, caretaking and management of consequences (Landrine, Bardwell and Dean, 1988; Knapp, 1996; Capraro, 2000; Jersild, 2001: 91–125; West, 2001; Zailckas, 2005; Demant and Jarvinen, 2006; Lyons and Willott, 2008; Smith, 2011). These activities become widely public – a form of performance

---

[1] Use of classroom material and student quotes was determined to meet eligibility criteria for IRB review exemption authorized by 45 CFR 46.101, category 4 by the Institutional Review Board of the University of Pennsylvania. All names, places, institutions and events have been altered to protect the identity of the students and those observed.

art as psychological development – through storytelling and social media. Indeed, students often claim that their use is both juvenile and adult; juvenile because they know they can't drink the same way when they 'enter the real world' and adult because they also know they must learn to drink 'like an adult' in order to navigate that 'real world'. Drinking to excess becomes a last hurrah of childhood while remaining an important bridge to adulthood. The tension created by such differing developmental tasks might be partly to blame for the abuse of alcohol in campus settings. Students wish to simultaneously retain and celebrate their youth while also mastering the tricky yet rewarding world of adult sociality, and alcohol is viewed as an essential component of both developmental realms.

Text analysis of the party reports and diaries reveal that some of the most prominent and prevalent observations were about gender and identity construction and performance (management of the strategic self), the facilitation of sexual and social encounters, accomplishment narratives including caretaking behaviors and status display, and the use of intoxication to overcome social anxieties. The sample consists of 139 ethnographic observations of college-age parties (the students were required to be sober at the event) collected from 2002 through 2010, and semester-long weekly diaries of alcohol observations from 57 students collected from 2008 through 2010. The diaries were not always the product of sober observation and resulted in a few shocking stories and a number of 2am emails to the professor along the lines of "OMG YU wouldn't bleive wht I just saw!!!!!" The course used a harm reduction paradigm to encourage students to examine their beliefs about alcohol use, and the purpose of the writing exercises was to raise awareness of drinking behaviors so that the students could better understand the consequences of intoxication.

The diaries reveal a high frequency of alcohol-laced social events and emphasize the episodic nature of students' drinking habits (Tremblay et al., 2010). While most students described two or three evenings a week devoted to parties or bar-hopping, athletes were less likely to indulge during their seasons because of team-enforced dry periods. As a result, when athletes were able to drink they often attempted to 'make up for lost time', a phrase used repeatedly in the diaries and party ethnographies. Restrictions created episodic binge behaviors in a significant number of student-athletes while other students moderated their intakes but drank more frequently. That does not mean, however, that non-athletes were drinking any less or any less dangerously, merely that the athletes were more likely to describe their drinking behaviors, when they could drink, as designed to cause intoxication. The student athletes also provided more sober diaries and ethnographies, since they were very conscious of the intake proscription and mused upon how it affected their participant observation of parties and bar scenes.

Being Social with Alcohol: Relieving Anxiety and Releasing the 'Drunk Self'

Students report that they drink because it creates social situations and gives them something to do. This might not make sense to adults, who probably view the daily freedom of college as a time in which a plethora of sober leisure activities could occur, but many students are not as pro-active about exploring the world around them as are older and more secure adults. Above all, it is important to remember that students are 'emerging adults' (Arnett, 2004) who are learning adult roles rather than firmly established in them. Much of student identity is still connected to peers who help to establish a sense-of-self through group affiliation – and since alcohol is often a factor in social activities it provides an excuse for students to spend time together (Borsari and Carey, 2006; Kremer and Levy, 2008; Dement and Jarvinen, 2011; Lange et al., 2011). There is a strong belief among students that only alcoholics drink alone, and if a student wishes to take advantage of some of the stress-reducing features of intake he or she *must* find a partner or a party for companionship. This is demonstrated in this quote from a diary:

> "My roommate invited me to drink and I agreed to have a couple of drinks with him. I was not in our room when he started drinking and John had already drank four shots by himself. John immediately told me to take two shots so that I could 'catch up' to him so that he wouldn't feel so bad for having drunk by himself; at one point he even said that he felt like an alcoholic because he had been drinking alone and because he was bored."

The more prevalent reason for drinking together is that it promotes social interactions and relaxes young adults who might be insecure about their social capacities. Alcohol is used to relieve the stress caused by being social, which is not unexpected given that students are thrown into large social groups with peers from a wide variety of backgrounds, classes, countries and cultures. Alcohol is used by adults to reduce stress and to bolster self-identity in social situations (Horton, 1943; Bacon, 1945; Robbins, 1973), but students use intake specifically to overcome social anxieties because they are still learning how to interact with others (Orcutt, 1993; Burke and Stevens, 1999; Beccaria and Guidoni, 2002; Borsari and Carey, 2006; Ham et al., 2010; Smith and Berger, 2010; Smith, 2011: 122–123). Alcohol has also been accused of replacing the emotional and communicative work needed to develop strong friendships since it creates a reason for sociality and functions as a short-cut to feelings of similarity, inclusion and belonging (Winlow and Hall, 2006: 53–57 and 89–92). The power of alcohol to smooth over social fears is clear in the following quotes, as is its ability to promote instrumental and shallow associations:

> "A girl in my pledge class (AG) attended a pre-game. It was her mission to get drunk before the mixer with the frat. AG threw back shots at an aggressive rate. She kept complaining, 'uggg I don't understand what the point of sober sisters is, I can't even imagine being there sober. That frat isn't even cool, I'll shoot myself if I have to talk to any of the brothers in their fraternity sober. There is NO way I am showing up there without being wasted. These stupid mixers are only fun when you are drunk. I have to get drunk, quickly.'"

> "I came to a very scary realization the other night during a conversation with a friend. We concluded our generation is incapable of forming lasting, meaningful relationships. Specifically I mean male–female romantic relationships, but likely other relationships are suffering as well … In our technology-saturated, self-absorbed, arguably reckless lives 'dating' consists of a text invitation to a house party, pre-gaming, an extra drink or two upon arrival at the party, some grinding on the dance floor, public or private make-out (depending on the level of drunkenness) and the date finally ends with either a walk home or a walk upstairs. What happens when we're 23 and don't know how to ask someone out to coffee in person? What about when we go out to dinner and can't keep conversation going past the first course without a few drinks?"

> "Normally, while drunk, I would have no qualms about making conversation with new people, but I found myself acting very reserved while my inebriated friends easily chatted and mingled with the other attendees. Something that troubled me throughout the evening was that I did not know what to do with my hands. I have never experienced this before, because at parties, I always have a drink to hold. I found myself crossing my arms, holding my hands out in front of me, or holding my purse, with each change becoming more awkward."

> "It was obvious that there was no point in staying at the apartment when there was no longer any alcohol; the notion of having social relations without an alcoholic beverage in hand was just too terrifying."

Some students have said that they "only had drunk friends" and that their social connections were entirely constructed through reliance on alcohol. One student told a story of having a date with a very attractive young man who didn't drink. Because she wasn't drinking she felt that she had no way to talk to or interact with this fascinating but scary new person, and became convinced that she was boring to him simply because she couldn't show him her 'fun personality' unleashed through intoxication. She was particularly bothered by the silences that occurred during the date because she felt that for a social encounter to be successful people had to talk and be funny all the time. By the end of the evening she was miserable and never wanted to see him again, but was also worried that he hated her for being boring and insecure. When I explained that these were very common first-date fears, she was incredulous because she was convinced that everyone else was "so secure, so popular, so together." I asked her if she thought it would be a good idea for the college to teach social skills and she said yes, but that students would be afraid to go openly because they believed people were supposed to be 'super-social' naturally and if you weren't born with those skills you were a loser. She was surprised to hear that many people practiced their social skills in order to feel less nervous when meeting new people. As a result of this and similar conversations, my harm reduction class shifted to include discussions about how to attend a party without drinking and how to feel comfortable being social. We discuss tricks to evade peer pressure to drink (carry a red solo cup of water or juice since no-one ever assumes it's anything but alcohol) and tricks to appear socially adept (ask questions, have an amusing self-deprecating anecdote, talk about movies, books or travel, etc.). When I discuss Dale Carnegie and similar lessons for sociality the students express amazement that each generation has to learn how to be comfortably social – that it's not an inborn skill. These in-class discussions have revealed students' deep insecurities and one of the reasons alcohol can become a necessity for college social gatherings.

Negotiating the Gendered Self with Alcohol

Alcohol also allows students to experiment with social identities and to play with how they behave while being social. Students sometimes refer to this personality shift as the 'Drunk Self', an acknowledgement they are consciously playing with identities while using alcohol. The Drunk Self allows students to displace responsibility for consequences ("I'm always so mean when I'm drunk – I just lash out and then have to apologize later, but people understand") but is mostly used to establish the self as a fun-loving person. Given the 'work hard, play hard' mythos of many students, the Drunk Self allows a temporal shift in personality and action and the creation of a 'time-out' persona (Vander Ven, 2011: 135). The importance of alcohol to provide the break between work and play is illustrated in this quote: "The mentality my friends and I have is that if you go out then you are going out to drink; the only excuse for not drinking is staying in to do work." Because many students believe that they have to be perfect in all realms of life, the Drunk Self is a manifestation of a deeply compartmentalized self-image that allows them to reconcile the contradictions between being a high-achieving student as well as a successful social player; to be smart as well as popular. There is a strong element of performance in drinking as well as the management of what might be considered the strategic self. Students use the absence of alcohol to define a daytime self who is hard-working and aspirational just as they use alcohol intake to construct a night-time/leisure self who is social, popular and fun. That neither or both might be a real or authentic element of their personalities they do not ponder in their essays; nor do they question why they happily wear sweats and pajamas to class while playing a 'hard working and aspirational' role but would never wear anything but well-put-together, fashionable and attractive clothing when out at night. Nor do they consider the possibility that these day/night and disparate personalities might be two manifestations of a greater and more integrated whole.

The conscious use of alcohol as both a time-out instigator and a time-out personality creator is particularly apparent in this first quote:

> "In a way, it was disconcerting that the insecurities that haunt me all during the day when I am sober were invading my party time. I wasn't singing or dancing because I was afraid of what people would think. I wasn't initiating conversation with anyone besides my housemates. I wasn't really enjoying the party. My roommates were trying to pull me onto the dance area, but I kept gazing around wondering how I appeared to everyone in the room. I was unable to relax fully with myself during play time and I resented it. What I realized as I saw Susan going for her fourth refill of the night was that the party animal identity she assumes is dependent on alcohol. I am usually right there with her, but I couldn't 'let loose' like she did because I didn't have a drink in hand. She was kidding when she made the comment but it did make me realize that 'letting loose' really was centered on drinks despite the fact that we never consciously make that connection."

> "Hank casually remarked, 'I wish I was drunk all the time.' We all laughed, since it was such a ridiculous thing to say. Later, I asked him what he meant by his comment. 'I just like myself drunk. I like my drunk self. I think my drunk self is funny.'"

> "They were using alcohol mixed with caffeine as a social lubricant, a way to convince themselves that they could be the exciting, witty and intelligent student they were expected to be. I watched my friends lie to themselves about why they were pre-gaming a basketball game to avoid the reality that maybe they are somewhat shy when not intoxicated."

> "I could always have seen Ted being in a fraternity. However, I never expected that he would turn into one of the loud, obnoxious, drunken rude and hyper-masculine characters one sees at traditional frat parties."

And, as the last quote demonstrates, how a student acts when drunk is a performative construction of gender beliefs and identity. Alcohol use has always been gendered historically and cross-culturally; no culture that uses alcohol expects the same reaction from males as from females, and all cultures seem to have very strong belief systems about how alcohol should be used by each gender. Women often are expected not to drink, and most drinking establishments have traditionally been masculine enclaves. Fossey (1994: 203–204) argues that from an early age children absorb a cultural belief that female drinking is improper and abnormal and that as a result girls grow up to feel shame in drinking. That males are more readily accepted as drinkers is clear; intake, especially heavy public intake, is primarily a male activity in most cultures and often one that defines masculinity (Singer et al., 1992; McDonald, 1994; Macdonald, 1994; Dragadze, 1994; Purcell, 1994; Suggs, 1996; Perez, 2000; Abad, 2001; Turmo, 2001; Mitchell, 2004; Gamburd, 2008; Measham, 2008; Pine, 2009; Mager, 2010). Regular drinking has been problematic for respectable American women of all ages (Murdock, 1998; Rotskoff, 2002), while public intoxication is sometimes considered not only a male rite of passage but a college male right of behavior (Landrine, Bardwell and Dean, 1988; Giles, 1991; Capraro, 2000; West, 2001; Harnett et al., 2000; Peralta, 2007).

"Kelly is very quiet and is consumed by her eating disorder, but when she is drunk she emerges from her shell. It is as though the girl within her she is constantly trying to suppress due to her insecurities, emerges and she is starving."

In the college setting, however, drinking has become normalized for young women, and is used to challenge gender norms as well as to preserve them. Young women can perform gender two ways with alcohol: they are able to usurp male power by behaving like males when intoxicated and can perform normative heterosexual femininity by upholding drinking norms that expect women to be dainty, sexually alluring and in control. These two positions are paradoxical, mutually exclusive and must be manipulated strategically. Women more frequently adopt the gender-challenging drunken comportment when in same-gender groups (Sheehan and Ridge, 2001; Montemurro and McClure, 2005; Eldridge and Roberts, 2008) but also acknowledge that drinking heavily conveys power and perceived equality with males (Young et al., 2005; Lyons and Willott, 2008). For some events, particularly heterosexual mixers such as fraternity parties and Greek date events, they prefer to remain classically feminine. Female students are aware of the inconsistencies in their beliefs and behaviors, which is probably one of the reasons they mention these gendered drinking norms in essays.

Some examples that demonstrate how women appropriate male drinking behaviors and attitudes to display personal and social power follow:

"Girls these days, on top of drinking, play beer games to prove to guys that they too can drink and play their games. Guys define their male identity through how much they drink and how they drink. I see guys trying to act like real men by chugging beers and going back for more. The only thing that differentiates a girl from other girls is clothing."

"Alcohol consumption in college, in any context, results in the construction of certain power relationships. The first is a gender relationship and the second is a relationship of social control. At this party, I watched a game of Beirut where a pair of fraternity members competed against two girls. While the men were intent on winning the game the girls were relaxed and focused on grabbing the men's attention by teasing them and provocatively dancing with each other."

This second quote highlights a common linguistic motif in these writings: females are often labeled 'girls' but males are called 'men'. Sometimes the terms 'boys' and 'girls' are used by female writers, but male writers more typically use 'guys' and 'girls'. The message is clear: women are infantilized and linguistically de-powered in the arena of drinking, while males retain their adult gender status. Similarly, women may adopt derogatory male characterizations to describe themselves, as these quotes demonstrate:

"I picked Friday to be sober because I had to be up early the next day. I had to rationalize it to some of my housemates who were chiding me, 'Well I just want to be in good enough shape for the real party Saturday night.' After a few jokes about me being lame and a 'dirty slutbag,' they agreed that it would be all right for one night if I didn't drink. I reside with eight other girls. We are known as a party house, and there is rarely a weekend that we do not hold some sort of social gathering. We refer to ourselves as 'bitches' and are very proud of the fact that often times we can out-drink boys. As one male visitor described our house this past weekend 'You girls are awesome! You drink like boys, you think like boys, but you are hot.' I never really attended one of our house events completely sober … I just always drink at our house. I sometimes drink a lot. I never saw our behavior as terribly odd … until Army Navy Weekend when I was sober and for the first time was my actual self at a party."

"At the party I saw a lot of people shot-gunning beers, where you chug a whole beer by punching a hole in the side of the can towards the bottom, popping the top and letting the contents drain into the mouth.

One failing to complete the shot gun was berated and her performance qualified because 'she's a girl.'"

In these examples, female writers rely on the male gaze to describe female actions and characteristics; there is no irony or anger over gender bias. While appropriating terms such as 'slutbag' and 'bitches' in self-description may seem empowering – if it is consciously used to overturn and reverse negative meanings – in these examples the writers seem to accept that males have the right to label females, and that the labels may conflate gender, sexuality and denigration without comment or resistance.

Gender categories extend to types of alcohol and ways of drinking. Different kinds of alcohol frame social behavior and social identity among collegians. In the essays and diaries there is an opposing relationship between beer and wine, males and females, in-control drinking and out-of control drinking and adult vs. non-adult patterns of use and behavior – a characterization decades old, apparently (Landrine, Bardwell and Dean, 1988). These dichotomies are so definitively accepted that they determine the gender understood to be in control of a social situation; beer and shots signal male space and being 'out of control' while cocktails and wine signify female social control and adult, responsible drinking behaviors. Clothing is a manifestation of these categories, since female-oriented drinking events require jackets and dresses while male-oriented events are casual: t-shirts, jeans and flip-flops or sneakers. The latter style of dressing encourages high-end drinking, intoxication and bad behavior. The students assume that as they 'grow up' they will change from the male pattern of drinking to an adult female one just as they will wear suits to work instead of shorts and t-shirts. These conceptual categories reverse the linguistic terminology used in the papers: men are childish drinkers while women become adults because they drink wine and dress professionally. This belief can drive drinking patterns, encouraging both males and females to abuse in an effort to perform age-appropriate gender. Some quotes illustrate these beliefs:

"Already, however, the girls I am with are silently challenging gender roles. They are all drinking beer, a typical 'guy's drink' and drinking lots of it. They will not be prissy girls sipping their Malibu pineapples. They are tough, they are strong, and they will drink their beer."

"The students always had a drink in hand. For girls, it was mixed drinks. Most of them sipped their fruity concoctions through a slim straw, while almost every guy in the room drank beer. The men not only drank beer as an indication of their masculinity, but the manner in which they drank is just as important, as it is for girls. The guys were not seen sipping a beer, instead they had to gulp or chug it."

"Having a semi-formal party changed behaviors between the guys and girls. Many of the guys chatted with the girls for extended periods of time and even asked for their phone numbers instead of ignoring them until the girls were drunk and then trying to just get them to go upstairs for a hookup as they would at a frat party."

"The types of alcohol served – wine and mixed drinks – and the semi-formal dress deterred people from taking shots, and several students even swirled, sniffed and sipped from their plastic cups. Even though there was music few people danced because suits and dresses were inappropriate attire for 'grinding'… A male guest said 'yes, I guess this whole party feels more adult than a frat. I wouldn't talk about this stuff standing around a keg but I'm drinking wine in a suit – I'm not exactly going to start grinding and hooking up with some chick.' The drinking culture created by the atmosphere was somewhat of a mock-adult environment. Guests mingled and conversed in a manner consistent with 'typical' college parties; however, as all *were* college students, the environment they created represented their *ideas* about adult cocktail parties. These were the same people who would 'grind' and take shots at a keg party, but altered their behavior according to a more 'sophisticated' standard because they perceived that wine and suits required the change."

DeSantis explores gender identity performance in his 2007 examination of Greek life on college campuses (Desantis, 2007). His gender themes and beliefs illustrate many of the observations made in the papers and diaries. He argues that the Greek system's reliance on dichotomized gender patterning reflects Pan-Hellenic social activities because masculine and feminine are perceived as starkly divided and deeply oppositional. To be male is to be not-female, and the characteristics of each gender are separate and defining. The five male gender qualities are heterosexual promiscuity, toughness and assertiveness, imposing physical bodies, relational independence and professional orientation. The five female characteristics are symmetrically matched and opposite: monogamy and virginity, nurturing and caring, petite physical bodies, relational interdependence and domestic orientation. These ideationally paired characteristics are on display during frat parties and other drinking events designed to promote male/female interactions. When the above dichotomies of male/female, beer/wine, in-control/out-of-control and childish/adult are added to DeSantis' oppositional pairings a conceptual behavioral pattern for male drinking emerges, one that corresponds with Connell's description of hegemonic masculinity (Connell, 1995). A properly masculine college male is an entitled, sexualized, physically imposing and assertive beer drinker who is out of control and not really an adult – and therefore not responsible for his actions. Such a performative norm ensures that alcohol-induced violence against unaffiliated males and women is excused, expected and common because true masculinity is aggressive (DeSantis, 2007: 77–104). Within these belief systems, males are exhibiting their true natures and personalities when they behave badly when drinking.

"During the party, a friend of mine made Alex a cosmopolitan drink. And one of his friends, Samuel, tried for five minutes to get him to not drink the cosmopolitan stating that it was a girly drink. He repeated told Alex that he would lose 'man points' if he drank the cosmopolitan and the he might as well turn gay. And during those five minutes Alex argued that 'it had alcohol in it, and that's all that mattered.' Alex eventually drank the cosmopolitan, but to make it more 'manly' he chugged it. Samuel, who still was disappointed that Alex drank the girly drink, tried to 'bring Alex down' by announcing that Alex had drunk a cosmopolitan on Facebook."

In the diaries and essays bad male behavior was a frequent observation and some students considered drink-induced violence a natural way for young men to prove their masculinity. This is, of course, a common theme in cultural narrative from the ancient Greeks to Hemingway and recognized in academic studies (Capraro, 2000; West, 2001; Winlow and Hall, 2006; DeSantis, 2007; Dowdall, 2009; Peralta, 2007; Vander Ven, 2011: 104–110). Alcohol allows for time-out drinking that limits the social consequences of being violent and often allows young men to be excused from punishment – a 'night-time economy' performance in which carnavalesque crime/liminal leisure, as described by Presdee (2000: Chapter 8) and Rojek (2000: 147–150), is blended with gender identity. The participant observation papers and diaries listed incidences of violence, including fights, property destruction, theft and demeaning and rude behavior to waiters, school personnel, women and other males. Female writers recorded male attempts to steal belongings from house parties as a sign of male aggression and entitlement, while young males usually wrote about these episodes as pranks – and usually considered them to be amusing and of enjoyment to all, including the victims. One young man was particularly clueless about how badly he and his frat brothers were behaving at an up-market restaurant: they poured wine on middle-aged patrons at nearby tables while screaming 'uproariously' and climbing on tables. He interpreted this as a fun night and as a service to the victims, who thus were able to re-live their "own, fun-filled crazy college days" while "immersed in their current boring everyday lives." That the restaurant personnel then told the young men to leave he interpreted as "asshole behavior" and to punish the establishment they grabbed wine bottles from tables on their way out. This kind of casual violence (without consequences) was often not even recognized as such by the young men, who blindly assumed that they had the right to behave badly and to control the situation by telling service personnel what to do:

> "Rockets were set off by some of the guys while some of the other guys were dropping an old television set from the roof of the house. As soon as the TV hit the ground the guys that were at ground level started to bash the TV with sticks and poles that they had handy. Unfortunately, one of the guys on the team accidentally hit a friend on his back swing with a metal pole. The kid had to go to the hospital for stitches, but luckily nothing really serious happened other than the fact that he had to get stitches."

> "Unfortunately, some random kid decided to kick the light post in front of the football house. The kid was obviously drunk because when one of the guys on the team asked him to stop the kid decided to throw a punch at one of our teammates. One of the guys proceeded to throw a beer at the kid to get his attention and then punch him so hard that he broke the kid's nose. All he was doing was protecting his teammate from getting hit by some kid that nobody knew. Some of the other guys on the team tried to stop it but the kid was so drunk he tried to fight everyone. Another wrong move, the guys on the team then dragged the kid on the sidewalk through the crowd while guys were just kicking him and beating him up. One of the guys that was walking on top of the cars so he would not be held up by the huge crowd jumped off the top and elbowed the kid, much like a wrestling move out of WWF, it was hysterical. Finally, the kid's friends dragged him out of the crowd and the guys on the team that were sober helped stop our drunken teammates from following them because the cops were coming."

> "My friend Ari ordered us blueberry vodka and sprite, an admittedly girly drink, but since it is clear and comes with a wedge of lime, is acceptable to drink in public. Ari then noticed four large pink hearts that were decorating the restaurant's bar and jokingly asked Jeremy to steal one. Jeremy, definitely intoxicated, thought that it was a great idea. He stood on a chair and grabbed one of the large hearts from on top of an antique armoire. A waiter told him to give back the heart. He argued for a few seconds and then agreed, although he must have said something sarcastic because the waiter pushed him. He pushed the waiter back, which alarmed the bartender, who started screaming at us. I told her to calm down and that we were leaving. Although I know Jeremy can be belligerent at times, I hadn't seen him do anything that warranted his removal. The bouncer pushed Jeremy and told him to get out. The bouncer made the mistake of continuously pushing Jeremy even after he conceded. Jeremy turned around and said 'I'm leaving, just stop pushing me.' The bouncer gave

him another quick push to which Jeremy responded, 'If you push me one more time, I'm going to fucking knock you out.' Apparently, the bouncer didn't like his face because he gave Jeremy one last push. Jeremy, being a man of his word, put his right fist into his left hand, and gave the bouncer a fierce right elbow to the jaw. The man's jaw clicked and he spit out a fair amount of blood as he hit the ground hard. Several other bouncers rushed over to tend to their wounded friend, and one especially large man actually picked up Jeremy and carried him outside. We hailed the nearest cab and rode back to campus."

"At the party, a frat brother I didn't know ripped a framed poster off our wall and started to carry it away. I stopped him and told him to give back the art and he threw the poster back against the wall, and the glass broke. Then he started laughing and said he was so fucked up. He was using alcohol as a way to excuse his destruction and theft of property and he was not expecting to be challenged, especially by a much smaller female. To me this perfectly reflected the gender roles expected in the context of alcohol use."

"I noticed a woman and a man playfully fighting with a spoon laden with Nutella; she appeared to be retaliating his attack that had left a sticky gob of Nutella on her cheek. Both laughing, he wrenched the spoon out of her hand and then his friend jumped in to help hold her back. One of the two males grabbed a bottle of chocolate syrup and as she saw it, she began to panic. Her struggling cries were mistaken for laughter and the first male started pouring syrup all over her until a group of her friends and I intervened. We followed her as she angrily stomped up the stairs to wash the chocolate that was well in her ear and all over her face, hair, and clothes. In the bathroom she started to cry unexpectedly, lashing out at the nature of drunk males and how 'they take things too far.'"

As seen in these quotes, alcohol also provides an excuse for violence against women, and this violence was sometimes unrecognized by both male and female writers. That alcohol is linked to sexual assault on campus is well known (Boswell and Spade, 1995; Abbey et al., 2001; Abbey, 2002), as is a correlation with misogynistic beliefs about women (Cracco, 2008; West 2001; DeSantis, 2007; Grazian, 2008: Chapter 5; Dowdall, 2009: 83–95). Several studies have demonstrated that college males believe that aggressive pursuit of females is expected and excused when drinking has occurred (Cracco, 2008) and Abbey et al. (2002) have shown that alcohol causes young men to misread women's cues during attempted seduction, which can encourage sexual assault and rape. One of the more horrifying essays in this collection was written by a young woman who described a very public sexual assault. The party was an elegant affair with cocktail dresses, wine and swanky appetizers. The hostesses had invited a number of 'boys and girls', with instructions to arrive nicely dressed and ready for an 'adult' evening. The guests were late, and some were already drunk when they arrived. Already the carefully constructed ambience of an elegant evening was breached, but as the atmosphere degenerated further the hostesses lost control of the party and a group of the guests, very drunk young men, talked the rest into leaving for a party at a frat house. As they left one of the young men pinned a female guest to the outside wall of the building and ripped the skirt of her cocktail dress, then demanded that she give him a blow job. When she said no he shook her, called her a "fucking cocktease," and tried to rip off her dress. The hostesses and the other guests pulled the young man away from the young woman and the entire group continued on to the next party. My student was disturbed because the party had ended badly – she felt that the guests had read the frame of the party incorrectly and behaved as if they were attending a frat party rather than an elegant and grown-up cocktail party. I was disturbed because my student failed to interpret the attack as a sexual assault or, indeed, as any kind of behavior out of the ordinary. Over the course of several meetings she began to understand that the behavior was an assault, but the core of her unhappiness was that the guests had transposed behavior acceptable for one type of party to something entirely different, and in the process ruined her evening. She repeatedly assured me that this behavior was expected of young men, and that the real crime had been the mis-reading of the party themes and expectations.

Candy Is Dandy but Liquor Is Quicker

Alcohol and sexuality are linked in more positive ways as well, especially since many students rely on 'Dutch Courage' to be able to make a move on someone they find attractive. But researchers tend to focus on assault rather than the connection between mutually consensual sex and alcohol. Alcohol and alcohol events encourage sexual search and play for both males and females, and intoxication certainly decreases the psychological barriers to intimacy, even if, according to Shakespeare, it "provokes the desire, but it takes away the performance" (Macbeth, Act II Scene 3). As one female writer reported: "at fraternity parties there is a reason why guys want girls to drink more and get drunk. The entire environment harbors male hormonal thought." Women also use alcohol as a convenient excuse to explore their sexuality and to engage in activity that might otherwise provoke self-consciousness. Young women recognize that a sexual double-standard still functions, as illustrated by DeSantis' paired gender dichotomies, but they also wish to explore their sexuality and to display equality with males through adopting male sexual mores. The tension generated by these oppositions can be excused and explained away in a socially appropriate manner by blaming alcohol for questionable behavior.

"'Lizzie, you know you aren't going to get any ass if you don't drink.' I can't help but notice that there is a lot of physical touching going on. It is possible that the touching has to do with the fact that there are sailors on leave at our house. However, looking at the room from a sober viewpoint I notice that the touching going on is not something I want to take part in due to the overwhelming sense of shyness that usually is present in my everyday life. As these girls are not looking for a seriously committed relationship, alcohol seems to be doing a nice job of letting them relax from their usual boundaries."

"I remember being a freshman and feeling invincible at fraternity parties because I had access to alcohol, older men, and decreased inhibitions."

"It is not that girls only want to have sex or talk to boys when they have alcohol, it's that alcohol allows them to engage in sexual relations without actually dealing with the emotional aspects of the relationship. Without the empowerment of a buzz, for the first time I did not feel at ease at my own party."

"In the cab ride on the way back to campus, one girl said, 'I'm so drunk … I really don't want to get taken advantage of.' She said this while she danced on her date's lap."

"The most important and prevalent finding was the shedding of the female sex role. Girls grinding with each other, Jessie kissing everyone, and Emily kissing on the dance floor all reinforced an abandonment of feminine sexual reserve and modesty. These college women were able to leave behind the ideals that they humor in American culture and trade them for others in this drinking culture."

And from the male perspective:

"It generally wasn't until most drinkers had a few drinks under their belts that they broke the gender lines and launched conversations with those of the opposite gender. Many will admit that they feel more comfortable, or loosened up and more confident in making conversation after sucking down a few drinks."

"In the brief time that we spent there, Bill managed to pick up a girl. This was quite the surprise since he is a pretty awkward guy, to the extent that he can barely manage conversation with most girls. He walked the girl home, while Hank, a friend of Bill's girl and I lagged behind. The friend of Bill's girl explained the secret to his success: indicating Bill's hook up, she said, 'At this point, she'd fuck anything.'"

Alcohol works for students because it encourages a goal – sexuality – while diminishing fears about attaining that goal. For males, alcohol helps to assuage fear of rejection; the drive toward sex is considered normal and natural. For females, alcohol decreases concerns about being sexual, since having sex or engaging in sexual activities are morally fraught due to a gendered double-standard. Alcohol gives a woman permission to act and provides an excuse for doing so; she can always excuse her 'bad' behavior by claiming intoxication. Sexuality becomes an element of the time-out period facilitated by drunkenness and as such ceases to exist in the light of day, as do the moral and social consequences of sexual activity.

Accomplishment, Caretaking and Performance of Adulthood

Thomas Vander Ven maintains that 'getting wasted' (the title of his ethnography) allows students to accomplish important developmental tasks. Some of these we have discussed; alcohol encourages events that promote sociality and decreases the nervousness related to these encounters, from meeting new people to seduction. But Vender Ven also maintains that alcohol permits students to experiment with adult roles, caretaking behaviors and management of risk while building networks of trusted friends. His description of Drunk Support is insightful (Vander Ven, 2011: 83–94) because he identifies how each gender performs supportive behaviors and how they enhance social credibility within the college arena. Taking care of drunken, sick and upset friends promotes emotional development that prepares students for more nurturing adult roles with spouses and children. He argues that many of the self-care and management tasks that earlier generations would have assumed at younger ages are now being done by 'helicopter' parents. This phenomenon – one well known to all college professors – involves parental management of day-to-day responsibilities such as homework, scheduling and decision-making. This leaves students unsure of their competence and ability to resolve problems effectively. Caring for drunk and disorderly friends is a means to practice care of others, learn new life management skills, gain confidence to handle problems and reason through appropriate and inappropriate interpersonal actions. And students can learn (what seem to be) appropriate gendered patterns of management: young women care for friends by physically keeping them safe and performing "drunk counseling" (ibid.: 171) while young men often manage the more physical side of consequences such as protection, aggression in the face of danger and cleaning up.

Students plan for drinking events by assigning a sober person to look after the rest of the group, or by a tacit acknowledgment that the person who customarily drinks the least would take care of anyone who was seriously ill due to alcohol (ibid.: 91). It is more likely that a 'sober sister' will be negotiated if the drinking group ventures off-campus to bars or clubs outside of the campus bubble. These tasks include functioning as a wingwoman (or wingman) to make sure friends don't hook up with the wrong person or while too drunk to make a good decision about sexual activity, and making sure drunks get home safely. Holding heads (and hair) when vomiting, rubbing the distressed person's back and shoulders, feeding water and other non-alcoholic liquids and verbal comfort are all part of the mothering activities that the responsible friend assumes.

"When I went over at 10pm, Hank was very drunk. By 11, Hank was so drunk, he had passed out on the bar. His tab for the night: $150. Bill and I spent the rest of the night taking care of him. At 12, Hank was coherent enough (relatively speaking) that we could get him home. Bill and I walked him home the five blocks from the bar through the snow and put Hank to bed, even as he drunkenly berated us. The next morning he apologized. I told him not to worry about it, since he's a good friend, but that there would come a time when I wouldn't be willing to deal with it anymore."

"While we were heading back to my dorm, Taylor kept complaining that she had to use the bathroom … she said she could not wait any longer, running to some shrubs where she vomited all of the contents in her stomach. I held her hair away from her face and rubbed her back as she finished vomiting."

"During the game of 'Beirut', Victoria became inebriated and began vomiting. Victoria was surrounded by a group of her friends who were making sure that she was OK. They brought her water, tissues, made sure that she was coherent, held her hair while she threw up, etc. And it was not only Victoria's friends who were concerned for her, several other people at the mixer began offering to help with Victoria: they offered to walk her home and/or a place to stay the night if she 'couldn't make it home.' The game did not resume until Victoria stopped vomiting and was taken home."

"After the mixer, when everyone was getting ready to leave, the main questions asked were 'Where do you live?' and 'How are you going to get there?' The rules for going home were 1) you walked home with a group (people most likely who lived in the same college house) 2) if you were a girl, you were accompanied by a guy or two girls and 3) if you were a guy, you were fine to walk home alone unless you were inebriated; then you would walk home with a group or accompanied by another male."

"Well some of my friends were trying to get her to drink water before she passed out. And it was interesting to see the various techniques people used to try to get her to drink water. One of her friends, a girl, was talking to her in a motherly voice and my other roommate was using a combination of jokes and 'here comes the choo-choo train' technique. In the end putting the cup in her hand and forcing her to drink the water did the trick."

The need for caring behaviors occurs in response to physical illness caused by extreme drunkenness or because of the consequences of extreme drunkenness. Consequences range from the unpleasant but relatively harmless (such as forgetting something at a bar, or saying something later regretted) to serious problems including property damage, police intervention, accidents, injuries and death. Students describe these consequences as a 'Shit Show', which means anything from a really wild party with lots of interpersonal drama to an event that results in more serious and dangerous outcomes (Vander Ven, 2011: 79–119). My students have used this phrase, and their diaries and essays reveal the same attitudes and mirror the theme of accomplishment in handling risky outcomes as do the students Vander Ven describes. In these narratives drunken consequences can be viewed as accomplishments because students are able to practice coping skills by handling the outcome of parties gone awry. They are then able to model accomplishment and capacity to others, often through storytelling and morning-after discussions (ibid.: 139).

Shit Show narratives range from discussions about consequences and how they were minimized, rationalized or excused to descriptions of how problems were solved:

"Nick revealed that since his freshman year at Penn, whenever he got blackout drunk he would wake up covered in his own urine, and it would often be on his floor as well. John mentioned that before winter break he had been wasted and was walking home alone and he accidently walked into their next door neighbor's house – which was unlocked – and passed out on the kitchen floor. These stories were told with little embarrassment because 'everyone who gets drunk has embarrassed themselves like this in some way.'"

Girl: "So Katie told me you were being so mean and yelling at her last night"

Guy: "Hahahaha, I don't remember that at all"

Girl: "Yea, that's what I told her it's fine!"

Guy: "So how was the rest of your night?"

Girl: "Well I was so blackout before you guys even got there! I should not have been doing shots with you guys! I slept in Robby's bed!! I must have just passed out there"

Guy: "Robby's bed?!! WHAT?!"

Girl: "Hahah, I know! Joe came in this morning and was like you get up, what are you doing here and I noticed all the posters were different!"

Guy: "Where was Robby?"

Girl: "In the hallway! Robby was asleep on the floor"

Guy: "Hahah, oh wow! That's so funny!!"

Girl: "Yea haha, it was crazy, so much fun!"

"My friend Tim disappeared from the party around 2:30 am and passed out on Jamie and Kara's floor an hour or so later. He woke up in his own vomit the next morning with handfuls of candy in his pocket with no idea how they got there. My friend Joe took his shirt off at the party and started dancing on tables. He vomited in and then passed out on one of the guy's beds. The guy whose bed it was was too drunk to notice at the time and passed out there as well. Our friend Katie vomited on a couch with some coats on it, and then in the bed of one of the guys who lived in the house that she had been hooking up with for a couple of weeks. My new nose ring fell out somehow at some point and I had to go get a new one today. The cops came later on in the night because of a noise complaint. Despite (or because of?) all of this, everyone seemed to have a great time and called the party a 'Shit Show' and success."

Most of the accomplishment narratives recorded involved complicated and lengthy accounts of helping friends make it home, make bail or get to the emergency room safely. Two stories were notable because their authors spent many sentences explaining why and how they cared for someone else or how they cleaned up a mess. In the first account, several young men lost sight of a very drunk friend at a bar but later discovered him on the sidewalk covered in vomit and blood; he had fallen on to a parked car and gashed his scalp. Even though they were all quite drunk, they "sobered up fast" (or thought they did) and called 911. When the ambulance came two friends accompanied him to the ER and the others went home to get his room ready for his recovery. Each action was described in great detail and the author was clearly proud of how well they had managed the event and ensured their friend's safety. The other mishap involved alcohol, a balcony and a trip to the hospital. During a party in a high-rise apartment a very drunken young man fell from a fifth floor balcony. The others watched in intoxicated horror, thinking that he had fallen to his death. Fortunately, he'd managed to grab the railing on the balcony a floor below, although he was cut up, had broken some ribs and had to go to the hospital. The student who recorded this event provided a step-by-step account of how the rest of the participants responded to the crisis, and was quite shocked that after putting him into the ambulance they all went back to the original apartment to drink some more. She was the only sober person at the party and was deeply affected by the experience. All of the accounts of consequences read as accomplishment narratives because they detail the choices made and actions taken, and emphasize how the students managed to make the situation go away or get better. They provide a narrative arc that poses the self and others as effective grown-ups and problem-solvers who learn from mistakes made and are ready to move on, into larger roles and responsibilities. They function as coming-of-age stories.

Even tales that seem to lack educational and salvation discourses serve as accomplishment stories. Simply re-telling an embarrassing event reiterates that one has survived it, learned and can move forward. Embedded in the drunken story is the message that the protagonist has accomplished something important – even if only to amuse others with a joke on the self. Sharing stories about 'the night before' cements friendships and promotes a shared sense of common concerns and behavioral norms (Sheehan and Ridge, 2001). Tales of Shit Show adventures are shared over breakfast with housemates and friends from the night before and traded as cultural currency on Facebook:

> "Sunday afternoon is the best time to Facebook. By late afternoon, the photos of the weekend's escapades have been put up by those further procrastinating. For some reason, pictures of one's family vacation or sober gatherings do not necessitate the rapid posting, tagging, de-tagging and comment ritual that characterize so many lazy Sundays across campus. An even odder phenomenon is the extremely public nature of the photographs. I doubt that I am alone in flipping through the album of a distant friend or long-lost high school pal. I think this says a lot about our generation and growing up in the technology age. The rise of digital cameras allows people to capture memories anywhere they go, even in situations that they may not remember the next day, and Facebook facilitates the easy sharing of these sometimes racy, usually hysterical, photos. I can't think of another forum where it would be socially acceptable to post photos of underage kids drinking, a round of shots, a keg stand, or strangers making out. The photos of peace signs, 'gangsta' poses, and double fisting red cups would not make it into the family photo album, but they do become immortalized in cyberspace and paint a fairly accurate picture of a large portion of college social life. It is albums like these that serve as social cues for acceptable drunken college behavior. For example, somewhere along the way it became cool to throw up a sideways peace sign in a photo, but this only applies when intoxicated, and now every album likely has at least one such shot. Facebook photo albums eternalize the drunken nights, and set a standard for 'fun'. A good set of pictures symbolizes a fun night, too few pictures is disappointing, and an album of too many 'de-tags' represents the sloppiest of nights that really should never occur.

Regardless, they are all online, and all afternoon students will be clicking away during those all too frequent study breaks."

"Well after she began throwing up and we got her to drink water everyone began telling her how funny she was and that they were going to be making fun of her for this 'stunt' for a while. It was interesting to see this switch in attitudes so sudden, as though someone had flipped on a switch. Everyone went from being 'ancy' to joking around and making fun of Ashlee puking in a trash can. I guess one could consider this a 'bonding moment' for the fact a bunch of us worked together to get Ashlee back safely and make sure that she would be ok for the rest of the night."

"Much of what happened would not have occurred if we were all sober. Of course, the party could still have been fun without any alcohol, and most of the time we do have plenty of fun without intoxicants, but it would have been a different kind of fun. There is fun and there is intoxicated fun, each appropriate at its own time and place. The best part of the intoxicated fun is the laughable stories, the Facebook photo albums, and the bonding that occurs during a few hours on your hands and knees scrubbing the floor."

Time-out Drinking, Stress and Control

A final theme found in drinking accounts is that of using alcohol for relief from a stressful academic schedule. Many college students experience their lives as stressful, filled with responsibilities far beyond those of adults. Alcohol provides the easiest shortcut to stress reduction. According to many students (and reminiscent of Lefebvre's arguments about cultural rhythms of work, rest and reward) stressful periods that require strong self-control such as midterms and finals can only be overcome through an equal and opposite investment in out-of-control debauchery. Time-out drinking styles were explored thoroughly in a previous chapter, so the reasons for such beliefs should be clear. What makes college drinking time-outs more psychologically rational is that students are less likely to have control over their stress and less likely to be able to regulate their schedules. Assignment due-dates are created by professors and rarely provide a regular pattern within an individual student's schedule (outside of clear midterm and finals periods), which may increase stress because responsibilities are perceived to be simultaneously exogenous and beyond personal control. While students' overall responsibilities may pale in comparison to those of adults with jobs and families, lack of control over the rhythm of their lives may increase real feelings of stress.

Many diaries and party ethnographies report episodes of drinking designed to overcome 'a stressful week'. The rhythm of college drinking events makes these time-outs rational and easier to accomplish; weekday and week drinking is largely frowned upon as evidence of incipient alcoholism, while Thursday-Saturday drinking is considered normal. Other periods in which drinking is expected are immediately after test periods, during Spring Break and during a three-day period called 'Spring Fling' marked by concerts, social activities and campus rituals.

TIME-OUT DRINKING

"Particularly the line 'Time isn't wasted when you're getting wasted' rings so true. In passing discussion about weekends, the 'Oh it was boring I didn't really do much or get any work done' is viewed as so much more wasted than the 'Oh my gosh, it was so fun, we went out 3 nights! Didn't finish that paper or study for my exam, but oh well!' While both are some-what exaggerated, generalized statements, I'd be willing to bet that most students would regard a weekend of partying less of a wasted weekend than one sitting in the library sipping coffee and studying – weekends are, after all, a time for relaxation and fun, that must occur even in addition to the many other breaks that college students grant themselves during the regular workweek."

"The atmosphere at a college party is unlike anything else. During college, both responsibilities to the 'real world' and supervision by authority figures are at a minimum. The Spring Festival weekend is a time of further relaxation of the standards of discipline, and is seen by most students as a 48-hour period of drunken debauchery. This belief is reinforced by the actions and statements of police which reportedly include, 'Well, if you're going to drink, at least get off the sidewalk' and 'you're either going to have to dump those beers or chug them.'"

SPRING BREAK DRINKING

"I noticed Charles lying on a blanket with vomit all around him. I asked my friends who were with him the night before what happened, and they told me that he had not stopped drinking since 8am the morning before. Not only had he been drinking enormous amounts, he decided that consuming actual food was not as important as getting a large frozen drink. I could see it from the faces of the girls who were telling me the story that they were annoyed, and embarrassed for him. It was okay to be a drunken fool the night before, but when a person acts that way in broad daylight, it is exposed for everyone to see and it is unacceptable."

"While preparing for the night, Denise and Sandra ended up taking four shots before we left, and both seemed to be tipsy but coherent. At the club, we all began dancing with each other and other people, and men began taking interest in Denise. Several men would take her to the bar and buy her a drink, and she, not realizing her current state, would accept. After two Cosmos and a Bahama Mama, Denise was obviously drunk. The man who she was talking to was kind enough to order her a couple of waters, but by that time she was very sick and we were forced to leave the club. The next morning, it was apparent from Denise's face that she was ashamed. We all were laughing about the situation, but Denise did not hesitate to apologize profusely. I asked her why she accepted all those drinks, she explained that she liked the attention she was receiving from the men and that it was Spring Break, so 'what happens in Miami, stays in Miami.'"

STRESS DRINKING

"Her response was 'I really don't care, as long as I get some alcohol in me I am fine.' I then tried to find out the cause for these feelings. It turns out that she had had a rough week and was looking for nothing more than to forget it. However she had not eaten all day because she had been running around all day and had woken up late as well. When we arrived at the bar she immediately sat down and demanded a drink. There was not really any more margarita mix, so what we ended up doing was joining the rest of our drinks so that she could get some alcohol in her. In total, this added up to 3 drinks. She downed them in 20 minutes. And that is how Kara forgot her horrible week."

This type of time-out, carnavalesque drinking has a deep history, as established in earlier chapters. What makes college drinking more challenging (especially for parents and university administrators) is the regularity of such events. Unlike adult periods of accepted excess such as Mardi Gras and holiday parties, students seem to celebrate weekly, episodically and according to a calendrical cycle. Drunken students are visible because they are usually in large crowds and can be obnoxious. The reasons behind college drinking are many, and some have been explored in this chapter. In essays and interviews students frequently rationalize this excess by referencing how controlled they are during the week and when they have deadlines. My students are indeed a self-controlled, high-achieving group who turn in good-quality assignments on time while also managing to pack in after-school sports and drama activities, volunteer work and jobs. They are exactly the sort of students – conscientious, driven, Type-A over-achievers – expected at a well-respected school. In other words, it's possible that their perceived need for release is linked to their need for self-control in response to schedules beyond their control, and that the shifting yet tight schedules they keep may increase desire to binge (Vander Ven, 2011: 135).

In a series of interviews conducted at Mardi Gras in New Orleans, Davis Redmon hypothesized that those with low self-control would engage more frequently in activities of 'normative deviance' during Mardi Gras and that low self-control personality characteristics would correlate with wilder and more abandoned behavior. However, he found the opposite – that the more scheduled and controlled people, those who profess adherence to strong beliefs about morality and behavior (the more obviously respectable!) tended to behave with greatest abandon while in New Orleans (Redmon 2002 and 2003a and b). Arguing from Bakhtin (1968) that during carnival periods the body is emphasized over the higher intellectual or spiritual realms, Redmon hypothesizes that the everyday adherence to self-control in highly structured and moral people impels the inverse during periods of cultural release: that there is a psychological and cultural reason for 'what happens in New Orleans stays in New Orleans'. He chronicles comments such as "it's just for fun, for the thrill of doing something I can't do back home!" to explain why "the beliefs they hold during everyday life are suspended during Carnival, especially if their beliefs only pertain to the context in which they are relatively situated as opposed to a normative definition of beliefs" (Redmon, 2002: 381). These periods allow for play and exploration, and the trying on of roles and personae that may directly oppose everyday self-image (Redmon, 2003a). Rituals of reversal are simply that; they encourage the opposite of normative comportment and provide a venue for enacting such behaviors, especially in cultures with a 'work hard, play hard' ethos (Sexton, 2001). Most students strongly identify with being in control of the self, working hard and preparing for a professional future. But they also inhabit a liminal period between the social controls of the childhood family and the professional controls of employment, and so the 'work hard, play hard' mantra combines with time-out drinking opportunities to normalize rhythmic periods of intoxicated excess.

Conclusions

The 'College Bubble' is marked by geographic space, bounded time and social rhythm to construct a time-out period in which youth can experiment with identity while learning adult roles. Alcohol encourages playing with identity during rapid psychological and physical development and provides an excuse when experiments go awry. The search for – or development of – an 'authentic self' is paramount for psychological growth but can seem an overwhelming and frightening task. One student wrote: "alcohol is used as a means to mask a lack of honesty with oneself. It is not easy to wake up every morning and lie to oneself about who we are, but alcohol blurs the lines and makes these lies seem plausible." This perfectly illustrates the developmental tasks important to the college years as well as the fears that incite alcohol use. Alcohol is not a problem when the individual and communal consequences are minimal and students and campuses remain safe. Unfortunately, this is not the case with some drinking events, and the need to teach moderation is obvious. A harm reduction approach acknowledges that students drink, and recognizes that keeping them safe (rather than abstinent) is the goal of intervention. Because alcohol clouds perceptions it is difficult to teach boundaries and limits since the student may understand when sober, but when drunk will ignore the cues. And that remains the greatest problem with alcohol moderation for drinkers of all ages.

Alcohol plays a central role in social events. Because students can use drunk narratives as proof of accomplishment there is little desire to decrease consequences since overcoming the Shit Show is a performance of self-identity and learned maturity. Students are aware of the dangers of intoxication, but often lack the skills to recognize or read internal cues of abuse. Student drinking styles also encourage fast intakes that quickly increase the blood alcohol content. These characteristics of student drinking have led to specific harm reduction lessons in my classes. First, we discuss what 'adult' drinking looks like, and how they will integrate alcohol into their professional and adult personal lives (if they choose to drink). We discuss the dangers of drinking at work events, and how to moderate intake when it's important to drink with others but stay sober. We use phone applications to calculate BAC based on drink types, student weight and intake timing as a way to learn how to reach – and not exceed – a safe buzz. Students don't always understand that there is a lag between a drink and its full effect so they tend to overshoot their intoxication goal; I want them to use alcohol safely by accepting its effects and understanding how to enjoy them appropriately. We spend time talking about how each student reaches his or her comfort zone – the state of inebriation that makes them happy but keeps them from doing something stupid. After these boundaries are understood we discuss how to stay in the comfort zone. Students share tricks for decreasing intake or avoiding it completely, such as making sure to carry a cup filled with water, resist peer pressure, beg off drinking through acceptable excuses ("I'm on antibiotics!"or "I have a game tomorrow") and how to explain a desire not to drink when someone is really insistent. We discuss what is and what is not appropriate behavior in public, especially in professional circles, and how to deal with friends who have stepped over the line. These tricks of the drinking trade are often new to students, since they have rarely thought about drinking norms outside of their peer groups.

Very few students feel that they 'know how to drink', or how to moderate intake while having fun in a safe and appropriate manner. Their drinking styles have been learned among similarly underaged and furtive peers who drink as much as possible when granted intermittent access to alcohol. When alcohol is freely available they might not be able to shift intake behaviors and so they drink too much, too fast. Very few students report that parents or other adults taught them how to drink or counseled them in anything other than avoidance. Parents, in turn, are counseled to rely on temperance messages to discourage intake because it's not culturally appropriate to acknowledge to themselves or to other parents that their teens might use alcohol. But teens do drink, and they turn into college students who drink, who morph into adults who drink. And those adults, much like college students, sometimes drink too much. They become adults who haven't learned how to drink in a healthy and responsible manner because their culture has never been comfortable acknowledging that in a society that uses alcohol, individuals have to learn how to drink safely.

8

CONCLUSION

Why Do People Drink?

SCENE ONE

In the late 1980s I spent a couple of months in Indonesia and made many friends among the women of Bali. One night my landlady told me that she and some other women were going to go to the local temple to do a special women's moon ceremony, and would I like to come? That night she and I walked the mile or so to the 'big temple' and joined a small group of women who were sitting in a circle talking. Some spoke English for my benefit and others translated for me. The typical glasses of hot lemon water were offered all around, and the ladies drank. And so did I, expecting the soothing taste of citrus and sugar. To my surprise, the glass held lemon, yes, but also *arak*, a fiery grain alcohol that is harsh, unforgiving and best avoided. My throat screamed, my eyes stung, and I coughed while trying to swallow. Man, it hurt going down! The ladies looked at me and roared with laughter. The joke was on me, but also with me … because Balinese women don't drink. Many times I had been told by local ladies that I couldn't be a Westerner since I didn't smoke and drink "like the Australians do." As a woman traveler in 'Eastern' lands I rarely drank unless I was with other Westerners, since few women in South-East Asia drink in public. This marked me as being different than other tourists to the ladies of Bali and hastened our friendships, since they told me that I was "more like a Balinese woman." While that probably wasn't the case, my public abstinence singled me out from the sometimes-intoxicated tourists they encountered. So you can imagine my shock when given a tumbler full of *arak*, since I had never seen a Balinese woman drink alcohol.

The night wore on, and we chatted and told jokes for several hours, all the while sipping our lemon- infused *arak*. No-one got drunk, although we were all a little tipsy and we giggled a lot. There also wasn't any evidence of a ritual, although gifts of elaborately arranged food were left at the altar. To this day I don't know if there is a moon ceremony (the anthropologists who know Bali look puzzled when I ask them) or if it was merely an elaborate ploy for a ladies' night out. I do know that a gentle joke was played on me, but it was a kind and friendly one – the ladies were laughing with me, not at me. I was included in their group of friends and trusted to keep their secret – a very transgressive one involving alcohol – a ritual of reversal of gendered Balinese habits.

SCENE TWO

A few years ago we had a terrible accident at the university. During a party a young man fell over the railing of a stairway and was badly hurt. We devoted a significant part of the next class to a discussion of the accident, and it was an especially difficult conversation because several of his friends were in the course and had been at the party when he fell. The students were horrified by what had happened, especially since they all agreed that he wasn't "a big drinker" and was "a good kid." No-one thought he had been all that drunk before he fell and he wasn't in the habit of getting out-of-control drunk at parties. As we continued the discussion, I realized that the students were searching for a narrative that would explain why the accident had happened. The trajectory of action that led to his fall simply didn't fit into their understandings about how and why bad things happen with alcohol use. Furthermore, they had no Shit Show narrative with which to share the occurrence, and felt horrified that they hadn't been able to cleverly manage the outcome. In short, the accident cut through their understandings of alcohol use: it is fun, wild and crazy, the downstream of the Shit Show can be managed by the competent student and that part of demonstrating success in college and life is managing the Shit Show. They were horribly aware that this time they had not been competent, that a really bad thing had happened, and that they were powerless to make it better. It negated their normative stories about alcohol use and left them searching for answers – and doubting themselves, their maturity and their capacity to 'be in control' and 'high powered and successful' students and future corporate leaders. They were faced with the ultimate philosophical and theological conundrum: "Why do bad things happen to good people?" and had almost no tools with which to reason it through. They were contemplating the reality of an unfair and potentially nasty universe, a vision that simply didn't agree with their ethos of personal strivings and success.

In contrast, a few years earlier a drunken alumnus had fallen from the roof of a fraternity house and died. That accident had caused an immediate cessation of all university parties and the campus was declared dry for several months. The university convened committees of faculty, health education staff and students to revamp the campus alcohol policy, which resulted in a number of thoughtful and reasonable regulations designed to make sure that students were as safe as possible, even at parties. But the reaction in my class was very much different than it was with the later incident, since the students didn't know the person who died and were more concerned with the lockdown on social activities than on the events that led to his death. They felt that they were being punished because an outsider – someone they didn't know and who wasn't in their group or like them – had done something stupid and died. Their narrative was that older people couldn't handle their booze, it was the alumnus' fault for having an accident, and the accident didn't really have anything to do with them or their university life. Since in their experience deaths didn't happen at college parties it must be an anomalous situation tied to the individual rather than the social system: "he must have been an alcoholic" they collectively agreed.

Why, I wondered, had the response been so different? After talking with students it seemed to me that the disconnect was tied to two factors: their understanding of the consequences of college alcohol intake were tied to manageable Shit Show narratives and they associated alcohol accidents with driving under the influence. Because the MADD Public Service Announcements linking drunk-driving to accidents and death had been ubiquitous throughout their youth, they became the primary, and often the only, negative consequence in the minds of these students. Few of them had encountered other types of consequences (such as falls) so they reasoned that as long as you weren't driving you were probably safe to drink. And because the Shit Show narratives allowed them to define reaction to consequences as accomplishment they couldn't contemplate that alcohol might cause serious harm when not behind the wheel. The success of the MADD campaign messages have contributed to a sense of false safety in youth drinkers.

I provide these tales for two reasons: they are experiences that have caused me to reflect on the meaning of drinking (mine and that of other people) and illustrate the good and bad sides of alcohol use. Alcohol can promote friendship and provide a liquid symbol of inclusion and amity. In Bali, the ladies used alcohol to let me know that they wanted to be friends and to demonstrate their trust in me. It was a transgressive act and it would have been very unpleasant had I told others (in Bali) of my experiences; the ladies would have lost face in their society. They also used alcohol to enhance a social occasion and to accentuate feelings of good fellowship. No-one became intoxicated, we all had a fine time, and barriers were broken down through the disinhibiting effect of alcohol. I suspect the ladies were keen to have me join them so they could ask many questions about women's lives in the United States, since that is what happened. We spent the night (and most of the early morning) telling stories about how we lived, East and West. I learned much about Balinese life and they learned much about my life; to the normally reticent Balinese woman these questions would have seemed rude or intrusive if asked over coffee in the afternoon.

Similarly, the story about the accidents at college demonstrates the negative side of alcohol, and the difficulty of affixing boundaries to problem behaviors.

One of my brightest students once told me that I should concentrate on consequences if I wanted to encourage moderate use of alcohol among college students. I replied that I thought that the messaging focused too much on consequences; to which she agreed but countered with the observation that the consequences discussed were always too extreme and were rejected by youth. Few young people (fortunately) knew someone who was killed in a drunken car wreck, so focusing on that consequence encouraged young people to think "oh, that won't happen to me." Indeed, another student demonstrated this when she wrote that her best friend's brother was put in prison after killing several people while driving drunk on the weekend after he finished medical school. She was horrified that all of his smarts and efforts were going to waste, that he had done something so stupid that scarred his life forever and caused others' deaths. She wrote that "people like us don't do this kind of thing. We know better – how could this have happened?". And here again, there is a boundary crossed, the idea that 'our kind of people' don't have or cause these problems and consequences. Others might – the old, the non-college educated, the addicted, the less than successful – but we who can manage the Shit Show and are smart, accomplished, in-control and on the path to success do not have serious consequences when we drink. And those boundaries are, of course, as false as the beliefs that provide comfort in creating differences between 'us' and 'them'.

Why Do People Drink?

So why do people drink? This book has illustrated many of the reasons for the popularity of alcohol, including its power to augment social occasions and demonstrate inclusiveness, economic power, status and gender role expectations. Alcohol is deeply embedded in cultural habits and can signal the timing and tenor of social rhythms and events. "It's Miller Time!" means the worker becomes the free citizen able to do as he wishes, when he wishes, where he wishes and with whom he wishes. Use of alcohol, in America, is a semiotic text that screams 'Freedom!' to the user and to all who observe him ... and the concept of 'freedom' is a cornerstone of American self-identity. Alcohol also signals sociality, since most cultures classify it as something that should not be taken alone. Because it is evanescent and often expensive, using and sharing is a way to demonstrate status and economic power to the self and others. As a consumption item in a consumerist world, it helps to define the self vis-à-vis branding. And, also as a consumer item, it is a very important economic product that creates millions of jobs worldwide in farming and viticulture, brewing, distilling, sales and marketing, and restaurant service. Alcohol provides the profit margin for most restaurants and is essential to the bottom line in the nightlife and entertainment industries. Alcohol use is also a site of contested morality and every culture has specific rules about appropriate use and behavior. As shown in the Balinese example, drinking with someone reveals much about that person – and her culture.

Alcohol drinking is also deeply pleasurable, when taken in moderation. The feeling of a slight buzz has been celebrated by poets, writers and artists for millennia. From the lyric drama of the Greeks to the gentle poetry of early Chinese philosophers, wine has freed the mind, unbound the soul and given words wings to flow freely. From Li-Po to Baudelaire the gifts of intoxication have been celebrated, and often compared to love. Omar Khayyam famously wrote "Here with a loaf of bread beneath the bough, a flask of wine, a book of verse – and thou – beside me singing in the Wilderness – and Wilderness is Paradise enow" which was, perhaps, an echo of the Song of Solomon: "Let him kiss me with the kisses of his mouth: for thy love is better than wine." And we must not forget Ben Jonson: "Drink to me only with thine eyes, And I will pledge with mine; Or leave a kiss within the cup, And I'll not ask for wine." The intrinsic connection of wine and love references not only the giddy feelings of love so like intoxication, but also the age-old linkage of alcohol and love. "Candy is dandy, but liquor is quicker" has a naughty air, yet describes a reality played out on college campuses daily. It is no wonder that Valentine's Day is celebrated with chocolate and champagne.

We shy away from the pleasures of alcohol when we dwell on its excess. The pleasure becomes furtive, and the furtive always is rushed. Like teenagers hastily swigging from dad's vodka bottle we forget to enjoy the slow languor of a glass with friends, to celebrate a festive occasion or toast a new marriage. We are ashamed, and being ashamed, we guzzle quickly and become drunk. Benjamin Franklin wrote of the glories of wine: "Behold the rain which descends from heaven upon our vineyards, there it enters the roots of the vines, to be changed into wine, a constant proof that God loves us, and loves to see us happy" (Isaacson, 2003: 374), but he also wrote about the dangers of over-indulgence: "Excess in all other Things whatever, as well as in Meat and Drink, is also to be avoided" (ibid.). Whenever a society faces tension, negotiated moral space and ambiguities, many rules and laws arise to manage this tension. Consequently, every society has a plethora of rules regarding drink: who, when, where, how much, why and with whom. The utilization of alcohol becomes culturally freighted because of this tension – intoxication tests human behavior morally and socially – and most cultures consider breaking a rule about alcohol a moral problem. Alcohol functions to test our characters, to test our capacities for appropriate social action and to test our knowledge of social rules. Part of enculturation is learning how to use intoxicants safely and appropriately. To quote an ancient Chinese proverb: "first the man takes a drink, then the drink takes a drink, then the drink takes the man." Somewhere between taking a drink and being taken by drink we must find our boundaries and teach them to our children.

One of the finest attributes of alcohol is that it is reliably dose-dependent. Please think about this for a minute; most intoxicants are far more unpredictable. The THC content of pot is variable, the quantity of actual cocaine present in the white powder purchased from a dealer often suspect, and who knows what is in the crystal meth or how it will affect the user. More frightening is that individual responses to most drugs and hallucinogens are wildly unpredictable and can cause negative consequences at quite low levels (Strassman, 2005). But alcohol has highly predictable, dose-response results (Sher et al., 2005) and, because we can usually sense the relative strength of what we drink, it is not too difficult to regulate effect. This is probably one reason why alcohol tends to usurp the place of other drugs in cultures that are introduced to it through trade or cross-cultural exchange (Sherratt, 1995). Alcohol allows for social intake in a way that other drugs do not. Certainly the heroin user can inhabit a shooting gallery with others, but he is not socializing with them while he takes his drug. Milder drugs such as pot allow for sharing but rarely promote the kind of interactions that alcohol allows; smokers tend to focus on individual responses to music, color or other stimuli, rather than contribute to the back and forth of conversation with others. Of course, at high dosages alcohol also promotes anti-social behaviors, from endless narcissistic babbling to violence, and that is probably why every culture has strong rules about how to drink. Cultural actors are expected to learn how to drink appropriately in order to augment a shared experience. The Greek Symposium is a perfect example of this phenomenon but every culture has its own version of 'learning how to drink'. Alcohol can be a safe social drug because it is dose-dependent when respected.

Unfortunately, modern beliefs about alcohol are quite different than those of earlier cultures, when wine or beer was the primary tipple. Prior to distillation alcohol provided safe liquids, needed calories and a means to store grain or fruit (grapes and apples) past harvest for leaner months. The calories available to those who drank may have ensured their health and reproduction due to better nutriture. In the Western world, there is a super-abundance of calories; we have become fat on industrial agriculture. And part of those calories, increasingly, are alcohol ... taken not as a necessary addition to a scant diet but in addition to a diet already rich and full. The hyper-production of carbohydrates propels our cars and allows ever-cheaper distilled alcohols. We are awash in alcohol, and just as we are encouraged to overeat during meals as well as between (Snack Attack!) so we are encouraged to have that frozen margarita when we dine at a restaurant. Hell, they're two for one, let's get four! Like jello, there is always room for more liquid. And more is always available, because even with the stringent liquor laws in place in most states, alcohol is everywhere and easily accessible to everyone.

The increasing production of grain and other carbohydrate sources promotes glut and price collapse unless the calories can be used to make something that can be stored, such as automotive ethanol or alcohol. This allows for ever-cheaper production of spirits and their trade throughout the global economy. Spirits were first used as medicine, then, in the form of French brandy (made from grapes), a tipple for the wealthy. With the rise of mechanization, industrial agriculture and a global trade system in the early modern period, distilleries became a favored way to use up excess grain and stabilize prices. Since the eighteenth century our agriculture has become ever more efficient at producing calories, and thus, ever more efficient at producing the raw ingredients for spirits. Even a typically expensive product like wine grapes can be converted into vodka when a glut occurs, as witnessed by the rise of the high-end French vodka Ciroc. Given that our industrial agriculture system is supremely capable of producing millions more calories than can be used in the West, we can only speculate on the future growth of distillation. It's safe to assume that our automobiles and bodies will absorb ever-growing quantities of alcohol products if production levels continue on the same trajectory.

Unfortunately, how we use alcohol can cause problems beyond mere obesity. As we have explored in this volume, it is often used in the United States as a time-out mechanism, a 'get out of jail free' card for bad or dangerous behavior. This construction only ramps up the furtiveness of drinking, and encourages over-use and abuse. Too many of our drinking narratives focus on extreme intoxication and its (usually humorous) consequences; it is shocking to realize that the film *The Hangover* seems destined to be a multi-series franchise since Part 2 made good box office. Part 3 is no doubt right around the orner, to celebrate bad behavior and blackouts on yet another continent. John Belushi is immortalized in *Animal House*, shown drinking a full fifth of Jack Daniels – yet rather than being a deterrent to the brand, that scene has inspired countless students to buy and chug along with John. Jack Daniels, a fine and historic American sipping whiskey, has been turned into a drug for frat brothers.

It is no accident that the discussion of excess should mention brands of alcohol. Alcohol is the perfect capitalist tool, a perfect engine of profitability. Whether industrial Britain, where the miseries of working-class life impelled drunkenness, or in the current day, when the lure of Miller Time compels the cubicle jockey to hit the bar every night, the supremacy of alcohol as release and reward is unchallenged. Alcohol can become a coping mechanism for the unfulfilled life; as John Berger argued, the lure of the dreamt future will always encourage a purchase that promises to transform the buyer into someone special, glamorous and enviable. And alcohol, because it provides solace from meaningless days, is the perfect antidote to the stresses of modern life and the ideal medium for forgetting the prosaic in favor of fantasy. As a creature of capitalism it is purchased, used up and gone; unlike a capital investment in education or property its use-value is delimited in time. Once drunk, the wine is gone, the vodka bottle drained, the whiskey jug empty. Buy more, or admit defeat, catch a cab and go home. The night is done.

Students learn to drink in this environment and as incipient adults they are products of this culture. Alcohol is restricted until the age of 21 and thus becomes a symbol of full adulthood. Unfortunately, while it might not be legal to drink during the teen years, alcohol is everywhere and readily available to youth. With little legal opportunity to learn how to drink moderately, student and youth culture creates new rituals and habits that encourage fast intakes such as pre-gaming and drinking games that force high-end drinking. With an 'all or nothing', time-out and 'work hard, play hard' cultural model it is no wonder that students drink excessively. But alcohol also allows students to accomplish other social and developmental tasks, including overcoming fear of social interactions, easing courtship rituals and demonstrating problem-solving skills. Unfortunately, these accomplishments can also create negative consequences, from unwanted sexual encounters and attacks to accidents and death.

Many people within the college environment now acknowledge that hardcore abstinence messages aren't working. In 2008 a group of college presidents created the Amethyst Initiative, a program designed to encourage responsible drinking by advocating a lower drinking age. The signers argued that it was time for social groups and government entities to reconsider the legal drinking age of 21 because it wasn't working and was contributing to youth binge drinking. The Amethyst Initiative was spearheaded by John McCardell, founder of Choose Responsibility, and was signed by 135 college presidents. Choose Responsibility (http://www.chooseresponsibility.org) advocates for a national discussion to lower the drinking age matched by

> a series of changes to treat 18, 19, and 20 year-olds as the young adults the law otherwise says they are … We support a series of changes that will allow 18–20 year-old adults to purchase, possess and consume alcoholic beverages. We propose a multi-faceted approach that combines education, certification, and provisional licensing for 18–20 year-old high school graduates who choose to consume alcohol. We envision an overarching program that combines appropriate incentive and reward for responsible, lawful behavior by adolescents, and punitive measures for illegal, irresponsible behavior
>
> http://www.chooseresponsibility.org/proposal/

In effect, Choose Responsibility advocates that adults recognize their responsibility to teach good drinking habits just as youth must recognize their responsibility to abide by such rules. This proposal encourages parents to accept that their children are probably already drinking, and to assume responsibility to make sure that they know the boundaries between enough and too much.

An astonishingly small percentage of my students tell me their parents have discussed the boundaries of drinking. Almost all of them tell me that their parents prefer to pretend that they don't drink at all. And indeed, most parents of teens tell me unequivocally "my kid doesn't drink – he's a good kid." We are sending a message that youth should drink on the down-low when we pretend it isn't happening. But this all-or-nothing attitude doesn't prepare young people to recognize when they have had enough or when their drinking is unsafe. Negotiating these boundaries is difficult to learn, and must be taught in advance of imbibing since alcohol clouds decision-making. By ignoring the reality of underage drinking we prevent youth from learning limits and boundaries and developing a sense of agency about use.

One year I decided to test students' ability to recognize and react to inappropriate use of alcohol. The course was team-taught with the alcohol counselor who handled infractions at the university, and we decided to share a bottle of wine during class to see what the students would say about our drinking. The night before class I emptied a bottle of red wine, re-filled the bottle with cran-grape juice and carefully recorked and resealed the bottle. The next day at 10:30am I nonchalantly placed two wine glasses on the podium. While continuing to lecture, I removed a corkscrew from my briefcase and removed the foil and cork from the doctored bottle. The cork made a very enthusiastic 'thunk' and sounded satisfyingly authentic. I poured a glass for my partner and one for myself and continued with my lecture. We finished our glasses, and started on our second glasses, which we also finished. The rest of the bottle was shared, a tad under a glass for each. We clinked, swirled and tossed 'em back. I finally looked up, and mid-sentence in lecture, said, "damn, the bottle's empty." During this time not one student asked us what we were doing, or questioned our actions. We were breaking almost every rule of appropriate American drinking: it was morning, we were working, we weren't sharing with everyone present, and we weren't drinking with a meal. But the students said nothing.

The next lecture we told them what we had done. They looked bemused, but no-one acknowledged that they had thought, at the time, that we might be fooling. Nor did they wonder if we were providing a lesson about drinking. We asked them to list rules for drinking appropriately and while they could tell us in great detail what was wrong for their age group and university peers, they were unable to explain the cultural (or adult) rules that might have labeled our behavior improper. They professed little knowledge of 'how to drink' in the adult world, and admitted that no adult had attempted to teach them basic boundaries of drinking. I realized that they were entirely unprepared to deal with alcohol outside of the relatively safe university setting; they had no skills to negotiate a cocktail party, a working dinner with wine or the office Christmas party. They didn't even know how to say 'no' to a drink. I was reminded of this last year when a student told me the sad tale of a friend who, during a Wall Street recruiting interview, took advantage of the free bar to become quite drunk. He vomited during the dinner (and at the table) and, needless to say, did not get the job. The student finished the tale with "and he was a straight-A business student!"

So let us finish with a thought exercise. Imagine that you were a student in my class, watching me drink wine at 10:30 in the morning. What would you have done? And now, after reading this book, what do you think you should do in similar situations? What will you do when next you see a friend use alcohol inappropriately?

BIBLIOGRAPHY

Abad, Luis Cantarero (2001). "Gender and Drink in Aragon, Spain." In: De Garine, Igor, and De Garine, Valerie (Eds.). *Drinking: Anthropological Approached.* New York and Oxford: Berghahn: 144–157.

Abbey, Antonia (1998). "Alcohol-Related Sexual Assault: A Common Problem among College Students." *Journal of Studies of Alcohol* 14: 118–128.

Abbey, Antonia, Pam McAuslan, Tina Zawacki, A. Monique Clinton, and Philip O. Buck (2001). "Attitudinal, Experiential, and Situational Predictors of Sexual Assault Perpetration." *Journal of Interpersonal Violence* 16(8): 784–807.

Aertgeerts, Bert, and Frank Buntinx (2002). "The Relation between Alcohol Abuse or Dependence and Academic Performance in First-Year College Students." *Journal of Adolescent Health* 31: 223–225.

Aldridge, Judith, Fiona Measham, and Liz Williams (2011). *Illegal Leisure Revisited.* London and New York: Routledge.

Ames, Genevieve (1985). "American Beliefs about Alcoholism." In: Genevieve Ames and Linda Bennett (Eds.). *The American Experience with Alcohol.* New York and London: Plenum Press: 23–39.

Ames, Genevieve M. "Middle-Class Protestants: Alcohol and the Family." In: Genevieve Ames and Linda Bennett (Eds.). *The American Experience with Alcohol.* New York and London: Plenum Press, 1985: 435–458.

Amouretti, Marie-Clare (1999). "Urban and Rural Diets in Greece." In: Jean-Louis Flandrinand Massimo Montanari (Eds.). *Food: A Culinary History.* New York: Penguin, 1999: 79–95.

Aneirin (1969). *The Gododdin* (Kenneth Hurlstone Jackson, Trans.). Edinburgh: Edinburgh University Press.

Arnett, Jeffrey (2004). *Emerging Adulthood: The Winding Road from the Late Teens through the Twenties.* Oxford and New York: Oxford University Press.

Arnold, Bettina (1999). "Drinking the Feast: Alcohol and the Legitimization of Power in Celtic Europe." *Cambridge Archaeological Journal* 9(1): 73–93.

——— (2001). "Power Drinking in Iron Age Europe." *British Archaeology* 57(Feb). Available from http://www.britarch.ac.uk/ba/ba57/feat2.html.

Arthur, T. S. (1877). *Strong Drink: The Curse and the Cure.* Philadelphia: Hubbard Brothers.

Atkin, Charles, and Martin Block (1981). *Content and Effects of Alcohol Advertising.* Virginia: Bureau of Alcohol, Tobacco and Firearms.

Atwell, Katie, Charles Abraham, and Theodora Duka (2011). "A Parsimonious, Integrative Model of Key Psychological Correlates of UK University Students' Alcohol Consumption." *Alcohol and Alcoholism* 46(3): 253–260.

Austen, Jane (1800). "November 20, 1800". Electronic Text Center, University of Virginia Library. Available from http://etext.lib.virginia.edu/etcbin/toccer-new2?id=AusLett.sgm&images=images/modeng&data=/texts/english/modeng/parsed&tag=public&part=all.

Bacon, S. D. (1945) "Alcohol and Complex Society." *Alcohol, Science and Society:* 179–200. Yale Summer School of Alcohol Studies. New Haven: Quarterly Journal of Studies on Alcohol.

Bakhtin, Mikhail (1984). *Rabelais and His World*. Bloomington: Indiana University Press.

Banks, Fay (1997). *Wine Drinking in Oxford, 1640–1850: A Story Revealed by Tavern, Inn, College and Other Bottles; with a Catalogue of Bottles and Seals from the Collection in the Ashmolean Museum*. Oxford: Oxford University Press.

Barnes, Donna M., and Peter G. Rose (2002). *Matters of Taste: Food and Drink in Seventeenth-Century Dutch Art and Life*. Syracuse: Syracuse University Press.

Baron, Stanley Wade (1962). *Brewed in America*. New York: Little Brown & Company.

Barr, Andrew (1999). *Drink: A Social History of America*. New York: Carroll and Graf Publishers, Inc.

Baudrillard, Jean (1985). "The Ecstasy of Communication." In: Hal Foster (Ed.). *Postmodern Culture*. London: Pluto Press: 126–133.

Baumeister, Roy F., and John Tierney (2011). *Willpower: Rediscovering the Greatest Human Strength*. New York: The Penguin Press.

Beccaria, Franca, and Odillo Guidoni (2002). "Young People in a Wet Culture: Functions and Patterns of Drinking." *Contemporary Drug Problems* 29 (Summer): 305–334.

Berger, Arthur Asa (2007). *Ads, Fads and Consumer Culture*. 3rd ed. New York: Rowman and Littlefield Publishers.

Berger, John (1972). *Ways of Seeing*. London: British Broadcasting Company and Penguin Books.

Blair, Lawrence (1940). *English Church Ales: With a Note on Church Fairs*. Ann Arbor: Edwards Brothers, Inc. GT2890 B55.

Booth, Alan (1991). "The Age for Reclining and Its Attendant Perils." In: William J. Slator (Ed.). *Dining in a Classical Context*. Ann Arbor: The University of Michigan Press, 1991: 105–120.

Boswell, A. A., and J. Z. Spade (1996). "Fraternities and Collegiate Rape Culture: Why Are Some Fraternities More Dangerous Places for Women?" *Gender & Society* 10: 133–147.

Bowie, E. L. (1995). "Wine in Old Comedy." In: Oswyn Murray and Manuela Tecusan (Eds.). *In Vino Veritas*. London: The British School at Rome: 113–125.

Bradford, William (1856). *History of Plymouth Plantation*. Vol. 2. 2 vols. Boston: Massachusetts Historical Society.

Brears, Peter (1993a). "Brewing at Hicketon." In: *Liquid Nourishment: Potable Foods and Stimulating Drinks*. Edinburgh: Edinburgh University Press: 60–69.

——— (1993b). "Wassail! Celebrations in Hot Ale." In: *Liquid Nourishment: Potable Foods and Stimulating Drinks*. Edinburgh: Edinburgh University Press: 106–141.

Breed, W., and J.R. Defoe (1981). "Themes in Alcohol Advertisements; a Critique." *Journal of Drug Issues* 9: 5–10.

Brothwell, Don, and Patricia Brothwell (1969). *Food in Antiquity*. Baltimore and London: Johns Hopkins University Press.

Budd, Jim (2003). "The Greek Wine Renaissance." *Wine Business Monthly*. Available from http://www.winebusiness.com/wbm/?go=getArticle&dataId=27899.

van Bueren, Thad (2002). "Struggling with Class Relations at a Los Angeles Aqueduct Construction Camp." *Historical Archaeology* 36(3): 28–43.

Burke, R. S., and R. S. Stevens (1999). "Social Anxiety and Drinking in College Students: a Social Cognitive Theory Analysis." *Clinical Psychology Review* 19: 513–530.

Burnett, John (1999). *Liquid Pleasures*. London and New York: Routledge.

Butler, Edward R (1993). "Alcohol Use by College Students: A Rites of Passage Ritual." *NASPA Journal* 31(1): 48–55.

Cantrell III, Philip (2000). "Beer and Ale." *The Cambridge World History of Food*. Cambridge: Cambridge University Press.

Capraro, Rocco L. (2000). "Why College Men Drink: Alcohol, Adventure, and the Paradox of Masculinity." *College Health* 48: 307–315.

Carleton, Will (1871). *Farm Ballads*. New York: Harper and Brothers.

Carmichael, Zachary (2009). "Fit Men: New England Tavern Keepers 1620–1720". Master's dissertation, Miami University. Available from http://utexas.academia.edu/ZachCarmichael/Papers/335034/Fit_Men_New_England_Tavern_Keepers_1620-1720.

Carson, Gerald (1983). "Watermelon Armies and Whiskey Boys." In: Roger Lane and John J. Turner Jr. (Eds.). *Riot, Rout and Tumult: Readings in Social and Political Violence.* 70–79.

Cashman, Sean Dennis (1981). *Prohibition, the Lie of the Land.* New York: Macmillan Publishing Company.

Cashmore, Ellis (2006). *Celebrity/Culture.* New York: Routledge.

de Certeau, Michel (1984). *The Practice of Everyday Life Volume One* (Stephen Rendall, Trans.). Berkeley: University of California Press.

——— (1998). *The Practice of Everyday Life Volume Two* (Timothy Tomasik, Trans.). Minneapolis and London: University of Minnesota Press.

Chalfont, Harry Malcolm (1920). *Father Penn and John Barleycorn.* Harrisburg Pennsylvania: The Evangelical Press.

Charters, Steve (2006). *Wine and Society: The Social and Cultural Context of a Drink.* Amsterdam: Elsevier.

Chartres, John (2002). "The Eighteenth-Century English Inn: A Transient 'Golden Age'?" In: Beat Kumin and Ann Tlusty (Eds.). *The World of the Tavern: Public Houses in Early Modern Europe.* Burlington Vt.: Ashgate: 205–226.

Chatterton, Paul, and Robert Hollands (2003). *Urban Nightscapes: Youth Cultures, Pleasure Spaces and Corporate Power.* London and New York: Routledge.

Chrzan, Janet (2010). "Binge Drinking." *Alcohol in Popular Culture.* Santa Barbara, Denver and Oxford: Greenwood Press.

CIA World Factbook (2010). *Greece.* Online. CIA. Available from https://www.cia.gov/library/publications/the-world-factbook/geos/gr.html.

Clark, Norman (1976). *Deliver Us From Evil: An Interpretation of American Prohibition.* New York and London: W. W. Norton and Company. Available from http://www.questia.com/PM.qst?a=o&d=102117203.

Clark, Peter (1983). *The English Alehouse: A Social History 1200–1830.* London: Longman.

Cole, Harry Ellsworth (1997). *Stagecoach and Tavern Tales of the Old Northwest.* Louise Phelps Kellogg (Ed.). Carbondale and Edwardsville: Southern Illinois University Press.

Connell, Raewyn Connell (1995). *Masculinities.* Berkeley: University of California Press.

Conroy, David W (1995). *In Public Houses: Drink and the Revolution of Authority in Colonial Massachusetts.* Chapel Hill: University of North Carolina Press.

Cool, H.E.M. (2006). *Eating and Drinking in Roman Britain.* Cambridge: Cambridge University Press.

Core Institute (2010). *Core Alcohol and Drug Survey 2006–2008 National Data.* Carbondale: Core Institute: Southern Illinois University.

Coughtry, Jay (1981). *The Notorious Triangle: Rhode Island and the African Slave Trade 1700–1807.* Philadelphia: Temple University Press.

Cracco, Elizabeth J. (2008). "Sexual Aggression in Bars: What College Men Can Normalize." *The Journal of Men's Studies* 16(1): 82–96.

Crane, Rev. J. T. (1871). *Arts of Intoxication: The Aim, and the Results.* New York: Carlton and Lanahan.

Craven, Pamela Elizabeth (2007). *The Final Feast: An Examination of the Significant Iron Age Amphora Burials in North-west Europe in Relation to the Mediterranean Symposium and Feasting Ritual.* BAR International Series 1605. Oxford: Hadrian Books Ltd.

Crawford, Lizabeth, and Katherine Novak (2006). "Alcohol Abuse as Rite of Passage: The Effect of Beliefs About Alcohol and the College Experience on Undergraduates' Drinking Behaviors." *Journal of Drug Education* 36(3): 193–212.

Crowley, John W. (Ed.) (1999). *Drunkard's Progress: Narratives of Addiction, Despair and Recovery.* Baltimore and London: Johns Hopkins University Press.

Csikszentmihalyi, Mihaly (1968). "A Cross-Cultural Comparison of Some Structural Characteristics of Group Drinking." *Human Development* 11: 201–216.

Cunliffe, Barry (1988). *Greeks, Romans and Barbarians: Spheres of Interaction.* New York: Methuen.

Curtis, Wayne (2007). *And a Bottle of Rum: A History of the New World in Ten Cocktails.* New York: Three Rivers Press.

Dalby, Andrew (2003). *Bacchus: a Biography*. Los Angeles: The J. Paul Getty Museum.

Dalby, Andrew, and Sally Grainger (1996). *The Classical Cookbook*. Los Angeles: The J. Paul Getty Museum.

Davidson, D. Kirk (2003). *Selling Sin: The Marketing of Socially Unacceptable Products*. 2nd ed. WestPort, Connecticut: Praeger.

Davidson, James (1997). *Courtesans and Fishcakes*. New York: St. Martin's Press.

Dawson, Mark (2009). *Plenti and Grasse: Food and Drink in a Sixteenth-Century Household*. Blackawton, Devon: Prospect Books.

Day, Ivan (2002). "Bridecup and Cake: The Ceremonial Food and Drink of the Bridal Procession." In: Laura Mason (Ed.). *Food and the Rites of Passage*. Leeds Symposium on Food History: Food and Society. Blackawton: Prospect Books: 33–61.

Dement, Jakob, and Margaretha Jarvinen (2006). "Constructing Maturity through Alcohol Experience – Focus Group Interviews with Teenagers." *Addiction Research and Theory* 14(6): 589–602.

—— (2011). "Social Capital as Norms and Resources: Focus Groups Discussing Alcohol." *Addiction Research and Theory* 19(2): 91–101.

DeSantis, Alan D. (2007). *Inside Greek U.: Fraternities, Sororities, and the Pursuit of Pleasure, Power and Prestige*. Lexington, KY: The University Press of Kentucky, 2007.

DeSimone, Jeff (2009). "Fraternity Membership and Drinking Behavior." *Economic Inquiry* 47(2): 337–350.

Dietler, Michael (1990). "Driven by Drink: The Role of Drinking in the Political Economy and the Case of Early Iron Age France." *Journal of Anthropological Archaeology* 9(4): 352–406.

—— (1995). "Early 'Celtic' Socio-political Relations: Ideological Representation and Social Competition in Dynamic Comparative Perspective." In: Bettina Arnold and D. Blair Gibson (Eds.). *Celtic Chiefdom, Celtic State*. Cambridge: Cambridge University Press: 64–72.

—— (1996). "Feasts and Commensal Politics in the Political Economy: Food, Power and Status in Prehistoric Europe." In: Polly Wiessner and Wulf Schiefenhovel (Eds.). *Food and the Status Quest: An Interdisciplinary Perspective*. Providence: Berghahn, 1996.

—— (2006). "Alcohol: Anthropological/Archaeological Perspectives." *Annual Review of Anthropology* 35: 229–249.

Dillon, Patrick (2003). *Gin: The Much-Lamented Death of Madam Geneva*. Boston: Justin, Charles and Co.

Dodgshon, Robert A. (1995). "Modelling Chiefdoms in the Scottish Highlands and Islands Prior to the '45." In: Bettina Arnold and D. Blair Gibson (Eds.). *Celtic Chiefdom, Celtic State*. Cambridge: Cambridge University Press: 99–109.

Dollard, John (1945). "Drinking Mores of the Social Classes." In: *Alcohol, Science and Society*. New Haven: Quarterly Journal of Studies on Alcohol: 95–104.

Douglas, Mary (1987a). "A Distinctive Anthropological Perspective." In: Mary Douglas (Ed.). *Constructive Drinking: Perspectives on Drink from Anthropology*. Cambridge: Cambridge University Press: 3–15.

Douglas, Mary (Ed.) (1987b). *Constructive Drinking: Perspectives on Drink from Anthropology*. Cambridge: Cambridge University Press.

Dowdall, George W. (2009). *College Drinking: Reframing a Social Problem*. WestPort, CT: Praeger.

Dragadze, Tamara (1994). "Gender, Ethnicity and Alcohol in the Formers Soviet Union." In: Maryon McDonald (Ed.). *Gender, Drink and Drug*. Oxford and New York: Berg: 145–152.

Drummond, J. C., and Anne Wilbraham (1959). *The Englishman's Food: A History of Five Centuries of English Diet*. London: Readers Union – Jonathan Cape.

Duff, Cameron (2003). "Alcohol Marketing and the Media: What Are Alcohol Advertisements Telling Us?" *Media International Australia, Incorporating Culture & Policy* 108(Aug): 13–21.

Duis, Perry R. (1983). *The Saloon: Public Drinking in Chicago and Boston 1880–1920*. Urbana and Chicago: University of Illinois Press.

Durkheim, Emile (1997). *Suicide: A Study in Sociology*. New York: Free Press.

Dyer, Christopher (1989). *Standards of Living in the Later Middle Ages: Social Change in England c. 1200-1520.* Cambridge: Cambridge University Press.

Dyer, Gillian (1988). *Advertising as Communication.* London and New York: Routledge.

Earnshaw, Steven (2000). *The Pub in Literature: England's Altered State.* Manchester University Press: Manchester and New York.

Economist, The (2011). "Alcohol in Africa: Keep on Walking." *The Economist,* October 1.

Eldridge, Adam, and Marion Roberts (2008). "Hen Parties: Bonding or Brawling?" *Drugs: Education, Prevention and Policy* 15(3): 323–328.

Elliott, Stuart (2011). "In New Campaign, a Vodka Promotes 'Balance'." *New York Times.* October 3, Business Section: B4.

Engs, Ruth (1977). "Drinking Patterns and Drinking Problems of College Students." *Journal of Studies on Alcohol* 38(11): 2144–2156.

——— (1995). "Do Traditional Western European Drinking Practices Have Origins In Antiquity?" *Addiction Research* 2(3): 227–239.

——— (2001). "Past Influences, Current Issues, Future Research Directions." In: Eleni Houghton and Anne M. Roche (Eds.). *Learning About Drinking.* Philadelphia: Brunner-Routledge: 147–166.

——— (2002). "Drinking Practices and Patterns Among Collegians." *SPSS Newsletter* 33(3).

Enright, Michael J. (1996). *Lady with a Mead Cup: Ritual, Prophecy and Lordship in the European Warband from La Tene to the Viking Age.* Portland, Oregon: Four Courts Press.

Epstein, Barbara Leslie (1981). *The Politics of Domesticity: Women, Evangelism, and Temperance in Nineteenth-Century America.* Middletown, CT: Wesleyan University Press.

Eriksen, Sidsel (1990). "Drunken Danes and Sober Swedes? Religious Revivalism and the Temperance Movements as Keys to Danish and Swedish Folk Cultures." In: Bo Strath, (Ed.). *Language and the Construction of Class Identities. The Struggle for Discursive Power in Social Organisation: Scandinavia and Germany after 1800.* Gothenburg: Gothenburg University: 55–94.

Euripides (1906). *The Bacchae* (Gilbert Murray, Trans.). Second ed. London: George Allen.

Ewen, Stuart (1990). "Marketing Dreams: The Political Elements of Style." In: Alan Tomlinson (Ed.). *Consumption, Identity and Style: Marketing, Meanings and the Packaging of Pleasure.* London: Routledge: 41–56.

Field, Edward (1897). *The Colonial Tavern: a Glimpse of New England Town Life in the Seventeenth and Eighteenth Centuries.* Providence: Preston and Rounds.

Field, Peter B (1962). "A New Cross-Cultural Study of Drunkenness." In: David J. Pittman and Charles R. Snyder (Eds.). *Society, Culture and Drinking Patterns.* New York and London: John Wiley and Sons: 48–74.

Fielder, Robyn, and Michael Carey (2010). "Predictors and Consequences of Sexual 'Hookups' Among College Students: A Short-term Prospective Study." *Archives of Sexual Behavior* 39: 1105–1119.

Fleming, Stuart (2001). *Vinum: The Story of Roman Wine.* Glen Mills, PA: Art Flair.

Fossey, Emma (1994). *Growing Up with Alcohol.* London: Routledge.

Foster, Robert J (2005). "Commodity Futures: Labor, Love and Value." *Anthropology Today* 21(4): 8–12.

Fowles, Jib (1976). "Advertising's Fifteen Basic Appeals." In: Michael Petracca and Madeleine Sorapure (Eds.). *Common Culture: Reading and Writing About American Popular Culture.* Upper Saddle River: Prentice Hall.

Fuller, Robert C. (1996). *Religion and Wine: A Cultural History of Wine Drinking in the United States.* Knoxville: The University of Tennessee Press.

Furnham, Adrian (2004). "Binge Drinking: Causes, Consequences and Cures." In: Malcolm MacLachlan and Caroline Smyth (Eds.). *Binge Drinking and Youth Culture: Alternative Perspectives.* Dublin: The Liffey Press: 21–70.

Gamburd, Michele Ruth (2008). *Breaking the Ashes: The Culture of Illicit Liquor in Sri Lanka.* Ithaca, NY: Cornell Press.

Gately, Iain (2008). *Drink: A Cultural History of Alcohol.* New York: Gotham Books.

van Gennep, Arnold (1960). *The Rites of Passage* (Monika B. Vizedom and Gabrielle L. Caffee, Trans.). Chicago: University of Chicago Press.

Giles, Geoffrey (1991). "Student Drinking in the Third Reich: Academic Tradition and the Nazi Revolution." In: Susanna Barrows and Robin Room (Eds.). *Drinking: Behavior and Belief in Modern History.* Berkeley: University of California Press: 132–146.

Girouard, Mark (1984). *Victorian Pubs.* New Haven and London: Yale University Press.

Glassman, Tavis, Virginia Dodd, Jiunn-Jye Sheu, Barbara Rienzo, and Lex Wagenaar (2010). "Extreme Ritualistic Alcohol Consumption Among College Students on Game Day." *Journal of American College Health* 58(5): 413–423.

Goffman, Irving (1959). *The Presentation of Self in Everyday Life.* New York: Doubleday Anchor Books.

——— (1976). *Gender Advertisements.* New York: Harper Colophon Books.

Goldman, Robert, and Stephen Papson (2011). *Landscapes of Capital.* Cambridge: Polity Press.

Graves, Robert (1960). *Greek Gods and Heroes.* New York: Dell.

Grazian, David (2008). *On the Make: The Hustle of Urban Nightlife.* Chicago: University of Chicago Press.

Grey Goose (2007). "Grey Goose Vodka 2007 Advertising Campaign". Available from http://designtaxi.com/news/11358/Grey-Goose-Vodka-2007-Advertising-Campaign/.

Gunter, Barrie, Anders Hansen, and Maria Touri (2010). *Alcohol Advertising and Young People's Drinking: Representation, Reception and Regulation.* London: Palgrave McMillan.

Gusfield, Joseph (1986). *Symbolic Crusade.* Second. Urbana and Chicago: University of Urbana Press, 1986.

——— (1987). "Passage to Play: Rituals of Drinking Time in American Society." In: Mary Douglas (Ed.). *Constructive Drinking: Perspectives on Drink from Anthropology.* Cambridge: Cambridge University Press: 73–90.

——— (1991). "Benevolent Repression." In: Susanna Barrows and Robin Room (Eds.). *Drinking: Behavior and Belief in Modern Society.* Berkeley: University of California Press: 399–424.

Hadfield, Phil (2006). *Bar Wars: Contesting the Night in Contemporary British Cities.* Oxford: Oxford University Press.

Hagen, Ann (2006). *Anglo-Saxon Food and Drink.* Frithgarth, England: Anglo-Saxon Books.

Hale, Sarah Josepha (1996). *The Good Housekeeper.* 2nd ed. Mineola, NY: Dover.

Ham, Lindsay, Byron L. Zamboanga, Janine Olthuis, Hilary Casner, and Ngoc Bui (2010). "No Fear, Just Relax and Play: Social Anxiety, Alcohol Expectancies, and Drinking Games Among College Students." *Journal of American College Health* 58(5): 473–479.

Hamilton, Carl (1994). *Absolut.* New York and London: Texere.

Harnett, Robert, Betsy Thom, Rachel Herring, and Kelly Moira (2000). "Alcohol in Transition: Towards a Model of Young Men's Drinking Styles." *Journal of Youth Studies* 3(1): 61–77.

Harrison, Brian (1973). "Pubs." In: H.J. Dyos and Michael Wolff (Eds.). *The Victorian City: Images and Realities*, 1. London: Routledge and Kegan Paul: 161–190.

Hayes, William Allen (1866). *Selected Songs Sung at Harvard College 1862 to 1866.* Cambridge, MA: John Wilson and Sons. Available from http://books.google.com/books?id=_D8BA AAAYAAJ&pg=PR5&lpg=PR5&dq=harvard+college+drinking+songs&source=bl&ots=6 FiHGNl2mZ&sig=KHhoiRta5UBdqF4hJJlt0Jd0yrY&hl=en&sa=X&ei=Prp4T5PbDqTx0g Hk6dmZDQ&ved=0CEsQ6AEwBQ#v=onepage&q=harvard%20college%20drink-ing%20songs&f=false.

Hayward, Keith, and Dick Hobbs (2007). "Beyond the Binge in 'Booze Britain': Market-led Liminalization and the Spectacle of Binge Drinking." *The British Journal of Sociology* 58(3): 437–456.

Heaney, Seamus (2008). *Beowulf* (Seamus Heaney, Trans.). New York: W.W. Norton and Company.

Heath, Dwight B (1987). "Alcohol Use 1970–1980." In: Mary Douglas (Ed.). *Constructive Drinking: Perspectives on Drink from Anthropology.* Cambridge: Cambridge University Press: 16–69.

———— (2000). *Drinking Occasions: Comparative Perspectives on Alcohol and Culture.* International Center for Alcohol Policies Series on Alcohol on Society. Philadelphia: Taylor and Francis.

Heath, Dwight B. (Ed.) (1986). *Mourt's Relation: A Journal of the Pilgrims at Plymouth.* Bedford, MA: Applewood Books.

Heather, Nick, Susan Partington et al. (2011). "Alcohol Use Disorders and Hazardous Drinking Among Undergraduates at English Universities." *Alcohol and Alcoholism* 46(3): 270–277.

Hensley, Paul B. (1992). "Time, Work, and Social Context in New England." *The New England Quarterly* 65(4): 531–559.

Hingson, R. W., T. Heeren, M. Winter, and H. Wechsler (2005). "Magnitude of Alcohol-Related Mortality and Morbidity Among US College Students Aged 18–24: Changes from 1998–2001." *Annual Review of Public Health* 26: 259–279.

Hingson, R. W., T. Heeren, R. C. Zakocs, A. Kopstein, and H. Wechsler (2002). "Magnitude of Alcohol-Related Mortality and Morbidity Among US College Students Aged 18–24." *Journal of Studies on Alcohol* 63(2): 136–144.

Hofstadter, Richard (1955). *The Age of Reform: From Bryan to F.D.R.* New York: Knopf. Available from http://proxy.library.upenn.edu:2731/2027/heb.00652.0001.001.

Holt, Mack (2006). "Europe Divided: Wine, Beer and the Reformation in Sixteenth-Century Europe." In: Mack Holt (Ed.). *Alcohol: A Social and Cultural History.* Oxford: Berg: 25–40.

Holt, Thomas (2005). "How Societies Desire Brands." In: S. Ratneshwar and David Glen Mick. *Inside Consumption: Consumer Motives, Goals and Desires.* London and New York: Routledge: 273–291.

Horton, Donald (1943). "The Functions of Alcohol in Primitive Societies: A Cross-Cultural Study." *Quarterly Journal of Studies of Alcohol* 4: 199–320.

Huang, Jiun-Hau, William Dejong, Laura Gomberg Towvin, and Shari Kessel Schneider (2008). "Sociodemographic and Psychobehavioral Characteristics of US College Students Who Abstain From Alcohol." *Journal of American College Health* 57(4): 395–410.

Hunt, Geoffrey, Molly Moloney, and Kristin Evans (2010). *Youth, Drugs and Nightlife.* London and New York: Routledge.

Hunter, Judith (2002). "English Inns, Taverns, Alehouses and Brandy Shops: The Legislative Framework, 1495-1797." In: Beat Kumin and Ann Tlusty (Eds.). *The World of the Tavern: Public Houses in Early Modern Europe.* Burlington, VT: Ashgate: 65–82.

Isaacson, Walter (2003). *Benjamin Franklin: An American Life.* New York: Simon and Schuster.

Jersild, Devon (2001). *Happy Hours: Alcohol in a Woman's Life.* New York: HarperCollins Publishers.

Joffe, Alexander (1998). "Alcohol and Social Complexity in Ancient Western Asia." *Current Anthropology* 39(3): 297–322.

Joffrey, R (1979). *Le Tresor De Vix: Histoire Et Portee D'une Grand Decouverte.* Paris: Tallandier, 1979.

Johnson, Hugh (1989). *Vintage: The Story of Wine.* New York: Simon and Schuster.

Johnson, Paul (2004). *A Shopkeeper's Millennium: Society and Revivals in Rochester, New York, 1815–1837.* 25th Anniversary ed. New York: Hill and Wang.

Katz, Solomon, and Fritz Maytag (1991). "Brewing an Ancient Beer." *Archaeology* 44(4): 24–33.

Katz, Solomon, and Mary Voight (1986). "Bread and Beer." *Expedition* 28(2): 23–34.

Keeling, Richard (2000). "The Political. Social, and Public Health Problems of Binge Drinking in College." *Journal of American College Health* 48: 195–198.

Kelly-Blazeby, Kelly (2006). "Kapeleion: Casual and Commercial Wine Consumption in Classical Greece". (Doctoral dissertation, University of Leicester, 2006).

Kidd, I. G. (1999). *Posidonius: Volume III. The Translation of the Fragments.* Cambridge: Cambridge University Press.

Kitsantas, Panagiota, Anastasia Kitsantas, and Tanya Anagnostopoulou (2008). "A Cross-Cultural Investigation of College Student Alcohol Consumption: A Classification Tree Analysis." *The Journal of Psychology* 142(1): 5–20.

Knapp, Caroline (1997). *Drinking: A Love Story.* New York: Dell Publishing.

Koch, John T. (1997). *The Gododdin of Aneirin: Text and Context from Dark-Age Britain*. Cardiff: University of Wales Press.

Konstantakos, Ioannis (2005). "The Drinking Theater: Staged Symposia in Greek Comedy." *Mnemosyne* LVIII(2): 183–217.

Kovacs, Maureen (Trans.) (1985). *The Epic of Gilgamesh*. Stanford: Stanford University Press.

Kremer, Michael, and Dan Levy (2008). "Peer Effects and Alcohol Use Among College Students." *Journal of Economic Perspectives* 22(3): 189–206.

Kumin, Beat (2007). *Drinking Matters: Public Houses and Social Exchange in Early Modern Central Europe*. New York: Palgrave Macmillan.

Kuo, Meichun, Henry Wechsler, Patty Greenberg, and Hang Lee (2003). "The Marketing of Alcohol to College Students: The Role of Low Prices and Special Promotions." *American Journal of Preventive Medicine* 25(3): 204–211.

Landrine, Hope, Steve Bardwell, and Tina Dean (1988). "Gender Expectations for Alcohol Use: A Study of the Significance of the Masculine Role." *Sex Roles* 19(11/12): 703–712.

Lange, James E., Loraine Devos-Comby, Roland S. Moore, Jason Daniel, and Kestrel Homer (2011). "Collegiate Natural Drinking Groups: Characteristics, Structure, and Processes." *Addiction Research and Theory* 19(4): 312–322.

Lathrop, Elsie (1926). *Early America Inns and Taverns*. New York: Rovert M. McBride and Company.

Lears, Jackson (1994). *Fables of Abundance A Cultural History of Advertising in America*. New York: Basic Books (Harper Collins).

Leemon, Thomas A. (1972). *The Rites of Passage in a Student Culture*. New York and London: Teachers College Press, Columbia University.

Lefebvre, Henri (2004). *Rhythmanalysis: Space, Time and Everyday Life*. London and New York: Continuum.

Leigh, Barbara, and Christine Lee (2008). "What Motivates Extreme Drinking?" In: Marjana Martinic and Fiona Measham (Eds.). *Swimming with Crocodiles: The Culture of Extreme Drinking*. New York and London: Routledge: 53–78.

Lemert, Edwin M (1962). "Alcohol, Values and Social Control." In: David J. Pittman and Charles R. Snyder (Eds.). *Society, Culture and Drinking Patterns*. New York and London: John Wiley and Sons, 1962: 553–571.

Lender, Mark Edward, and James Kirby Martin (1987). *Drinking in America: A History*. 2nd ed. New York: The Free Press.

Levine, Harry Gene (1978). "The Discovery of Addiction." *Journal of Studies on Alcohol* 39(1): 143–174.

——— (1983). "The Good Creature of God and the Demon Rum: Colonial Americas and 19th Century Ideas About Alcohol, Crime and Accidents." In: *Alcohol and Disinhibition: Nature and Meaning of the Link*, Research Monograph 12. National Institute on Alcohol Abuse and Alcoholism. Washington D.C.: U.S. Department of Health and Human Services: 111–161.

——— (1984). "The Alcohol Problem in America: From Temperance to Prohibition." *British Journal of Addiction* 79(1): 109–119.

——— (1993). "Temperance Cultures: Alcohol as a Problem in Nordic and English-Speaking Cultures." In: Malcolm Lader, Griffith Edwards, and D. Colin Drummon. *The Nature of Alcohol and Drug-Related Problems*. New York: Oxford University Press: 16–36.

Levine, Robert (1997). *A Geography of Time*. New York: Basic Books (Harper Collins).

Linn, Susan (2004). *Consuming Kids*. New York and London: The New Press.

Lissarrague, F. (1990). "Around the Krater: An Aspect of Banquet Imagery." In: Oswyn Murray (Ed.). *Sympotica: A Symposium on the Symposion*. Oxford: Clarendon Press: 196–209.

Lotman, Yuri (1977). *The Structure of the Artistic Text* (G. Lenhoff and R. Vroon, Trans.). Michigan Slavic Contributions. Ann Arbor: University of Michigan.

Lyons, Antonia C., and Sarah A. Willott (2008). "Alcohol Consumption, Gender Identities and Women's Changing Social Positions." *Sex Roles* 59: 694–712.

MacAndrew, Craig, and Robet B. Edgerton (1969). *Drunken Comportment*. Chicago: Aldine Publishing Company.

Macdonald, Sharon (1994). "Whisky, Women and The Scottish Drink Problem. A View from the Highlands." In: Maryon McDonald (Ed.). *Gender, Drink and Drugs*. Oxford and New York: Berg: 125–144.

MacNish, Robert (1828). *The Anatomy of Drunkenness*. Glasgow: W. R. McPhun.

Mager, Anne Kelk (2010). *Beer, Sociability and Masculinity in South Africa*. Bloomington and Indianapolis: Indiana University Press.

Makela, Klaus (1983). "The Uses of Alcohol and Their Cultural Regulation." *Acta Sociologica* 26(1): 21–31.

Mandelbaum, David G. (1965). "Alcohol and Culture." *Current Anthropology* 6(3): 281–293.

Manning, Paul, and Ann Uplisashvili (2007). "'Our Beer': Ethnographic Brands in Post-Socialist Georgia." *American Anthropologist* 109(4): 626–641.

Marchant, W.T. (1888). *In Praise of Ale: Or, Songs, Ballads, Epigrams and Anecdotes Relating to Beer, Malt and Hops*. London: George Redway.

Marcus, Anthony (2005). "Drinking Politics: Alcohol, Drugs, and the Problem of US Civil Society." In: Thomas M. Wilson (Ed.). *Drinking Cultures*. Oxford and New York: Berg: 255–276.

Marmot, Michael, Johannes Siegrist, and Tores Theorell (2006). "Health and the Psychosocial Environment at Work." In: Michael Marmot and Richard G. Wilkerson (Eds.). *Social Determinants of Health*. Second ed. Oxford: Oxford University Press: 97–130.

Marshall, Mac (1983). "'Four Hundred Rabbits': An Anthropological View of Alcohol as a Disinhibitor." In: *Alcohol and Disinhibition: Nature and Meaning of the Link*, Research Monograph 12. National Institute on Alcohol Abuse and Alcoholism. Washington D.C.: U.S. Department of Health and Human Services: 186–204.

Martens, Matthew P., Tracey L. Rocha, Jessica Martin, and Holly F. Serrao (2008). "Drinking Motives and College Students: Further Examination of a Four-Factor Model." *Journal of Counseling Psychology* 55(2): 289–295.

Martin, A. Lynn. "Fetal Alcohol Syndrome in Europe, 1300-1700." *Food and Foodways* 11: 1–26.

——— (2006). "Drinking and Alehouses in the Diary of an English Mercer's Apprentice, 1663–1674." In: Mack Holt (Ed.). *A Social and Cultural History of Alcohol*. Oxford and New York: Berg: 93–105.

——— (2009). *Alcohol, Violence and Disorder in Traditional Europe*. Kirksville, Missouri: Truman State University Press.

Martin, Scott C. (2002). *Devil of the Domestic Sphere: Temperance, Gender and Middle-class Ideology 1800–1860*. Dekalb: Northern Illinois University Press.

Mass Observation (1943). *The Pub and the People: A Worktown Study*. London: Victor Gollancz Ltd.

Mattingly, Carol (1998). *Well-Tempered Women: Nineteenth-Century Temperance Rhetoric*. Carbondale and Edwardsville: Southern Illinois University Press.

Mauss, Marcel (1924). *The Gift: The Form and Reason for Exchange in Archaic Societies*. 1990 [1924] ed. New York: W. W. Norton.

McDonald, Maryon (1994). "A Socio-Anthropological View of Gender, Drink and Drugs." In: Maryon McDonald. *Gender, Drink and Drugs*. Oxford and New York: Berg: 1–32.

McGovern, Patrick (2003). *Ancient Wine: The Search for the Origins of Viniculture*. Berkeley: University of California Press.

——— (2009). *Uncorking the Past: The Quest for Wine, Beer, and Other Alcoholic Beverages*. Berkeley: University of California Press.

Meacham, Sarah Hand (2009). *Every Home a Distillery: Alcohol, Gender and Technology in the Colonial Chesapeake*. Baltimore: Johns Hopkins University Press.

Measham, Fiona (2008). "A History of Intoxication: Changing Attitudes to Drunkenness and Excess in the United Kingdom." In: Marjana Martinic and Fiona Measham (Eds.). *Swimming with Crocodiles: The Culture of Extreme Drinking*. New York and London: Routledge: 13–36.

Megaw, J. V. S. (1966). "The Vix Burial." *Antiquity* XL: 38–44.

Milton, Katherine (2004). "Ferment in the Family Tree: Does a Frugivorous Dietary Heritage Influence Contemporary Patterns of Human Ethanol Use?" *Integrative and Comparative Biology* 44: 304–314.

Mitchell, Tim (2004). *Intoxicated Identities: Alcohol's Power in Mexican History and Culture.* New York and London: Routledge.

Montemurro, Beth, and Bridget McClure (2005). "Changing Gender Norms for Alcohol Consumption: Social Drinking and Lowered Inhibitions at Bachelorette Parties." *Sex Roles* 52(5/6): 279–288.

Mumford, Lewis (1963). *Technics and Civilization.* New York: Harbinger Press.

Murdock, Catherine Gilbert (1998). *Domesticating Drink: Men, Women and Alcohol in America, 1870–1940.* Baltimore and London: The Johns Hopkins University Press.

Murray, Gilbert (Trans.) (1906). *Euripides, The Bacchae.* New York: P.F. Collier & Son.

Murray, Oswyn (1983). "The Greek Symposion in History." In: E. Gabba (Ed.). *Tria Corda: Scritti in Onore Di Arnaldo Momigliano.* Como: New Press.

——— (1991). "War and the Symposium." In: William J. Slator (Ed.). *Dining in a Classical Context.* Ann Arbor: The University of Michigan Press: 83–103.

Nahoum-Grappe, Veronique (2008). "Beyond Boundaries: Youth and the Dream of the Extreme." In: Marjana Martinic and Fiona Measham (Eds.). *Swimming with Crocodiles: The Culture of Extreme Drinking.* New York and London: Routledge: 37–52.

National Institute on Alcohol Abuse and Alcoholism (2002). *A Call to Action: Changing the Culture of Binge Drinking on Campus.* Rockville, MD: National Institutes of Health.

——— (2004). *NIAAA Council Approves Definition of Binge Drinking.* NIAAA Newsletter. Bethesda, MD: National Institutes of Health, Winter.

Neighbors, Clayton, Casey Spieker, Laura Oster-Aaland, Melissa Lewis, and Rochelle Bergstrom (2005). "Celebration Intoxication: An Evaluation of 21st Birthday Alcohol Consumption." *Journal of American College Health* 54(2): 76–80.

Nelson, Max (2005). *The Barbarian's Revenge: A History of Beer in Ancient Europe.* London and New York: Routledge.

Nemeth, Zsofia, Robert Urban, Emmanuel Kuntsche, and Emilio Moreno San Pedro (2011). "Drinking Motives Among Spanish and Hungarian Young Adults: A Cross-National Study." *Alcohol and Alcoholism* 46(3): 261–269.

Nicholls, James (2008). "Vinum Britannicum: The 'Drink Question' in Early Modern England." *Social History of Alcohol and Drugs* 22(2): 190–208.

Nuwer, Hank (1999). *Wrongs of Passage: Fraternities, Sororities, Hazing, and Binge Drinking.* Bloomington and Indianapolis: Indiana University Press.

O'Callaghan, Michelle (2004). "Tavern Societies, the Inns of Court, and the Culture of Conviviality in Early Seventeenth-Century London." In: Adam Smyth (Ed.). *A Pleasing Sinne: Drink and Conviviality in Seventeenth-Century England.* Cambridge: D. S. Brewer: 37–51.

O'Guinn, Thomas, and Albert Munoz (2005). "Communal Consumption and the Brand." In: S. Ratneshwar and David Glen Mick (Eds.). *Inside Consumption: Consumer Motives, Goals and Desires.* London and New York: Routledge: 252–272.

O'Reilly, Mike, and Mike Tennant (2009). *The Age of Persuasion: How Marketing Ate Our Culture.* Berkeley: Counterpoint.

Okrent, Daniel (2010). *Last Call: The Rise and Fall of Prohibition.* New York: Scribner.

Oldenburg, Ray (1989). *The Great Good Place.* New York: Paragon House.

Oldfather, C. H. (Trans.) (1933). *Diodorus Siculus: Library of History,* Volume I, Books 1-2.34. Cambridge MA: Loeb Classical Library.

Orcutt, James D. (1993). "Happy Hour and Social Lubrication: Evidence of Moodsetting Rituals of Drinking Time." *Journal of Drug Issues* 23(3): 389–407.

Peck, Garrett (2009). *The Prohibition Hangover.* New Brunswick: Rutgers University Press.

Pellizer, Ezio (1990). "Outlines of a Morphology of Sympotic Entertainment." In: Oswyn Murray (Ed.). *Sympotica: A Symposium on the Symposion.* Oxford: Clarendon Press: 177–184.

Pennington, Janet (2002). "Inns and Taverns of Western Sussex, England, 1550-1700: A Documentary and Architectural Investigation." In: Beat Kumin and Ann Tlusty (Eds.). *The World of the Tavern: Public Houses in Early Modern Europe*. Burlington, VT: Ashgate: 116–135.

Pennock, Pamela E. (2007). *Advertising Sin and Sickness: The Politics of Alcohol and Tobacco Marketing 1950–1990*. Dekalb, IL: Northern Illinois University Press.

Peralta, Robert (2007). "College Alcohol Use and the Embodiment of Hegemonic Masculinity Among European American Men." *Sex Roles* 56: 741–756.

Perez, Ramona L. (2000). "Fiesta as Tradition, Fiesta as Change: Ritual, Alcohol and Violence in a Mexican Community." *Addiction* 95(3): 365–372.

Pine, Adrienne (2008). *Working Hard, Drinking Hard: On Violence and Survival in Honduras*. Berkeley: University of California Press.

Pollan, Michael (2001). *The Botany of Desire*. New York: Random House.

Presdee, Mike (2000). *Cultural Criminology and the Carnival of Crime*. London and New York: Routledge.

Presley, C. A., A. Leichliter, and P. W. Meilman (1998). *Alcohol and Drugs on American College Campuses: A Report to College Presidents*. Carbondale: Core Institute: Southern Illinois University.

Purcell, N. (1985). "Wine and Wealth in Ancient Italy." *The Journal of Roman Studies* 75: 1–19.

Purcell, Nicholas (1994). "Women and Wine in Ancient Rome." In: Maryon McDonald (Ed.). *Gender, Drink and Drugs*, Oxford and New York: Berg: 191–208.

Putnam, Robert (2000). *Bowling Alone: The Collapse and Revival of American Community*. New York: Simon and Schuster.

Reckner, Paul E., and Stephen A. Brighton (1999). "'Free From All Vicious Habits': Archaeological Perspectives on Class Conflict and the Rhetoric of Temperance." *Historical Archeology* 33(1): 63–86.

Redmon, Davis (2002). "Testing Informal Social Control Theory: Examining Lewd Behavior During Mardi Gras." *Deviant Behavior: An Interdisciplinary Journal* 23 (2002): 363–384.

———— (2003a). "Examining Low Self-Control Theory at Mardi Gras: Critiquing the General Theory of Crime Within the Framework of Normative Deviance." *Deviant Behavior: An Interdisciplinary Journal* 24: 373–392.

———— (2003b). "Playful Deviance as an Urban Leisure Activity: Secret Selves, Self-Validation and Entertaining Performances." *Deviant Behavior: An Interdisciplinary Journal* 24: 27–51.

Robbins, Richard (1973). "Alcohol and the Identity Struggle: Some Effects of Economic Change on Interpersonal Relations." *American Anthropologist* 75: 99–122.

Roche, Ann M. (2001). "Drinking Behavior: A Multifaceted and Multiphasic Phenomenon." In: Ann M. Roche and Eleni Houghton (Eds.). *Learning About Drinking*. Philadelphia: Taylor and Francis: 1–34.

Rojek, Chris (2000). *Leisure and Culture*. New York: St. Martin's Press.

Room, Robin (2004). "Drinking and Coming of Age in a Cross-Cultural Perspective." In: R.J. Bonnie and M. J. O'Connor (Eds.). Reducing *Underage Drinking: A Collective Responsibility*. Washington D.C.: National Academy Press: 654–677.

Room, Robin, and Klaus Makela (2000). "Typologies of the Cultural Position of Drinking." *Journal of Studies on Alcohol* 61: 475–483.

Rorabaugh, W. J. (1979). *The Alcoholic Republic: An American Tradition*. New York and Oxford: Oxford University Press.

Rose, Peter G. (2009). *Food, Drink and Celebrations of the Hudson Valley Dutch*. Charleston and London: The History Press.

Rosler, Wolfgang (1995). "Wine and Truth in Greek Symposion." In: Oswyn Murray and Manuela Tecusan (Eds.). *In Vino Veritas*. London: The British School at Rome: 106–112.

Rotskoff, Lori (2002). *Love on the Rocks: Men, Women and Alcohol in Post-World War II America*. Chapel Hill and London: The University of North Carolina Press.

Royall, Anne (1969). *Letters from Alabama*. Birmingham: University of Alabama.

Rozik, Eli (1997). "Pictorial Metaphor in Commercial Advertising." In: Winfried Noth (Ed.). *Semiotics of the Media: State of the Art, Projects and Perspectives.* New York: Mouton de Gruyter: 159–173.

Rush, Benjamin (1790). *An Inquiry into the Effects of Spirituous Liquors on the Human Body and the Mind.* Boston: Thomas and Andrews. Available from http://www.librarycompany.org/.

Saffer, Henry (2002). "Alcohol Advertising and Youth." *Journal of Studies of Alcohol* 14(Supplement): 173–181.

Salinger, Sharon V (2002). *Taverns and Drinking in Early America.* Baltimore and London: Johns Hopkins University Press.

Sande, Allan (2002). "Intoxication and Rites of Passage to Adulthood in Norway." *Contemporary Drug Problems* 29(Summer): 277–303.

Sander, Fredrik (1893). *Edda Samund Den Vises.* Stockholm: P. A. Norstedt and Soner.

Schachtman, Tom (2006). *Rumspringa: To Be or Not to Be Amish.* New York: North Point Press.

Schatzki, Ted (2009). "Timespace and the Organization of Social Life." In: Elizabeth Shove, Frank Trentmannand Richard Wilk (Eds.). *Time, Consumption and Everyday Life: Practice, Materiality and Culture.* Oxford and New York: Berg: 35–48.

Schivelbusch, Wolfgang (1993). *Tastes of Paradise* (David Jacobson, Trans.). New York: Vintage Books.

Scott-Sheldon, Lori A. J., Michael Carrey, and Kate Carrey (2010). "Alcohol and Risky Sexual Behavior Among Heavy Drinking College Students." *AIDS Behavior* 14: 845–853.

Sexton, Rocky L (2001). "Ritualized Inebriation, Violence, and Social Control in Cajun Mardi Gras." *Anthropological Quarterly* 74(1): 28–38.

Sheehan, Margaret, and Damien Ridge (2001). "'You Become Really Close... You Talk About the Silly Things You Did, And We Laugh': The Role of Binge Drinking in Female Secondary Students' Lives." *Substance Use and Misuse* 36(3): 347–372.

Sher, Kenneth J., Mark D. Wood, Alison E. Richardson, and Kristina M. Jackson (2005). "Subjective Effects of Alcohol I: Effects of the Drink and Drinking Context." In: Mitch Earleywine (Ed.). *Mind-Altering Drugs: The Science of Subjective Experience.* Oxford: Oxford University Press: 86–134.

Sherratt, Andrew (1995). "Alcohol and Its Alternatives." In: Jordan Goodman, Paul E. Lovejoy and Andrew Sherratt (Eds.). *Consuming Habits: Global and Historical Perspectives on How Cultures Define Drugs.* Second ed. London and New York: Routledge: 11–45.

Shove, Elizabeth (2009). "Everyday Practice and the Production and Consumption of Time." In: Elizabeth Shove, Frank Trentmann and Richard Wilk (Eds.). *Time, Consumption and Everyday Life: Practice, Materiality and Culture.* Oxford and New York: Berg: 17–34.

Simmons, Amelia (1798). *American Cookery.* Hartford CT: Simeon Butler. Available from http://digital.lib.msu.edu/projects/cookbooks/html/books/book_01.cfm.

Singer, Merrill, Freddie Valentin, Hans Baer, and Zhongke Jia (1992). "Why Does Juan García Have a Drinking Problem? The Perspective of Critical Medical Anthropology." *Medical Anthropology* 14(1): 77–108.

Singman, Jeffrey (1999). *Daily Life in Medieval Europe.* WestPort, CT: Greenwood Press.

Skene, William F. (1868). *The Four Ancient Books of Wales.* Edinburgh: Edmonston and Douglas.

Skiadas, P. K., and J. G. Lascaratos (2001). "Dietetics in Ancient Greek Philosophy: Plato's Concepts of Healthy Diet." *European Journal of Clinical Nutrition* 55: 532–537.

Smith, Christian (2011). *Lost in Transition: The Dark Side of Emerging Adulthood.* Oxford and New York: Oxford University Press.

Smith, Dennis E (2003). *From Symposium to Eucharist: The Banquet in the Early Christian World.* Minneapolis: Fortress Press.

Smith, Eliza (1994). *The Compleat Housewife.* 1758 ed. London: Studio Editions Ltd.

Smith, Frederick H (2008). *The Archeology of Alcohol and Drinking.* Gainesville, FL: University Press of Florida.

Smith, Margaret A., and Joseph B. Berger (2010). "Women's Ways of Drinking: College Women, High-Risk Alcohol Use, and Negative Consequences." *Journal of College Student Development* 51(1): 35–49.

Smith, Stacy L., and Ed Donnerstein (2003). "The Problem of Exposure: Violence, Sex, Drugs and Alcohol." In: Diane Ravitch and Joseph P. Viteritti (Eds.). *Kid Stuff: Marketing Sex and Violence to America's Children*. Baltimore and London: The Johns Hopkins University Press: 65–95.

Solomon, Jack (1988). *The Signs of Our Times*. Los Angeles: Jeremy P. Tarcher Inc.

Southerton, Dale (2009). "Re-ordering Temporal Rhythms." In: Elizabeth Shove, Frank Trentmann and Richard Wilk (Eds.). *Time, Consumption and Everyday Life: Practice, Materiality and Culture*. Oxford and New York: Berg: 49–63.

Sperber, Murray (2000). *Beer and Circus: How Big-Time College Sports Is Crippling Undergraduate Education*. New York: Henry Holt and Company.

Springer, Paul (2007). *Ads to Icons: How Advertising Succeeds in a Multimedia Age*. London and Philadelphia: Kogan Page.

Standage, Tom (2005). *A History of the World in 6 Glasses*. New York: Walker and Company.

Stearns, Peter N (1999). *Battleground of Desire: The Struggle for Self-Control in Modern America*. New York and London: New York University Press.

Strasberger, Victor (2002). "Alcohol Advertising and Adolescents." *The Pediatric Clinics of North America* 49: 353–376.

Strassman, Rick (2005). "Hallucinogens." In: Mitch Earleywine (Ed.). *Mind-Altering Drugs: The Science of Subjective Experience*. Oxford: Oxford University Press: 49–85.

Strauss, Robert, and Selden D. Bacon (1953). *Drinking in College*. New Haven: Yale University Press.

Strickland, Donald E., T. Andrew Finn, and M. Dow Lambert (1982a). "A Content Analysis of Beverage Alcohol Advertising. I. Magazine Advertising." *Journal of Studies on Alcohol* 43(7): 655–682.

—— (1982b). "A Content Analysis of Beverage Alcohol Advertising. II. Television Advertising." *Journal of Studies on Alcohol* 43(9): 964–989.

Suggs, David N. (1996). "Mosadi Tshwene: The Construction of Gender and the Consumption of Alcohol in Botswana." *American Ethnologist* 23(3): 597–610.

Syme, S. Leonard (2004). "Social Determinants of Health: The Community as an Empowered Partner." *Preventing Chronic Disease* January. Available from http://www.cdc.gov/pcd/issues/2004/jan/syme.htm.

Syrett, Nicholas (2009). *The Company He Keeps: A History of White College Fraternities*. Chapel Hill: University of North Carolina Press.

Szala-Meneok, Karen (1994). "Christmas Janneying and Easer Drinking: Symbolic Inversion, Contingency and Ritual Time in Coastal Labrador." *Arctic Anthropology* 31(1): 103–116.

Tchernia, André (1983). "Italian Wine in Gaul." In: Peter Garnsey, Keith Hopkins and C. R. Whittaker (Eds.). *Trade in the Ancient Economy*. Berkeley: University of California Press.

—— (1986). *Le Vin De l'Italie Romaine*. Rome: École Française de Rome.

Theall, Katherine P., William Dejong, Richard Scribner, Karen Mason, Shari Kessel Schneider, and Neal Simonsen (2009). "Social Capital In the College Setting: The Impact of Participation in Campus Activities on Drinking and Alcohol-Related Harms." *Journal of American College Health* 58(1): 15–23.

Thomann, G. (1887). *Colonial Liquor Laws: Liquor Laws of the United States; Their Spirit and Effect*. Vol. I and II. 2 vols. New York: The United States Brewers' Association.

Thompson, E.P. (1967). "Time, Work-Discipline, and Industrial Capitalism Time, Work-Discipline, and Industrial Capitalism." *Past and Present* 38(December): 56–97.

Thompson, Peter (1999). *Rum Punch and Revolution: Tavern Going and Public Life in Eighteenth-Century Philadelphia*. Philadelphia: University of Pennsylvania Press.

Thorson, Esther (1995). "Studies of the Effects of Alcohol Advertising: Two Underexplored Aspects." In: Susan E. Martin (Ed.). *The Effects of the Mass Media on the Use and Abuse of Alcohol*. Washington D.C.: U.S. Department of Health and Human Services: 475–480.

Tierney, J. J. (1959). "The Celtic Ethnography of Posidonius." *Proceedings of the Royal Irish Academy Section C* 60: 189–275.

Tlusty, Ann (2001). *Bacchus and Civic Order: The Culture of Drink in Early Modern Germany.* Charlottesville: University of Virginia Press.

Tomlinson, Alan (1990). "Consumer Culture and the Aura of the Commodity." In: Alan Tomlinson (Ed.). *Consumption, Identity and Style: Marketing, Meanings and the Packaging of Pleasure.* London: Routledge: 1–38.

Tremblay, Paul, Kathryn Graham, Samantha Wells, Roma Harris, Roseanne Pulford, and Sharon Roberts (2010). "When Do First-Year College Students Drink Most During the Academic Year? An Internet-Based Study of Daily and Weekly Drinking." *Journal of American College Health* 58(5): 401–411.

Triese, Debbie, Joyce Wolburg, and Cele Otnes (1999). "Understanding the Social Gifts of Drinking Rituals: An Alternative Framework for PSA Developers." *Journal of Advertising* 28(2): 17–31.

Truitt, W. J. (1912). *Know Thyself or Nature's Secrets Revealed.* Marietta, OH: The S. A. Mullikin Company.

Turmo, Isabel Gonzalez (2001). "Drinking: An Almost Silent Language." In: Igor De Garine and Valerie De Garine (Eds.). *Drinking: Anthropological Approached.* New York and Oxford: Berghahn: 130–143.

Turner, Victor (1967). *The Forest of Symbols.* Ithaca, NY: Cornell Press.

——— (1969). *The Ritual Process: Structure and Anti-Structure.* New York: Walter De Gruyter Inc.

Turrisi, Rob, Kimberley Mallett, Nadine Mastroleo, and Mary Larimer (2006). "Heavy Drinking in College Students: Who Is at Risk and What Is Being Done About It?" *The Journal of General Psychology* 133(4): 401–420.

Unger, Richard W (2004). *Beer in the Middle Ages and the Renaissance.* Philadelphia: University of Pennsylvania Press.

Vander Ven, Thomas (2011). *Getting Wasted: Why College Students Drink Too Much and Party So Hard.* New York: New York University Press.

Vasey, Daniel (1990). *The Pub and English Social Change.* New York: AMS Press.

Veblen, Thorstein (1899). *The Theory of the Leisure Class.* New York: A. M. Kelley.

Vetta, Massimo (1999). "The Culture of the Symposium." In: Jean-Louis Flandrin and Massimo Montanari (Eds.). *Food: A Culinary History.* New York: Penguin: 96–105.

Vicary, Judith R., and Chrstine M. Karshin (2002). "College Alcohol Abuse: A Review of the Problems, Issues and Prevention Approaches." *The Journal of Primary Prevention* 22(3): 299–331.

Ward, Christie L. (2001). "Norse Drinking Traditions". Alexandria, VA. Available from http://www.vikinganswerlady.com/resume/worksamples/NorseDrinkingTraditions.pdf.

Warner, Jessica (2002). *Craze: Gin and Debauchery in an Age of Reason.* New York: Four Walls Eight Windows.

——— (2008). *The Day George Bush Stopped Drinking: Why Abstinence Matters to the Religious Right.* Toronto: McClelland and Stewart.

Weaver, William Woys (2008). "The Medieval Origins of Commandaria." *Petits Propos Culinaires* 86(September): 15–62.

Wechsler, H., and S. B. Austin (1998). "Binge Drinking: The Four/Five Measure." *Journal of Studies on Alcohol* 59(1): 122–123.

Wechsler, H., A. Davenport, G. W. Dowdall, and S. Castillo (1995). "Correlates of College Student Binge Drinking." *American Journal of Public Health* 85: 921–926.

Wechsler, H., A. Davenport, G.W. Dowdall, B. Moeykens, and S. Castillo (1994). "Health and Behavioral Consequences of Binge Drinking in College, a National Survey of Students at 140 Campuses." *Journal of the American Medical Association* 272(21): 1672–1677.

Wechsler, H., G.W. Dowdall, G. Maenner, J. Gledhill-Hoyt, and H. Lee (1995). "Changes in Binge Drinking and Related Problems Among American College Students Between 1993 and 1997: Results of the Harvard School of Public Health College Alcohol Study." *Journal of American College Health* 47(2): 57–68.

Wechsler, H., and Bernice Wuethrich (2002). *Dying to Drink: Confronting Binge Drinking on College Campuses.* Emmaus, PA: Rodale.

Wechsler, Henry, Jae Eun Lee, Meichun Kuo, and Hang Lee (2000). "College Binge Drinking in the 1990s: A Continuing Problem." *Journal of American College Health* 48(March): 199–210.

Weitzman, Elissa, Toben Nelson, and Henry Wechsler (2003). "Taking Up Binge Drinking in College: The Influences of Person, Social Group, and Environment." *Journal of Adolescent Health* 32: 26–35.

Wells, Peter S (1980). *Culture Contact and Culture Change.* Cambridge: Cambridge University Press.

——— (1985). "Mediterranean Trade and Culture Change in Early Iron Age Central Europe." In: T. C. Champion and V. S. Megaw (Eds.). *Settlement and Society: Aspects of Western European Prehistory in the First Millennium BC.* New York: Palgrave Macmillan: 69–90.

——— (1995). "Settlement and Social Systems at the End of the Iron Age." In: Bettina Arnold and D. Blair Gibson (Eds.). *Celtic Chiefdom, Celtic State.* Cambridge: Cambridge University Press: 88–95.

West, Lois A (2001). "Negotiating Masculinities in American Drinking Subcultures." *The Journal of Men's Studies* 9(3): 371–392.

Wilk, Richard (2009). "The Edge of Agency: Routines, Habits and Volition." In: Elizabeth Shove, Frank Trentmann, and Richard Wilk (Eds.). *Time, Consumption and Everyday Life: Practice, Materiality and Culture.* Oxford and New York: Berg: 143–154.

Williamson, Judith (2005). *Decoding Advertisements: Ideology and Meaning in Advertising.* 15th ed. London: Marion Boyars Publishers Ltd.

Winlow, Simon, and Steve Hall (2006). *Violent Night: Urban Leisure and Contemporary Culture.* Oxford and New York: Berg, 2006.

Witt, Contanze Maria (1997). "Barbarians on the Greek Periphery?" (Doctoral dissertation, University of Virginia. Available from http://www2.iath.virginia.edu/Barbarians/first.html.

Wolburg, Joyce (2001). "The Risky Business of Binge Drinking Among College Students: Using Risk Models for PSAs and Anti-Drinking Campaigns." *Journal of Advertising* 30(4): 23–39.

World Health Organization (2011). *Global Status Report on Alcohol and Health.* Geneva: World Health Organization.

Wurst, LouAnn (1991). "'Employees Must Be of Moral and Temperant Habits' Rural and Urban Elite Ideologies." In: Randall H. McGuire and Robert Paynter (Eds.). *The Archeology of Inequality.* Oxford: Blackwell.

Young, Amy, Michele Morales, Sean Estaban McCabe, Carol J. Boyd, and Hannah D'Arcy (2005). "Drinking Like a Guy: Frequent Binge Drinking Among Undergraduate Women." *Substance Use and Misuse* 40: 241–267.

Zailckas, Koren (2005). *Smashed: Story of a Drunken Girlhood.* New York: Viking Penguin.

Zamboanga, Byron L., Janine Olthuis, Nicholas Horton, Elan McCollum, Jacqueline Lee, and Rebecca Shaw (2009). "Where's the House Party? Hazardous Drinking Behaviors and Related Risk Factors." *The Journal of Psychology* 143(3): 228–244.

Zerubavel, Eviatar (1985). *Hidden Rhythms: Schedules and Calendars in Social Life.* Berkeley: University of California Press.

INDEX

Figures in *Italic*; Tables in **Bold**